MUSIC IN THE WORLD OF ISLAM

A Socio-cultural study

Music in the World of Islam

A Socio-cultural study

Amnon Shiloah

Wayne State University Press   Detroit

U.S. edition published by
Wayne State University Press,
Detroit, Michigan 48201

Library of Congress Cataloging-in-Publication Data

Shiloah, Amnon
Music in the world of Islam: a socio-cultural study / Amnon Shiloah.
p. cm.
Includes bibliographical references and index.
ISBN 0-8143-2589-0
1. Music, Islamic—Arab Countries—History and criticism.
2. Music—Religious aspects—Islam. I. Title.
ML348.S56 1995
780'.917'671—dc20 94-47620
CIP
MN

Manufactured in England

Contents

Preface

This book represents the culmination of my long-standing research into the field of Near Eastern and Middle Eastern musical traditions. The first impetus was given to me more than three decades ago by the eminent scholar H. G. Farmer, who warmly encouraged me to explore an important source written by an eleventh-century author. His suggestion, as well as his specific and inspiring contributions, proved to be definitive in shaping my initial studies.

The journey into the fascinating world of medieval Arabic writings, and the attitudes of their authors toward fundamental problems of scholarship, had the effect on me of a personal spiritual encounter with men of the past and the glorious musical achievements of their respective epochs. However, hampered by the lack of concrete musical documents to tell us how the music of the past sounded, I addressed myself to the various living traditions. In them, I hoped to detect the threads by which they are linked to the classical music of the first centuries of Islam. The quest for the links between past and present, and for the affinities among the many and varied traditions established over a huge geographical area, has determined my basic approach in this book.

I am aware that by its very nature an analytical overview cannot possibly explore the multiple aspects of a topic of such magnitude, replete with so many significant events. Therefore, I have appended an extensive thematic bibliography, and I trust that anyone desiring further enlightenment on a given subject will turn to one or more of these additional sources. The bibliography has successive numbers and in the thematic sections the items are classified chronologically. The references in the text are presented in parentheses; they include the name of author cited or other works relevant to the matter treated, the corresponding number in the bibliography, and the page numbers preceded by a colon. We hope that this solution, and the avoidance of footnotes, will make the reading of the text more appealing. The bibliography is followed by a list of all the Arabic sources referred to in the text, the bulk of which are described in my book *The Theory of Music in Arabic*

Writings (see 76 in the bibliograpy). All the dates appearing in this list, as well as those in the text, are according to the Christian calendar.

Finally, I wish to express my gratitude to Shirley Shpira who edited the English text in a masterly and creative fashion. I would also like to thank Jane Singer for all her hard work and devotion in producing the book.

Amnon Shiloah
The Hebrew University of Jerusalem

Transliteration of Arabic Characters

The following is the system of transliteration used throughout this book:

ء	ʾ	ض	ḍ
ب	b	ط	ṭ
ت	t	ظ	ẓ
ث	th	ع	ʿ
ج	dj	غ	gh
ح	ḥ	ف	f
خ	kh	ق	q
د	d	ك	k
ذ	dh	ل	l
ر	r	م	m
ز	z	ن	n
س	s	ه	h
ش	sh	و	w
ص	ṣ	ي	y

Long vowels

ا ى	ā
و	ū
ي	ī

Diphthongs

و	aw
ي	ay
ة	a; at construct state
ال	(article) al- and 1 - even before the antero-palatals)

Introduction

There was a time, not too long ago, when a Westerner's initial encounter with Arab music hardly generated love at first hearing; exposure to this peculiar universe of sounds often reminded the uninitiated listener of a dog's howling. In August 1648, the French traveller M. de Monconys attended a dervish ceremony in Cairo, which he describes in gruesome terms:

> They all danced for more than an hour, shouting and screaming horribly; they whirled violently at such dizzying speed that their dance went beyond anything the wildest imagination can conceive of at a witches' sabbath . . . Their voices changed frequently from the screaming of enraged wolves to the barking of dogs.

This conclusion dovetails nicely with the judgement on Oriental music pronounced by the great composer Hector Berlioz in the second half of the nineteenth century: 'They call music that which we call *charivari*'. Of course, even in earlier times there were Westerners like Charles Fonton who had a more positive approach. In 1750 Fonton wrote a pamphlet on Turkish music severely attacking what today might be called the 'Eurocentrism' implied by his contemporary colleagues' judgement of the others' music.

Of more immediate concern, however, is whether traces of similar misunderstanding are still conceivable today; with the world shrinking into a 'global village,' exposure to practically all musical cultures is constant and almost unavoidable. Anyone seeking to acquire first-hand insight into those cultures has countless possibilities of doing so through the mass media, the vast quantities of recordings, and the many concerts held in major centres. In addition, extensive studies of various aspects of Near Eastern and Middle Eastern musical traditions are now available to whoever wishes to become acquainted with their characteristic forms of expression and attuned to their sounds. Nevertheless, there are still listeners who seek things in those musical traditions that are not there, while manifesting an inability to discern and appreciate the things that are there. They thereby ignore the fact that the concept of music is not the same everywhere.

In an article dealing with the question of uniformity of expression in the Persian traditional arts (*The World of Music* 1/1982), Jean During reports a discussion about music between a great contemporary Persian poet and some Westerners. Extolling the extraordinary richness of Western art music, the Occidentals compared it to an ocean in relation to which Persian music is only a miserable drop. On hearing this the poet said: 'Your music is indeed an ocean and ours in comparison is only a drop. But that ocean is only water while this drop, it is a tear'. Fully cognizant of the priceless value of the tear-drop, we have endeavoured in this book to single out and examine the way in which each culture conceives of and understands music and music-making.

A scholar wishing to embark on the arduous journey into the long, rich past of Arab music faces certain grave obstacles. Since its musical heritage was transmitted entirely by ear, it provides us with no musical documents prior to the first recordings, which were not made until the beginning of the twentieth century. Hence it is difficult to ascertain the extent to which current living musical traditions are descended from early classical musical traditions. The difficulty is exacerbated by changes that have affected the music in the course of time, particularly during our century, and by the relatively early emergence of loyalty to local features that began to characterize some of the major traditions flourishing in disparate cultural areas.

Although the absence of musical documents makes it impossible to establish definitively the nature of the music, quite a few fundamental questions can be clarified, with a high degree of probability, by consulting the many extant literary and theoretical sources, analyzing their contents, and juxtaposing them with the living traditions. Henry George Farmer, the scholar who for almost half a century defined and dominated this field of research and took full advantage of the known sources, has cleared the way for us with zealous persistence. In his major early study, *A History of Arabian Music*, published in 1929 but written in the early 1920s, Farmer was hampered by the paucity of preceding studies and the dearth of known sources.

The deliberations of the working committee headed by Farmer at the first Congress of Arab Music held in Cairo in 1932 were pervaded by an awareness that the quest for and discovery of new sources would be of prime importance in furthering our knowledge about the past. It was highly significant that the committee's terms of reference included both 'music history and manuscripts', two aspects that characterized the important contribution already made by Farmer himself. Furthermore, the Egyptian member of the committee, Muḥammad al-Ḥajjāj, argued that the study of old manuscripts would make it possible to understand the 'evolutionary' phases through which Arab music had passed. The committee's recommendations to locate, analyse, and publish manuscripts for the purpose of achieving a broader historical and cultural understanding of Arab music were only partially implemented. Subsequently, the most remarkable systematic contribution was that of Baron R. d'Erlanger who made a number of theoretical masterpieces available in French translation. The next generation of scholars exhibited a declining interest in the fascinating world of sources, and this has had a direct bearing on the quality of recent historical research on music. Few studies represent notable progress or demonstrate truly innovative approaches to the salient questions.

In conceiving this book we have aspired to present a comprehensive picture emphasizing the how and why – a picture drawn in the light of major historical and cultural events. We have endeavoured to present concepts about music, and conflicting attitudes towards it, as they prevailed in their time. To this end, we have taken the fullest advantage of the great number of sources now available. Indeed, in many instances a thorough analysis of known sources as well as of previously unexploited ones proved highly revealing; we found ourselves observing from new and unfamiliar vantage points that considerably enriched our knowledge and understanding.

The story of music told in these pages begins in pre-Islamic times with musical forms that bear strong imprints of the Bedouins' tribal way of life; these forms also show traces of refinement that indicate an affinity with the music of early or somewhat later civilizations within the same orbit. Pre-Islamic Arab music can be viewed as the forerunner of the art music that became defined and acquired a foothold after the advent of Islam. It was then, as the Arabs emerged from the Arabian Peninsula to conquer an empire, that their history became inextricably entwined with the musical traditions of the lands they conquered.

In general, the advent of Islam represents a turning point in the history of mankind; the Near East – where ancient civilizations flourished and the two other great religions, Judaism and Christianity, were born – became pre-eminently the land of Islam, the formative breeding-ground of its classical civilization. While its centre of gravity remained in this region, Islam spread over vast territories encompassing Arabia, the Fertile Crescent, Persia, Turkey, Central Asia, Afghanistan, Indonesia, parts of Africa, India and, for a while, Spain, Sicily, southern Italy and parts of Eastern Europe. Hence in this huge geographical area the overall term 'Arab music' covers a variety of musical styles and genres, from learned and sophisticated types of music elaborated in the context of supra-national Islamic civilization, to simple forms of sacred music and nomad or sedentary folk musical traditions.

It is clearly impossible to present a comprehensive survey of the music and musical life of such an immense geographical area over such a lengthy time-span, extending roughly from the fifth century to our days. The overview offered in the first eight chapters of this book therefore attempts to describe outstanding musical events and stylistic developments against the background of major historical and political happenings, and to indicate their relationship to other cultural fields. Following the lead of great Arab masters, who in times past examined music's role in human society, we have endeavoured to view all occurrences relevant to that role as an intertwining of ideas and trends closely associated with Islam's complex history and classical civilization. We have also tried to look upon musical elements as part of the value system that moulds an individual's world outlook. Hence the need to present a picture largely based on an interdisciplinary approach. In discussing issues relating to musical life and music-making, in dealing with theoretical speculations and concepts centred on music, special note is taken of artistic forms prevalent in classical civilization that were shared by the largest number of individuals and groups. Much emphasis is also placed on the search for typical styles and their eventual diversification into local musical traditions.

Our survey begins with an effort to pinpoint the emergence of classical forms of art music during the first and second centuries of Islam, a development that culminated in what is usually known as the 'Golden Age' of Islam's classical civilization. The process leading to the transformation of the conquerors' pre-Islamic, predominantly tribal music into sophisticated urbanized art music was particularly fascinating. It was distinguished by the consummate skill with which the new rulers succeeded in fusing dissimilar elements gleaned from old, prosperous civilizations; they managed to confer remarkable unity on the heterogeneous components. The merging of those diverse forms into a unique common style marked the advent of the Great Musical Tradition that gained favour throughout an extensive geographical area. Its immediate acceptance in the major centres of the Islamicized lands was undoubtedly decisive for its survival and perpetuation.

Some of the guiding principles and concepts of the Great Musical Tradition were still perceptible even after distinct autonomous styles began to appear – by the end of Islam's third century – in different parts of the Muslim empire. To a certain extent this development involved the Andalusian tradition, but first and foremost it impinged on the Persians and Turks who attained further heights of Islamic civilization and later produced musical styles of their own. Chapters 6 and 7 are devoted to the particular styles emanating from those countries, as well as to genres that flourished in Central Asia, Afghanistan and India. Particular attention is also paid to Andalusian musical traditions and their interrelation with European music.

The last four chapters deal with basic theoretical, formal and technical issues, such as scales, modes and rhythms; forms and genres; dance and folk music. This material often supplements the more general information treated in historical context in the earlier chapters.

To help the reader with the intricacies of historico-political issues referred to in the first eight chapters, we have provided a chronological table with a concise listing of outstanding relevant events.

Chronological table

c570	Birth of Muḥammad
622	The *hidjra* from Mecca to Medina; beginnings of the Muslim calendar
632	Death of Muḥammad; Abū Bakr appointed as first caliph
637–651	Conquest of Syria, Palestine, Iraq, Armenia, Egypt and Iran
661	Advent of the Umayyad caliphate
680	Battle of Karbalā and massacre of al-Ḥusayn, his family and supporters
705-715	Conquest of Bukhara and Samarkand; completion of conquest of North Africa
711–714	Conquest of most of Spain; invasion of Indus valley
750	Establishment of the ʻAbbāsid caliphate
751	Arabs defeat the Chinese army in Central Asia and Chinese paper makers captured
762	Foundation of Baghdad
789	Rise of the Idrisīd dynasty in Morocco
800	Aghlabid dynasty in Tunisia
821	Ṭāhirid dynasty in Khurasan
827	Conquest of Sicily
867	Saffārid dynasty in Eastern Iran
868	Ṭulīnid dynasty in Egypt
875	Sāmānid dynasty in Transoxiana
909	Rise of the Fāṭimid caliphate in Tunisia
929	ʻAbd al-Raḥmān III of Cordoba adopts the title of caliph
969	Fāṭimids conquer Egypt and found Cairo
ca 970	Seljuqs enter Islamic lands from the East
977	Ghazvanid dynasty in Afghanistan and India
1031	Fall of the caliphate of Cordoba and establishment of petty states in Spain
1060	The Normans conquer Sicily

1071	Seljuq Turks defeat Byzantines and occupy much of Anatolia
1085	Christians take Toledo in the framework of the reconquista
1091	Almoravid dynasty in Spain
1099	Crusaders capture Jerusalem
1145	Almohad dynasty in Spain
1171	End of the Fāṭimid caliphate
1187	Saladin takes Jerusalem
1219	Mongol Jinghiz khan invades Islamic lands
1249	Mamlūk dynasty in Egypt
1258	Mongols capture Baghdad, end of the ʿabbāsid caliphate; Il-khānid dynasty
1299	Emergence of Ottoman emirate
1370–80	Tīmūr becomes ruler of Central Asia; Tīmūrid dynasty
1392–1401	Tīmūr invades Western Iran, Mesopotamia, India, Georgia, Anatolia and Syria
1453	Ottomans capture Constantinople
1492	Fall of Granada—last Arab bastion in Spain
1502	The Safavid Ismāʿīl of Ardabil introduces Shīʿism as state religion in Persia; Safavid dynasty
1541	Subjugation of Hungary by the Ottomans
1556	Mughul dynasty in India
1570	Ottomans conquer Cyprus
1683	Ottomans before Vienna
1686	Ottomans lose Hungary
1739	Nādir Shāh of Persia takes Delhi
1770	War with Russia, annihilation of the Turkish fleet at Chesme
1789	Napoleon in Egypt
1811	Muḥammad ʿAlī wipes out the Mamluks in Egypt
1830	The French occupy Algeria
1869	Suez canal completed
1896	Greek-Turkish war

1 Pre-Islamic Music

The vast expanse of Arabia, within the boundaries of which the prophet Muḥammad founded Islam in 622, was not, as once thought, a country of rude barbarians living as nomadic or semi-nomadic warriors and rustics. It is true that the central and northern parts of the Arabian peninsula were largely desert, populated mainly by nomads and semi-nomads. In addition, however, there were settled villages and in the south and north there flourished an Arabian civilization of high achievement. There were also tribal market-places that displayed not only wares but works of the intellect as well. These were conceived in quite elevated fashion, reflecting inter-tribal social, cultural and behavioural codes, and the concepts they rested upon.

The Arabian peninsula was also far from isolated from the major civilizations around it; cuneiform inscriptions bear evidence of outside contacts as early as the Assyrian and Babylonian kingdoms. The earliest contacts were made primarily through caravans traversing overland trade routes, transporting commodities, the most important of which was frankincense. Indeed, the power and prestige of the flourishing southern kingdoms, also famous for their agriculture, rested on this trade. The Bedouin element throughout Arabia fulfilled an essential role in the traffic on the main routes from the Persian gulf to Syria and from Syria to Mesopotamia, Egypt and southern Arabia. Contact with the ancient Arabian civilization – cradle of many intellectual achievements, including music, musical theory and the development of musical instruments – grew closer and became more evident with the penetration of Christianity into the extreme south, the flourishing of Jewish communities and the establishment by the Byzantines and the Sassanians of vassal Arab kingdoms on the fringe of their respective empires.

The long and significant exposure in the pre-Islamic era to Babylonian, Egyptian, Greco-Roman and Indo-Persian civilizations undoubtedly left imprints, occasioning the interaction of musical ideas and sounds. However, as concerns music our insight is hampered at the outset – should we attempt to determine the exact nature of possible borrowings, influence or interaction – by the absence of actual musical documents. We have no tangible relics to facilitate investigation of the distant past. Nor, in our case, have we the relative advantage of the advanced Near Eastern civilizations in which the music's visible relics, in the words of C. Sachs, 'are dumb vision', that is to say they can be seen but cannot be heard (Sachs 99: 13). Arabian music does not provide us with iconographical musical scenes, or with instruments excavated from tombs. Except for some names and brief messages extant in graffiti on rocks, Bedouin culture was transmitted orally. Such pictorial art, limited though it was to rock drawings, nevertheless gives certain hints. Among the thousands of specimens in the style defined by specialists as style IV are three lyres engraved in rock near Najd Mussamma (present-day Saudi Arabia), dating from the third or second millennium BC. The engraving belongs to the last phase of style IV, which is the most widespread style to be found in all Middle East desert areas and includes many scenes of dancers accompanied by lyres, frame drums and, occasionally, double reed instruments associated with priests (Anati 123: 103–106). According to the specialists, this style also marks the earliest use of alphabets by Arabian groups in the peninsula. Also, at the advent of Islam, the lyre was among the instruments in use. It has survived through the ages and is still in vogue in coastal towns of the Red Sea area where it is played by fishermen in coffee houses (Shiloah 375). This example certainly illustrates Arabia's contacts with adjacent civilizations, but the state of our knowledge does not permit us to come to definitive conclusions as regards the nature and direction of these influences.

To this point, the bulk of our knowledge about music of the pre-Islamic age comes from later Islamic sources. Indeed, the earliest attempts to describe past musical events were made in the ninth century, when the Great Musical Tradition was at its height and had already gained wide acceptance among rulers and intellectuals. Much of the urbanized élite tended to consider pre-Islamic music as inferior and 'primitive'. To a large extent this view concorded with the Muslim hagiographic image of the pre-Islamic age in Arabia as backward and barbaric – *djāhiliyya*. In a similar spirit, historians tended to denigrate the simple folkloric nature of Bedouin music. In addition, traditions associated with pre-Islamic music might have suffered a degree of impairment as a result of their long oral transmission. The paper industry began to spread only in the second half of the eighth century, thanks to Chinese paper-makers who were taken prisoner when their army was defeated at Samarkand in 751. Thereafter the basis of Arab culture was transformed: from an exclusively oral tradition it became a genuinely literary one. The inferiority of Bedouin music was best defined by the great thinker and sociologist ibn Khaldūn (d. 1406): 'The Arabs did not know anything except poetry, because at that time, they practised no science and knew no craft. The desert attitude was their dominant trait'. He evaluates their songs as 'primary and simple types of tunes . . . that can be grasped by nature without any instruction'. While extolling the merits of classical poetry, ibn Khaldūn remarked that it was 'a small drop in the ocean of sound harmony' (Rosenthal 63: II, 401–402).

This having been the intrinsic quality of their music, Arab poetry served as a point of departure in the development of music before and after the advent of Islam.

The *djāhiliyya*

The Muslims call the period preceding the advent of Islam *djāhiliyya,* which means time of ignorance and backwardness. The same period, however, saw the flourishing of highly sophisticated poetry on the elevated level of discourse that marks the Golden Age of Arabism. It was the epitome of artistic achievement, the measure of Arab learning and the perfect expression of Arab wisdom. As this poetry was recited orally in public, the magic power of the spoken word bestowed the pleasure of sound and rhythm on its listeners. Some of its basic attributes continued to prevail long after the advent of the new faith.

The prevalent genre in this poetry – the *qaṣīda* – was based on a union of metre and rhyme, with the same rhythmical structure and rhymes repeated in each line (*bayt*) of the poem. The most distinctive unit in Arabic verse, the *bayt* was divided into two equal half-lines, or hemistiches. Every line consists of a certain number of feet. The metric system, which in essence is quantitative, is built on distinguishing clearly between the short and long syllables that comprise a word. Since Arabic philologists were not acquainted with the concept of syllable they adopted the distinction between quiescent and active components. For instance, the word *qad* represents a quiescent component which is equivalent to a long syllable, marked (–), and the word *laka* has two active components, equivalent to two short syllables, (marked ŭŭ). There are eight basic rhythmic feet which combine different patterns of quiescent and active 'syllables'; each foot is represented by a mnemonic word, derived from the root *f'l.* For example, the feet *fā'ilun* combine a sequence of quiescent–active–quiescent 'syllables' or long–short–long (–ŭ–). Al-Khalīl ibn Aḥmad (d. 791), a distinguished grammarian and musician who at a later period codified the metric system, assigned the graphic symbol o for an active or short 'syllable', and o / or o. for a quiescent (or long one). In this manner the feet *fā'ilun* would be o / o o / or o. o o. Thus, each of the 16 classical quantitative metres established by Al-Khalīl and designated by proper names, allocates a fixed number of feet to each line in a poem. Let us take as an example the *ṭawīl*, one of the metres favoured by the old poets and first in the Arab hierarchy. In accordance with the mnemonic words it has the following pattern: *fa'ūlun mafā'īlun fa'ūlun mafā'īlun* repeated twice (marked either: oo.o. oo.o.o. oo.o. oo.o.o. or: ŭ-- ŭ---ŭ--ŭ---). As this pattern recurs throughout the poem, its lines become absolutely symmetrical (CHAL 32: 15–18).

The defined rhythmic organization characterizing Arab quantitative metre tends to inspire rhythmic musical organization. Incidentally, the metric system soon became the model used by many music theorists when expounding the fundamentals of rhythm, including recourse to the aforementioned mnemonic words and graphic system (CHAL 32: 450-58).

Among the known classes of poetry were:

1. The short piece, *qiṭ'a,* consisting of seven or ten lines in *radjaz* metre whose basic feet --ŭ- are repeated three times in each hemistich. Pieces in *radjaz* and shorter variants were used in tribal war songs and other folk songs.
2. The *qaṣīda,* considered the highest achievement of Arabic eloquence. It has from ten to 100 lines, its standard pattern consisting of three sections, each one leading into the next.

The sections are an amorous prelude; a transitional section of disengagement, and the body of the poem containing its theme: that is, panegyry, satire, love, lamentation, glorification of the tribe, and words of wisdom (CHAL 32: 38–104). The best pre-Islamic *qaṣīdas* were the *Mu'allaqāt* (suspended poems) that number either seven or ten lines. They were called 'suspended' as it was customary to hang outstanding examples of the genre in the Meccan shrine – *Ka'ba*. These poems were chosen as the winners of poetry competitions held in the market place of 'Ukāz, near Mecca. The oldest was by the poet Imrū'l-Qays, a descendant of the ancient kings of Yemen; others were composed by the illustrious poets 'Amr ibn Kalthūm, 'Antara, Ḥārith ibn Ḥilliza, Labīd, Ṭarafa, Zuhayr, al-A'sha and Nābigha. Among the great bards were talented poetesses of whom al-Khansā' was the most celebrated; these gifted women excelled in elegiac art works, giving expression to grief in verse, song and dance (CHAL 32: 111–113).

According to the belief that prevailed among ancient Arabs, the poet (*shā'ir,* pl. *shu'arā'*), as the name implies, was thought to be endowed with supernatural knowledge and in rapport with spirits (*djinn*) from whom he received his magical powers; the *djinn* as an inspirational source re-emerged among some poets and musicians in Islamic times.

The magic of rhythm and word that epitomized classical poetry was enhanced by the chanting that underscored public recitations. This kind of recitation was given a special name: *inshād*, which originally meant raising the voice – *nishda* – from which is derived *inshād al-shi'r*, a protracted poetical recitation delivered in a loud voice. This meaning obviously gave rise to *nashīd,* a term that at a later period designated various musical forms. Originally this term also referred to the raising of the voice; its extended musical connotation probably derived from the melodious reciting of poetry in public as practised in pre-and post-Islamic times. Whether sung or declaimed, poetry was a symbol, a bond of unity between settled and nomadic tribes. It reflected the inter-tribal code of behaviour based on concepts of honour, blood-feud, jealousy over womenfolk, hospitality and defence of the weak, including women.

Generally speaking, there were three types of poetry: spontaneous poems that included short improvised pieces for dances and joyous social occasions, war songs, and ceremonial poems extolling the fundamental values of Bedouin society. The latter type generated sophisticated forms of art poetry that combined tribal and amorous aspects. The main consumers of this refined form were the upper classes in the Arab kingdoms of Ghassān and al-Ḥīra as well as in Mecca and Medina.

Music

In describing pre-Islamic music, Muslim historians, who were concerned only with their own civilization and its immediate forerunners, usually referred to the simple folk songs heard in the Bedouin encampments. One of the earliest complete and still extant works on music is the *Kitāb al-lahw wa'l-malāhī* (Book of Diversion and Musical Instruments) by the geographer Abū'l-Qāṣim 'Ubayd Allah ibn Khurradādhbih (d. 911). Part of the material in the book is presented as a dialogue between the Caliph al-Mu'tamid and ibn Khurradādhbih himself in *Murūdj al-dhahab wa ma'ādin al-djawāhir* (Meadows of Gold and Mines of Gems) by the famous historian and geographer al-Mas'ūdī, who died in 956. That the historian al-Mas'ūdī had recourse to ibn Khurradādhbih's work proves that the latter was long considered an important, authoritative source. Both sources record an anecdote describing the emergence of the first musical tunes. In the *Kitāb al-lahw* version it is said that Muḍar ibn Naẓar struck his servant's hands. The man cried out in pain: 'O my hands! my hands!' On hearing his sonorous voice, the camels were deeply moved. Al-Mas'ūdī's version reports that the same Muḍar fell from his camel and broke his hand. In his pain, Muḍar, who had a beautiful voice, cried out *yā yadāh* (O my hand!). Hearing this, the camels were impressed and invigorated. Both authors conclude that this was the origin of the first song genre, the *ḥudā'*(Shiloah 82: X, 112–16). Numerous texts repeat this story of the origin of the *ḥudā'* as well as the anecdote. As a caravan or camel song, the *ḥudā'* became identified with the *nawḥ* (lamentation or elegy). It is said that the *ghinā'* (lit. song) was derived from this rudimentary form of singing; in the Muslim era, *ghinā'* became the generic term for art music. We assume that in those early days it was loosely used as a generic term covering a whole range of songs in which the melodic and rhythmic components play separate roles.

The oldest and simplest type, the *ḥudā'*, was said to break the infinite silence of the desert, enheartening the lonely traveller and his mount. The melody of this simple song had a narrative, nostalgic character, based on a repeated melodic phrase. Other simple genres, such as songs performed during the watering of animals, were of similar character. The song sung while the animals were brought to drink seems to emphasize the importance of water in a dry area, and may have some kinship with the biblical 'Spring up, O well' (Numbers, XXI, 17), thought to be one of the oldest songs known, and most typical of ancient Israel's nomadic era.

Among the more musically developed forms were the variety of communal songs and dances that enhanced family celebrations, pilgrimages to holy shrines and to tombs of saints, as well as social evenings. On occasions that took place in the camps, male and female poet-musicians, each in his or her own group and in a pronounced nasal timbre, intoned tunes in light verses improvised on the spot. Perhaps because of their social function, those songs use many responsorial forms, the audience participating to a marked degree, singing, dancing, clapping hands and drumming. The number of 'new' melodies when compared with the frequent addition of 'new' texts was very limited. In a given genre one tune can be used for several texts.

Most of the enigmatic terms reported by later authors such as *naṣb*, *sanad-thaqīl*, *sanad-khafīf*, and *ahzādj* were probably related to the types mentioned above (Wright 132: 435–437).

The Lakhmides and Ghassānides: advent of a sophisticated musical style

In his concluding statement about the development of pre-Islamic music, al-Mas'ūdī writes:

> From the *ghinā'* Quraish (the tribe to which Muḥammad and the keeper of the Ka'ba shrine in Mecca belonged) knew only the *naṣb* (a simple song genre), until Naḍar-ibn al-Ḥārith went to the [Lakhmides kingdom] al-Ḥīra where he learned to play the *'ūd* (lute) and how to use it in accompanying art songs. Then he returned to Mecca and taught its people who consequently started to employ the *qaynāt* singers – *qayna* (a class of singing-girls) – to perform this new style'.

The *qayna*, who played an important role in the promotion of light music, were often extolled by poets and depicted as accompanying themselves on a lute called variously *mizhar*, *kirān* and *muwattar*.

The tradition related by al-Mas'ūdī touches on a crucial issue – it implies contacts between inhabitants of Arabia and the two major powers of Western Asia: the Iranian dynasty of Sassanians founded by Ardashir I in 224 AD, extending from Syria well into Central Asia, and the Christian

Byzantine empire, via the vassal Arab kingdoms, the Lakhmides and the Ghassānides.

The Lakhmides

In the third century the North Arabian Lakhmid dynasty, which had its centre in the city of al-Ḥīra, developed as an Iranian vassal state; its role was to help the Sassanians in their struggle with the Byzantine empire. The Lakhmids reached the acme of their power under King al-Mundhir III (503–554) and, like their protectors, were patrons of art and fostered Arabic poetry. Under al-Mundhir's successor ʻAmr ibn-Hind (554–569), al-Ḥīra became an important literary centre. Most of the famous poets of the time visited his court.

The Ghassānids

The Ghassānids, located in areas that are now part of Syria, Jordan and Israel, were the allies of Byzantium, serving as a buffer protecting the spice-trade route against Bedouin desert marauders. One of their kings, the Christian al-Ḥārith ibn Djabala (reigned 529–569), was instrumental in reviving the Syrian Monophysite church which taught – or was accused of teaching – that the Person of Jesus Christ embodied only one nature rather than two (divine and human). The Ghasānids, too, patronized Arab poets. One of them, Ḥassān ibn Thābit (563–683), who in his youth visited the court of the monarch Djabala ibn al-Ainam, has left us an interesting account reported by the tenth-century author al-Iṣfahānī in his *Kitāb al-aghāni* (Book of Songs). Ibn Thābit claims to have seen and heard ten singing-girls, five of them Byzantines, who performed songs of their country to the accompaniment of the *barbaṭ* (lute), and five from al-Ḥīra who sang their native songs. Arab singers used to come from Mecca and elsewhere to amuse the monarch.

Thus we see that in the courts of both kingdoms poets, musicians and poet-musicians such as the bard al-Aʻsha, known as *al-ṣannādj* (the 'harpist') brought the message of classical poetry to the Lakhmids and Ghassānids; with them pre-Islamic culture attained its highest development. From these centres, lyrical encomia in tribute to the fascinating charm and artistry of songstresses heard at court and in taverns were brought back to Mecca, Medina and the market-places.

The Sassanians

Music in al-Ḥīra flourished under the direct impact of the highly refined and strictly organized art music of the Sassanians. We have fairly rich information about the music in their Zoroastrian state church. Indeed, the earliest native Persian sources relating to music, musical life, instruments and names of celebrated musicians of this period have survived; significant echoes of this literature resounded in later Arabic works. The emerging picture indicates that music and musicians enjoyed an exalted status at the imperial court. The founder of the dynasty, Ardashir I, is reputed to have established an administrative system under which the king's entourage comprised seven bodies of officials, one of which included musicians. Thus it is altogether clear that the musicians in the Sassanian court occupied an elevated status in the king's retinue and were represented in the three hierarchic classes of courtiers. The important personage in charge of the curtain that separated the king from his ministers was also responsible for determining when and what to sing. To a large extent, this same hierarchical system would later be adopted by the 'Abbāsid caliphs in their courts. Such high rank conferred upon musicians found interesting expression in the credo of the communist-like Mazdakite movement. Named after Mazdak (489–531), it gained widespread popularity among the lower classes. Believing in the dualistic Zoroastrian religion (the struggle between the forces of good and evil for control of the world), the movement considered music to be one of the four spiritual powers surrounding the God of light, a hierarchy reflected on earth in the dominion of the king.

Among the known musicians referred to in the Sassanian source, the most famous was Barbad, court musician to King Khusrow Parwiz (reigned 590–628). He became legendary for his exceptional creativeness and fabulous virtuosity. He is credited with the invention of the seven *khosrovania* (systems or modes attributed to Khusrow the king) as well as the 30 characteristic melodies and 360 short compositions corresponding to the days of the week, month and year respectively. This important modal theory that goes back to the seventh century, as well as anecdotes extolling Barbad's achievements, were often cited in later Arabic writings, where he was sometimes referred to as Barbad and sometimes as Fihlīz. The author of *Kitāb al-aghānī*, for instance, relates an anecdote praising the rare virtuosity of Fihlīz which enabled the celebrated musician to play a lute that had gone badly out of tune while he was away (Barkechli 101).

As was the case in earlier Iranian periods, the Sassanians cultivated dance as a form of art. Iranian dancers, who had long been in great demand in India and China, maintained their reputation under Islam, despite the radical change in attitude toward all forms of dance; the treatise on art dance included in *Murūdj al-dhahab* by the famous Arab historian al-Mas'ūdī who died in 956, (Shiloah 356) is entirely founded on the dance tradition of the Sassanians (see Chapter 11). Another testimony refers to the Umayyad Caliph al-Walīd who wrote to the governor of Khorasan (Persia) asking him to send a group of female dancers to Damascus.

During this period instruments and instrumental music attained great perfection. Depictions of harps, lutes, shawms, trumpets and drums appear on rocks, in wood-carvings, ceramics, and iconographical sources.

2 The Rise of Islam

Muḥammad, founder of Islam, was born *circa* 570 AD in prosperous Mecca where the more settled population, influenced to some extent by both Judaism and Christianity, possessed an aura of *ḥilm* (urbanity). A great deal of the prestige and prosperity enjoyed by Mecca was undoubtedly due to the *Ka'ba* – the shrine. This small cube-shaped building with the celebrated black stone set in its south-east corner was said to have been built by Adam in replication of a celestial archetype. Under the powerful tribe of Quraish, the lords of the *Ka'ba*, the shrine had been elevated to the status of an Arabian pantheon, venerated by Arab tribesmen who came there to worship and to trade. Muḥammad belonged to the dissident Hashimite branch of the Quraishi clan; his prophetic message and revelations met with resistance among the Quraish leaders. In 622 AD he and his followers were forced to migrate to Yathrib, later called Medina (city) of the prophet. The migration (*hidjra*) of Muḥammad and the founding that same year of the Islamic community (*al-umma*) mark the beginning of the Islamic era. Thanks to his ability, strong personality and enthusiastic followers, in less than two years Muḥammad became the supreme leader. After Mecca had been subdued and the Meccans assured that their city would not suffer discrimination under the new religion, the way was open for the spread of Islam.

Following Muḥammad's sudden death in 632, Abū Bakr was elected as *khalīfa* (successor); he and his three elected successors: 'Umar (634), 'Uthmān (644) and 'Alī (656), were known as *rāshidūn* (Orthodox caliphs). Under their leadership the tribes summoned to the banners of Islam launched a formidable series of conquests. Within 12 years, the armies of Islam took possession of Syria, Iraq, Persia, Armenia, Egypt and Cyrenaica. At the same time, however, the growing dissension between the followers of the third caliph 'Uthmān and those of the fourth, 'Alī – Muḥammad's son-in-law – gave rise to the great religious parties that still exist: the *Sunnī* (originally followers of 'Uthmān) and the *Shī'ī* (who originally supported 'Alī).

Development of a new musical style in the cities of Ḥidjāz

Soon after the far-flung, rapid conquests of Islam, the two holy cities of Mecca and Medina, which were concentrations of political and religious power under the Orthodox caliphs' austere regimes, began to develop into important centres of rich musical life. This activity was instrumental in establishing the foundations of the future Great Tradition and was associated entirely with celebrating a life of pleasure. An aristocratic élite, enriched by booty and an influx of great wealth, avidly sought luxury and amusement best expressed in music and song. High society was thus indulging in a kind of escapism to help cope with the anxiety caused by the sudden dramatic changes. Another determining factor in the development of the new style was the presence of thousands of slaves who had been sent to Ḥidjāz; undoubtedly, there were many qualified artists and talented musicians among them. They brought their arts and crafts into captivity with them, transplanting the refined cultures of the conquered peoples. The combined circumstances of urbanization, economic expansion, a growing passion for music on the part of the Arab élite class and the presence of talented artists proficient in the arts of their previous cultural milieu, gave decisive impetus to the crystallization of a new art music suited to the new aspirations and values. Patronized and generously rewarded by the élite, the best singers and instrumentalists could thus demonstrate their finest achievements.

Despite the vehement attacks of the strict theologists, Medina became a centre of fashion, elegance, frivolous poetry and exciting music. Referring to this paradoxical development in the two holy cities, Pellat writes: 'Whereas one might expect the places where the Prophet had lived to produce a form of religious poetry paralleling the pious activities of their inhabitants, what the literature brings us is the celebration of a life of pleasure' (Pellat 28: 144). In fact the new religion does not seem to have been a source of inspiration for those who first adhered to it, except perhaps in folk creativity that is unknown to us. Patriotic, heroic or Islamic songs were non-existent in this period, and all energies were invested in one favourite theme – love. Love was sung in countless ways with the aim of stirring a whole gamut of feelings. This love poetry, set to appropriate melodies, had roots in the amatory prelude (*nasīb*) of the pre-Islamic *qaṣīda*. But the changes affecting the ancient poetry had repercussions not so much on its structure as on its content.

In this respect it should be remembered that the celebrated poets were still the Bedouins, whereas most of the musicians belonged to the conquered nations and naturally had less feeling for Bedouin culture. Consequently, though they endeavoured to satisfy their patrons' taste, the musicians were more open to change and to deviation from familiar musical norms. Then too, they could have influenced the transformation of Bedouin poetic themes into urban themes. On the other hand, there is no doubt that the support and encouragement of the idle amusement-seeking aristocracy played an important role in this development. It is interesting to note that the lion's share of patronage was extended by emancipated women of high society, who at that time were mixing freely with the opposite sex. Not yet totally cloistered, cultivated patronesses endowed with fine literary taste transformed their houses into salons where eloquence and extemporaneity reigned, and the greatest poets and musicians were encouraged to display their talent, competing with one another.

The salon was known under its Arabic appellation *madjlis,* which means both meeting-place and the session held there. This type of *madjlis,* was comparable to the Sassanian model but lacked its defined protocol. Regular entertainment sessions were organized, the assembled people giving themselves up to *ṭarab* (emotion and delight) evoked by the songs. Hence, at the salon the musician was an indispensable personality, capable of stirring the most blissful passions. Moreover, in addition to possessing a musical gift, he was perceived to be an agreeable conversationalist with a lively mind, and occasionally was a skilful poet.

It should be noted that most of the musicians, protégés of the Grand Ladies, belonged to the class of freemen-clients – *mawla* (pl. *mawālī*). The status of client was given to non-Arab Muslims by the noble tribes with a view to integrating them into the level of society that formed the Arabian ruling class. This was an extension of the principle of 'clientship' which had been practised by tribal society in pre-Islamic Arabia.

Many well-known female and male musicians of early Islam were *mawālī.* They were of varied origin, but most were Persians. After gaining their freedom, at least two of the known female musicians, 'Azza al-Maylā' (d. ca 705) and Djamīla (d. 720) established salons of their own in the manner of the high society patronesses. All Arab biographical sources concord in extolling 'Azza al-maylā's beauty, her supple waist and graceful walk, because of which she was called *al-Maylā'*. She belonged to the class of freed slaves and had great innate musical talent, enhanced by a superb voice and impressive skill in playing musical instruments. 'Azza studied with the songstresses Rā'iqa, Sīrīn and Zerneb from whom she learned the repertory of old Arab songs. She also learned Persian airs from Sā'ib Khāthir and Nashīṭ, both renowned performers of Persian music. Combining old and new in her art, 'Azza was called 'queen of singers' by her contemporaries (Caussin de Perceval 88: 401–409).

Djamīla was also a freewoman and, like 'Azza, was extolled not only for her high artistic achievements, but also as educator of celebrated male musicians. One of Djamīla's famous pupils, Ma'bad (d. 743), son of a negro, said of her: 'in the art of music Djamīla is the tree and we are the branches'.

Djamīla's pilgrimage from Medina to Mecca was the occasion of a great musical event which contemporary accounts commented on extensively. Her highly colourful cortege included all the principal musicians of the time, as well as 50 singing-girls. It is said about one of her distinguished pupils, ibn 'Ā'isha, who possessed a voice of extraordinary quality, that he so ravished the crowd attracted by his singing that the cortege was detained for a long time. On the way back to Medina there were three days of musical *fêtes* during which the travellers were regaled with songs of entertaining character that may not have been altogether compatible with piety (Caussin de Perceval 88: 453–545). They were probably very different from the proclamations and functional folkloristic songs typical of those performed during earlier pagan pilgrimages to the shrine of *al-Ka'ba*. Ibn Khaldūn (d. 1406) described that pre-Islamic chanting, generally called *tahlīl*, as *taghbīr* (religious cantillation).

The galaxy of musicians of this period includes such famous names as ibn Misdjaḥ who, after a *voyage d'étude* to Persia and Byzantium, proceeded to reform the art of music; his pupil ibn Muḥriz, who also studied with 'Azza al-Maylā'; Ṭuways, who claimed to have been the first male musician under Islam, and al-Gharīḍ, an effeminate artist (*mukhannath*) who had been taught by women to sing elegies and was known for his charming, heart-rending artistry. The particular attributes distinguishing the two latter musicians are significant in that they imply the emergence of a new type of artist, probably rare or entirely unknown in the pre-Islamic period. Here we find reference to the first male musician and then to the effeminate quality of a singer, due to his having been taught by songstresses. Since the latter was not an isolated case and the sources mention a class of effeminate artists known as the *mukhannathūn* (Farmer 95: 44–45), it may be assumed that the *qyayna*s art exerted a notable influence on this class of male musicians. Moreover, Farmer claims that 'during the "Days of Idolatry" music as a profession was for the largest part in the hands of the women-folk and slave girls, at any rate in al-Ḥidjāz and the peninsula generally'; he adds that the male professional musician 'was quite common in Persia and al-Ḥīra, whilst in Byzantium and Syria he had had a place from time immemorial' (Farmer 95: 44).

These musicians and others may be looked upon as contributing to the crystallization of the new art in which the Persian element was predominant. It is very likely that during this phase Persian influence was an extension of the living tradition in al-Ḥīra. In addition to the fact that Nashīṭ and Sā'ib Khāthir first sang in Persian, and 'Azza al-Maylā' as well as others learned from them, al-Ḥīra probably continued under Islam to be a musical centre that provided a model for musicians, poets and their patrons.

The bulk of our information on the music and musicians of this period comes from the monumental work: *Kitāb al-aghānī* (Book of Songs) by the

Arab historian, man of letters and poet Abū'l-Faradj al-Iṣfahānī who was born in Iṣfahān (Persia) in 897 and died in Baghdad in 967. The Book of Songs is one of the most celebrated works in all Arabic literature. By the author's own testimony he spent 50 years on the 21 volumes of this monumental work. It contains a collection of poems from the pre-Islamic period to the ninth century, all of which had been set to music, and includes biographical details about authors, composers, singers, instrumentalists and writers on music (Sawa 143: 20–32). He indicated the origin of each song and its melodic and rhythmic mode, referring to the modal theory of the *aṣābiʿ* (fingers) and *madjārī* (courses) attributed to the famous musician Isḥāq al-Mawṣilī (Farmer 453; Shawqi 73; Rajab 116; Shiloah 303: 30). The Book of Songs constitutes a mine of information on the history of music, musical life and musical aesthetics; the author also quotes long passages from earlier writers whose works have not been preserved for posterity. In addition to his *Kitāb al-aghāni*, al-Iṣfahānī wrote ten other works related to music, all unfortunately lost.

Distinctive concepts and aspects of the developing art

The urbanization that characterized the transitional period, as well as the high status enjoyed by musicians at that time, brought about the intensification and increased importance of musical activity which consequently started to develop its own means of expression.

An intimate link between poetry and music was still considered essential, but a shift took place in the balance between them. The earlier melodious recitation, chanting and simple melodic setting gradually evolved into more refined and sophisticated musical features that affected the quality of melody and rhythm as well as the instrumental accompaniment. Melodic instruments, mainly from the family of strings, were added to the rhythm marked by the drums and *qaḍīb* (a wand that stressed beat). However, the freedom henceforth given to the musician's imagination remained bound to restrictions imposed by the poetic text and its structure. The quest for an ideal new balance between the musical and poetic components therefore gave rise to conflicting tendencies leading to a quarrel, as it were, between *ancients et modernes*.

In this quarrel, the repercussions of which would be felt at a later period, musicians of different artistic views and temperaments were involved. Thus, for instance, the disagreement between Ibn Suraydj and al-Gharīḍ concerned the question of varying degree of refinement (*ẓarf)* which in its extreme form could subjugate poetry to music and disturb an ideal balance (Bencheich 124: 130). As against al-Gharīḍ's art which represented modernistic refinement with its predilection for light rhythms, Ibn Suraydj with his heavy style advocated the old ideals, expressed in his recourse to the archaic *ramal* rhythm that was similar to the *radjaz* and camel-song *ḥudā'*. His approach is summarized succinctly in his definition of an excellent singer. Mālik ibn abī'l-Samaḥ (d. ca 754) asked Ibn Suraydj what the qualities of the perfect musician were. He replied: 'The musician who enriches the melodies, has long breath, gives proper proportions to the measures, emphasises the pronunciation, respects grammatical inflections, holds long notes for their full value, separates short notes distinctly and, finally, uses the various rhythmical modes correctly; such a musician is considered perfect'. Mālik ibn abī'l-Samaḥ added: 'I reported this statement to Ma'bad, who declared: "If there were a Koran of music it could not be otherwise."' (Caussin de Perceval 88: 497–500).

The background to the quarrel was the adoption during this period of a more artistic musical genre called *al-ghinā' al-mutqan,* the introduction of which is ascribed to the Persian slave Nashīṭ. One of its innovative aspects seems to have been the application of rhythmic patterns and constructions that were independent of the poetic metre. Therefore, the question of degree of closeness to the metric principle and the possibility of blurring it was decisive.

Another important aspect was the growing awareness of the potential expressiveness of the human voice and its multiple nuances. There is good reason for the musical nomenclature that assigns various meanings to the term *ṣawt*; it may designate sound, voice or, occasionally, song; in the living traditions of the Persian Gulf, *ṣawt* indicates a musical genre. In pre-Islamic times, knowledge of the voice emitting magical sound through the myriad intonations of song, or even in solemn recitation, was instinctive. Now, however, the knowledge of voice became a major concern for both sacred and secular music. Symbolizing the life force and serving as a medium of communication between human beings, Arab authors considered the voice a reflection of the human soul's mysteries and feelings. For the mystics it symbolizes divine life, and puts man in vibrating resonance with the celestial and universal. A rich palette of timbres enables the musician's voice to express his diverse moods and the subtlety of his being (Shiloah 345: 92–93). Such an approach found particular emphasis in the recurring discussion and definition of the 'beautiful' voice (*al-ṣawt al-ḥasan*) in the literature of both secular and sacred music.

The powerful effect of a beautiful voice may even have medical properties. The Andalusian writer and poet ibn 'Abd Rabbih (d. 940), in the chapter on music in his encyclopedic work *al-'Iqd al-farīd* (The Unique Necklace), refers to the experts in medicine who claim that a beautiful voice infiltrates into the human body and flows in the veins, causing purification of the blood, delighting the heart and elevating the soul.

It should be remembered in this respect that song, combining both poetic and musical expression, was considered the summit of music's hierarchy. Hence, *ghinā'* (singing) became the general designation of art music, while the term *mūsīqī*, borrowed from the Greek, was reserved for the science of music. The primacy thereby given to vocal music has been a distinguishing mark of Arabian music throughout its history.

As noted previously, music is identified with the sweet tenderness of love, an emotion it expresses, imprinting its effect on the listener's soul. Among the various definitions of a perfect musician one finds: he who is moved and causes his listeners to be moved. Thus, in addition to a beautiful voice, tenderness and keen sensitivity often recur as basic qualities required from an excellent musician. An apt example is the anecdote praising the sweetness and tenderness that were characteristic of ibn Djāmi''s songs. It is said that the famous musician Isḥāq al-Mawṣilī, despite his good nature, suggested that the Caliph Hārūn al-Rashīd falsify a letter announcing the death of ibn Djāmi''s beloved wife who dwelt far away in Ḥidjāz. This would stir his profound love and elicit manifestations of his sorrow. The suggestion was accepted and such a letter was prepared. Upon learning the sad news, ibn Djāmi' was deeply afflicted. Confronted with his great suffering, the compassionate caliph told him that the letter had been sent in jest and asked him to sing. Ibn Djāmi' then sang in a manner that expressed all the pain he had experienced (Caussin de Perceval 88: 526–546).

The emotion stirred in the listener's soul, as well as its various effects, is called *ṭarab*. The term that had originally been used to designate emotion elicited by the fine recitation of a beautiful poem, was applied to the feelings roused by music. As such, it refers to a wide range of emotional reactions, from subtle delight to strong excitement and even ecstasy. In the course of time the term became synonymous with music and its derivatives: *muṭrib* (musician) and *'ālāt al-ṭarab* (musical instruments) (Shiloah 68: 213–214).

Voluptuous musical and poetic pleasure was a notable characteristic of Sassanian music, designated by a term that in Arabic is equivalent to *lahw* (pastime, amusement). The *lahw* in Arab literature is usually linked to its derivative *malāhī*, which figuratively signifies musical instruments, and in a broader sense is used as synonymous with music. Thus, associatively we reach an important concept that links art music to entertainment. This bond was largely exploited in attacks against music led by theologians and jurists – an important theme that we shall discuss in detail below.

A study of the sources reveals that the term *malāhī*, either alone or linked to *lahw*, appears in the title of eight musical works, seven of which appeared in the third/ninth century. It is interesting to note that, parallel to the positive use of these terms in connection with art music and instruments, they acquire the negative connotation of diversion or forbidden pleasure in the context of tracts opposing music. The work that became a model for following generations is *Dhamm al-malāhī* (The Condemnation of Malāhī) by Ibn abī'l-Dunyā (894). This is a diatribe against music, musical instruments, games and other kinds of amusement. The sharpest barbs in this attack were directed against the stringed instruments, which in the eyes of the theologians symbolized the new art and contributed to enhancing a life of pleasure (Robson 50). The two major instruments that paralleled the advent of professional musicians were the *ṭunbūr,* a long-necked lute and the *'ūd,* a short-necked lute that in the course of time became the symbol *par excellence* of Arab art music, being endowed with the title 'king of instruments'. The literature of that time describes this classical instrument as having four strings; the names given to them are indicative of the cultural fusion that occurred: the Persian names *zīr* and *bamm* were assigned to the first and fourth strings, and the Arabic *mathna* and *mathlath* to the second and third.

The foregoing can be represented as an equation: art music = urban milieu = prosperous and idle aristocracy = entertainment. This equation corresponds roughly to the theory advanced by the great historian and sociologist ibn Khaldūn. The following significant statement appears in the chapter on music of his *Muqaddima* (Prolegomena): '. . . It should be known that singing originates in a civilisation when it becomes abundant and (people) progress from necessities to conveniences, and then to luxuries. . . . It is in demand only by those who are free of all other worries and seek various ways of having pleasure' (Rosenthal 63: II, 401).

3 The First Dynastic Caliphate

In 661 the elective, orthodox caliphate came to an end, and the house of Umayya, the first dynastic caliphate, emerged; it moved the seat of the caliphate from Arabia to Syria. Under Umayyad rule the Islamic empire extended eastward as far as the borders of India and China, westward to the Atlantic and Pyrenees. In this new environment, which bore the impress of political and administrative traditions of the ancient Middle Eastern empires, the ground was propitious for the establishment of an imperial governmental system based essentially on the model of the empire Islam had superseded.

The first Umayyad caliph Mu'āwiya (661–80), knowing the value of maintaining a façade of princely living, shrewdly turned his capital Damascus into a centre of pomp and power. Being of literary and artistic tastes, Mu'āwiya opened the court to the most talented poets and musicians. Most of the succeeding Umayyad caliphs continued in the same vein; they encouraged and patronized poets and musicians and treated them with generous bounty. Those who particularly need mention in this respect are: Yazīd I (680–83), al-Walīd I (705–15), Yazīd II (720–24) and al-Walīd II (743–44); they were all absorbed in pleasure and had a passion for music. Known for his libertinage, Al-Walīd II was himself a poet, excellent singer, performer on the *'ūd* (lute) and drum as well as composer. One of his songs includes the following verses:

> There is no true joy but lending ear to music
> or wine that leaves one sunk in stupor dense.

Eulogy, that had been a distinguishing mark of pre-Islamic poetry, was firmly re-established as a major genre. The musicians were encouraged to set eulogies and other poems to music with the aim of augmenting their potency. As a result of the official support of the rulers and the nobility, the considerable reward showered on the musicians and their emulation of each other, the development of the new art was accelerated and it acquired a higher status. The rulers followed some of the procedures of the Sassanian kings, introducing among other customs the use of a thin curtain (*sitāra*) separating them from the performers. Some of the best known musicians turned their residences into schools of music where rich *dilettanti* came to develop their aptitude and where, in particular, talented slave girls who belonged to notables and wealthy men were trained in music and other cultural matters. Indeed the houses of the rich *bourgeoisie* competed with one another in attracting the best musicians to enhance their gatherings in which the singing-girls who lived in the house participated.

In the face of such eagerness for pleasure and things of the world, it is easy to understand the vexation of Muslim rigorists, who began to include music among the 'sins' of the Umayyads.

Whereas in Ḥidjāz contact with more advanced civilizations was usually via captives integrated as *mawālī* into the community of Muslims, in the new political and intellectual centres this contact expanded and became more direct. It accelerated and influenced the process of acculturation of both conquerors and conquered, due to the ethnic mixing resulting from increased intermarriage between Arabs and non-Arabs. Many qualified non-Arab converts were also indispensably involved in the administration and control of the conquered lands. In performing their duties, these converts had to comply with a stringent condition: they had to have good command of the official language – Arabic – even acquiring an expressive, artistic style exceeding the level of ordinary speech. On the other hand, the conquerors, despite their feeling of racial superiority as God's elect, were notable for a shrewdly pragmatic attitude toward adapting to and compromising with the cultures of the conquered. They thus abetted the transformation of the still disparate multinational and multireligious cultures into one unified and universally accepted civilization. In this spirit occurred improvements and innovations in the realm of music that affected song and singing techniques, melodic and rhythmic systems, instruments and instrumental accompaniments. The way was thus opened for the establishment of a Great Musical Tradition that crystallized under the Umayyads and reached its zenith under the 'Abbāsids.

The Great Musical Tradition

We borrow the concept of the Great Tradition from the study by R. Redfield and M. Singer, *The Cultural Roles of Cities*. This study propounds ideas concerning the part played by cities in the development, decline or transformation of cultures. A Great Tradition, according to the authors, 'describes a way of life and as such is a vehicle and standard for those who share it to identify with others in a common civilisation' (Redfield and Singer 386: 220). However, to envisage the transformation of what were by inference 'Little Traditions' of non-urban cultures into an explicit and systematic 'Great Tradition', is not an entirely applicable approach to the Great Musical Tradition that emerged in urban centres under Islam. Considering its syncretic nature, one should rather speak of skilful fusion of selected elements from the previous Great Tradition of the conquered peoples with elements from the homogeneous Arab 'Little Tradition'. This synthesis, effected in a spirit of compromise, resulted in successful 'new arrangements' so conceived as to be considered by both conquerors and conquered as outgrowths of the old, as well as representative of orthogenesis. However, unlike other well-known Great Traditions, the Islamic musical tradition did not achieve the perfect systematization that would facilitate identification and definition of an official art with universally acceptable, immutable norms. That is due primarily to the particular unity of religious and secular in Islam. The caliphs, commanders of the faithful who held absolute sway, were in the main enthusiastic supporters of art music, making it an integral part of their regal life and a model of inspiration for the upper strata of society. Yet, obligated as they were to obey the rules of Islam and the sacred law (*sharī'a*) which regulated social as well as religious life, they were in open conflict with the '*ulamā*', the learned expounders of Islamic religion and law who by virtue of their function were able to exercise considerable influence. Religious authorities from the beginning adopted a puritanical attitude, stressing scriptural revelation and observance of rules more than feelings. They disapproved of art music used to pass time, for entertainment and sensual pleasure. This disapproval diminished the prestige and distinction necessary for it to be accepted as an official systematized art.

It is interesting to note that the kind of systematization achieved in subsequent generations was rather of a philosophical, speculative and mathematical nature, owing to influence exerted by Greek theoretical writings translated into Arabic. The science of music to which these theoretical works were applied was classified among foreign areas of knowledge. Incidentally, in extolling music as a force for harmony and morality, philosophers were frequently led to denigrate its use as an agent with an intoxicating influence; in so doing they inadvertently gave support to similar views as expressed in attacks by religious authorities.

None of the sources provides us with pertinent analysis of the process that led to the establishment of what we have called the Great Tradition. However, reading the scattered evidence carefully, we do find references to the borrowing of elements from conquered cultures, and to the idea of fusion whereby the borrowed elements were grafted upon an Arabic tradition that had a character of its own. The best illustration of this is the account included in *Kitāb al-aghānī* concerning ibn Misdjaḥ (d. ca 169/785).

Often honoured as father of the new music under Islam, ibn Misdjaḥ travelled to Syria and Persia learning the theory and practice of Persian and Byzantine music; he incorporated much of this acquired knowledge into the Arabian song. Although he adopted new elements such as foreign musical modes, he rejected traits that were not suitable for Arabian music (Farmer 235: 236–239). Whether the account is authentic in all details or not, it can symbolize the process of fusion, the spirit of selectiveness and the very important process of Arabization that seems to have acted as a catalyst. In view of the great role played by Arabization as a general unifying factor in Islamic civilization, some clarification is needed, particularly as regards the musical aspects.

Arabization

It should be noted that during the epoch being discussed, there was a growing attachment among the urbanized conquerors to the past, to the things one carries in one's heart and wishes to preserve. This feeling was probably the source of the idea of Arabization as a means of cultural unification. One of its most prominent manifestations was the quest for and use of linguistic purity. This was a concern shared equally by readers of *Qur'ān*, grammarians and musicians. The trend was particularly notable at that time in the new garrison towns of Baṣra and Kūfa (Iraq). Unlike the old urban centres, these towns were dominated by Arabs who continued to lead a predominantly Bedouin life. Their famous market-places, similar to the pre-Islamic one in 'Ukāz, attracted admirers of classical poetry, philologists and musicians, flocking there to listen to poetry recited by *rāwīs* (reciters) who had prodigious memories.

The *rāwīs* institution goes back to the pre-Islamic era when every self-designated poet had his *rāwī*, who accompanied him everywhere, memorized his poems and handed them down to others, along with the circumstances of their composition. In this manner, the *rāwīs* ensured, to a large extent, the survival of ancient poetry through oral transmission, until the art of writing came into use at the beginning of the eighth century. After the advent of Islam, the *rāwīs*, instead of being attached to individual poets, began to form an independent class. Henceforth, the *rāwī* is a skilful reciter carrying in his memory thousands of various ancient verses. For instance, the well-known Ḥammād al-Rāwiya is said to have recited to the Caliph al-Walīd II, in one sitting, 2900 *qaṣīdas* by poets who flourished before Muḥammad. However, Ḥammād was accused by his contemporary Mufaḍḍal al-Ḍabī of having introduced verses of his own into genuine compositions. In any event, the surviving *rāwīs* were eagerly sought because, for practical reasons, during this period pre-Islamic poetry became a subject of great interest. The necessity of explaining the Sacred Text gave birth to the sciences of grammar and lexicography; philologists naturally found the best material in the pre-Islamic poems. The same held true for the musicians and the first readers of *Qur'ān* who sought to establish the rules of solemn recitation based on poetic language and its rendition. The musical expression that underlined the recitation through rhythmic accentuation, phonic relief, intensity and the establishment of the desired equilibrium between ideals and emotional values on the one hand and music and rhythm on the other, became a model for the experts in koranic reading and for composers of songs. The expressive, artistic manner of speech in many ways combined cantillation, art song and rhetoric (Talbi 209).

Their affinity is revealed in certain common terms. The root *gny* from which *ghinā'* (art song and music) is derived, signifies to sing and also to prolong the voice in psalmody and chant, to enrich or to renounce. The root *lḥn* from which *laḥn* (melody, rhythm and mode) is derived, also means to chant in a manner pleasant to the listener's ear, elucidating a word, singling out its meaning and also making mistakes in recitation. Arab lexicography gives the verb *laḥḥana* the meaning of lecture that stirs emotion or is rendered emotionally. A synonym for *laḥḥana* is *gharrada*; the *taghrīd* (noun of action) is defined as a sound including emotion. The fact that, according to the above definitions, the verbal expression generates the musical, should not be considered as merely a lexicographer's speculation or interpretation; it actually reflects one of the fundamental concepts of the Great Musical Tradition. The juxtaposition of poetic features, recitation with its vocal nuances and timbres, cantillation, composition and performance of art song was indeed decisive for the desired process of Arabization; concomitantly, it also gave rise to the *tadjwīd* that codifies the various rules of cantillation, and establishes art song norms of composition and performance. *Tadjwīd* and art song were united in their search for impressive richness of vocal emissions and timbres designed to ensure linguistic purity in the transmission of both sacred and poetic texts (Shiloah 345: 91–92). Ibn Suraydj's definition of a perfect singer, cited above, illustrates this tendency and concern clearly; we shall return to this in Chapter 4.

The refinement and proliferation of the Great Tradition under the 'Abbāsids

In 750 the Umayyads were overthrown by the 'Abbāsids, another branch of the prophet's family, who in 763 moved the capital from Syria to Iraq where they constructed a new city on the west bank of the Tigris – Baghdad. The advent of the 'Abbāsid's caliphate (750–1258) was rather more than a change of dynasty; it affected all aspects of life and culture in the Muslim empire. Due to the Persians' significant role in the revolution, they were privileged to occupy a prominent place in the new regime; their influence was strongly impressed on both government and culture. They played an important part in the new cosmopolitan group of Muslims of many races and they were decisive in the gradual termination of Arab racial supremacy within the empire. However, Arabic remained the official language and the medium of communication in government, commerce and education; it therefore remained a vital factor in the evolving culture.

The end of wars of conquest was another important factor that henceforth permitted much energy to be poured into economic expansion, trade, and the development of a sophisticated and diversified urban culture. The caliph exercised his authority through a vast and growing bureaucratic organization and, with a view to fostering cultural progress, he established the model of giving substantial support to a galaxy of *literati*, scholars, philosophers and talented artists. As a result von Grunebaum writes, 'the mere warrior ceases to be the ideal type, and the pen holds precedence over the sword' (von Grunebaum 19: 22). He added that, as a result of the changes, broad areas of psychological experience manifested themselves or became articulate, evoking more expansive and varied emotional experience in a richer and more comprehensive pattern.

The society wherein relationships were no longer dictated by tribal affiliation and there was a weakening of clientship bonds as well as rapid economic growth, gave rise to a wealthy class of genuine bourgeoisie. Like the sovereigns who adopted the model of the Sassanian court and ceremonies, the nobility and the new class of wealthy people became ardent patrons of the arts. During this epoch Baghdad attained its greatest magnificence as a city in which the arts and all areas of knowledge blossomed. Though it was not unique in this respect – many other great cities enjoyed splendid social life and intense cultural activities – Baghdad overshadowed all the others. This was particularly true under the brilliant, luxurious reigns of Hārūn al-Rashīd (786–809) and his son al-Ma'mūn (813–833), who was considered a great patron of learning.

Baghdad attracted many talented men from the provinces who were eager to make their mark on the new capital and to win fame and fortune. In this connection it should be noted that at the time the migration of artists, including of course musicians, was a major unifying factor. Indeed, whether seeking fame and better economic prospects, or invited by one of the many artistically inclined rulers, the migrating Arab and non-Arab artists helped both as performers and teachers to disseminate the new style and its fundamental norms. This extensive spread and diversification of the Great Musical Tradition via wandering artists differs from the process that marked the first phase of the new style in Ḥidjāz, where the new ideas came from non-Arab musicians brought in under coercion.

The ideal of learning

The portrait of the perfect musician as reflected in sources of the early 'Abbāsid period, known as the Golden Age, can be summarized as follows: he is gifted with an extraordinary natural bent for music, combining creative power and great ability as a performer; he is a singer and plays one or more instruments; he can write prose and verse; and, finally, he is a man of wide culture. The latter attribute conforms with the general deference to learning and the newly accepted standards for all human activities. This approach was outstanding particularly among the administrative secretaries – *kuttāb* (pl. of *kātib*) – who, during the first period of the 'Abbāsid caliphate, played an important role in the development of various aspects of culture, including music. The *kuttāb* controlled the economic and political management of the state and filled the high administrative positions. They were a dynamic element of the Persian-born establishment but tried to assimilate within the Arab aristocracy. This highly educated élite encouraged and patronized poets, *literati* and musicians; not a few of them also acquired fame in the world of letters and music. One of these, the qualified musician Yūnus al-Kātib (d. ca 765) who was a highly esteemed poet, wrote the first book on music: *Kitāb al-aghānī* (Book of Melodies).

The career of the *kātib* presupposed a solid education in all branches of knowledge, providing him with the intellectual tools necessary to accomplish his highly varied tasks. Hence a well-educated *kātib* signified a man imbued with the cultural pluralism reflected in the work known as *adab,* which integrated Arabic, Persian, Indian, Syriac and Hellenistic humanistic features. His cultural openness led him to embrace new literary and poetic orientations that to some extent disengaged themselves from the bonds of the traditional style.

The famous writer ibn al-Muqaffa' (d. ca 760), who started his career as a *kātib* under the Umayyads, was the author of a special cultural synthesis meant for the use of secretaries. He is chiefly remembered for his rendition in Arabic of a collection of the old Indian Fables of *Bidapai.*

For his Arabic translation, Ibn al-Muqaffa' used a Pahlavi, or Middle Persian adaptation of a work in Sanskrit made in the time of the Sassanian king Anushirvan Khusraw I (531–579). The work in its Pahlavi adaptation took its title *Kalilag u Dimnag* (rendered in Arabic *Kalīla wa-Dimna*), from corrupt forms of *Karataka* and *Damnaka*, the Sanskrit names of two jackals who dominate the opening narrative. The book was intended to instruct princes in the laws of polity by means of animal fables. The Arabic version of *Kalīla wa-Dimna*, one of the oldest prose works in the Arabic language, is regarded as a model of elegant style; it was also one of those books which inspired many Muslim artists whose miniatures illustrate a considerable number of manuscripts (CHAL 35: 50–53). Many such works are classified as *adab* (CHAL 35: 16–30), a term that embodies various meanings. It is applied to works of diverse character and form. Charles Pellat distinguishes three basic types: 'According to whether it aims to instil ethical precepts, to provide its readers with a general education, or to lay down guiding principles for members of the various professions' (CHAL 35: 83). The prolific prose writer and freethinker al-Djāḥiẓ (d. 868–9) is considered the originator of the genre and practitioner of all three types. It is noteworthy that the various early references to music are all conceived in the spirit of the *adab* genre.

Literary and anecdotal writings on music

Many of al-Djāḥiẓ's works include either random or more consistent references to music, primarily non-technical in nature. In his masterpiece *Kitāb al-ḥayawān* (The Book of Animals), an anthology based on animals and leading rather unexpectedly into theology, metaphysics, sociology, and so forth, there are several thoughtful observations on music, performance practice, musicians, the place of music in human and animal life, characteristics of sounds and the effect of music on the souls of men and animals. His treatise *Risālat al-qiyān* (On the Singing-Girls), a favourite topic with authors in the first centuries of Islam, became a model defending this class of female musicians and the ideal they embodied in their synthesis of music, beauty and love. The treatise also deals with famous singing-girl favourites of Persian and Arab kings. The classification of musicians who belong to a professional class, and the rank they occupy in it, constitutes the topic of his other treatise *Ṭabaqāt al-mughannīn* (Book of the Classes of Singers). Al-Djāḥiẓ's recourse to the term *ṭabaqāt* is quite significant since it was in common use with respect to different branches of knowledge during that period. It made its first and foremost appearance in the framework of the *ḥadīth* (Traditions of the Prophet) which in the course of time acquired the force of law (see Chapter 4). Each *ḥadīth* is composed of a basic text, *matn*, the authenticity of which was guaranteed by a chain of witnesses. Due to the importance of the verifying details concerning the transmitters, a sizeable literature flourished which classified the transmitters into hierarchical groups, categories and generations – *ṭabaqāt*. In its application to other fields, namely to poets and musicians, the genre adopted criteria emphasizing values of rank and merit, again having recourse to a chain of transmitters. Thus, in a biographical item about a male singer, instrumentalist, singing-girl, or in the presentation of collections of songs by one or more musicians, one would invariably find a recurring pattern: a series of modular traditions or a series of events that conform to the nature of the narrative material. Each is introduced by a chain of transmitters and deals with practical details rather than general rules.

Most of the writings on music that belong to this category, including the most outstanding, The Book of Songs by Abū'l-Faradj al-Iṣfahānī, use another significant term – *khabar* and the technique associated with it, which is the oldest form of Muslim historiography. It consists, as F. Rosenthal writes,

> of a well-rounded description of a single event. . . . It does not imply any fixed point in time, nor is it ever restricted to mean an organically connected series of events. Each *khabar* is complete in itself and tolerates no reference to any kind of supplementary material. In its formulation there is preference for dramatic situation and colour as against sober fact. It is, then, primarily an artistic form of expression. (Rosenthal 26: 66)

This way of describing the distinctive traits, primacy and exclusivity of exceptional artists, tends to give the musician a kind of mythical aura.

It is regrettable that many writings of this sort by famous musicians such as Isḥāq al-Mawṣilī, Yūnus al-Kātib, Yaḥya al-Makkī and his son, ʻAmr ibn Bāna and others, have not come down to us. We can however, learn something about them from the quotations included in *adab* and encyclopedic books, and particularly from the best and most comprehensive work of this kind – the *Kitāb al-aghānī* (Book of Songs) by the historian and man of letters Abū'l-Faradj al-Iṣfahānī. The inclusion of discussions on music and musicians in historical, encyclopedic, educational and entertaining writings of the epoch meant, above all, that in a society avid for knowledge the study of music became obligatory for every learned person; music was one of the topics frequently discussed by people in all walks of life. Moreover, such inclusion reflects the great passion of the ruling class, the nobility and wealthy people for music itself as an indispensable means of expression and communication. One may assume that these circumstances were among the major factors that led to the hostile attitude toward music adopted by not a few theologians and legalists, a topic that will be dealt with below.

The growing interest in written or oral discussions about music found expression in anecdotal and literary form, refined discussion at banquets, as well as in systematic, scientific treatment, which will be dealt with in Chapter 5.

The musician and his public

The courts of the caliphs and other sovereigns, the palaces of the nobility and the sumptuous houses of the wealthy bourgeoisie served as major venues in which the musician could display the best of his art. He was encouraged and highly rewarded by patrons fond of music and poetry, fine connoisseurs who were often proficient musicians themselves, such as the Caliph al-Wāthiq (842–47) and the prince Ibrāhīm ibn al-Mahdī – who after a brief reign (816–818) distinguished himself as one of the most important musicians of the age. The largest number of famous musicians simultaneously associated with one patron included 18 celebrities attached to the court of the legendary Caliph Hārūn al-Rashīd (786–809), not to mention the dozens of singing-girls who helped enhance the court's musical life. According to social conventions modelled after Sassanian etiquette, when performing, most of the musicians were separated from the caliph by the curtain *(sitāra)* mentioned above. Whenever an outstanding musician succeeded in stirring the caliph's emotions and curiosity, eunuchs would come from behind the curtain to learn more about the song and its performer, who would eventually be invited to a *tête-à-tête* with the caliph (Neubauer 114).

Such instances are recounted in a highly colourful manner in the *Kitāb al-aghānī*. According to one of them, ibn Djāmi' (d. 805) came all the way from Mecca to the court of Hārūn al-Rashīd in Baghdad in the hope of improving his economic situation. On the way he was charmed by the singing of a black woman who balanced a water jar on her head. He proceeded to spend all the money he had so that the woman would teach him the song. Before taking leave of him, she predicted that the song would bring him a thousandfold the amount he had spent on it. This prophecy comes true: after he repeats the song three times from behind the curtain, the Caliph Hārūn invites him to a *tête-à-tête* and favours him with a reward equal to a thousand times the amount he had given the black woman. This story may also symbolize the sweet tenderness that distinguished his art, which one of his contemporaries likened to honey (Caussin de Perceval 88: 526–546). As a court musician he was soon at odds with Hārūn's chief courtier and boon companion (*nadīm*) Ibrāhīm al-Mawṣilī (d. 804).

As regards the *nadīm* or drinking-partner, outstanding poets and musicians often became their patron's boon-companions as well as their entertainers and confidants, particularly when a patron developed a real interest in music or poetry. In works discussing the etiquette of wine and wine-parties, which necessarily included singing, playing on instruments and occasionally dancing, one finds the *nadīm's* code of conduct. There are also specialized treatises like the one written by the poet and astrologer Abū'l-Fatḥ Kushādjim (d. 971): *Kitāb adab al-nadīm* (Book on the Conduct of the Boon Companion). The fifth chapter in this treatise, which deals with the correct behaviour of a boon companion and features related to companionship, concerns listening to music in company and the resulting soul-satisfying pleasure.

Ibrāhīm al-Mawṣilī, who was elevated by Caliph Hārūn al-Rashīd to the foremost position and became his boon companion – hence his nickname, al-Nadīm – was considered the most versatile musician, singer and instrumentalist; he was also a prolific composer. He had 900 compositions to his credit and, inspired by superhuman spirits, the *djinns*, he introduced the rhythmic mode of a light character *al-mākhūrī* (Caussin de Perceval 88: 546–566). Ibrāhīm al-Mawṣilī was involved in an artistic controversy with ibn Djāmi‘, in which other court musicians took part. Among the supporters of Ibrāhīm were his son Isḥāq al-Mawṣilī (d. 850) and his brother-in-law Zalzal (d. 791), known as *al-ḍārib* (the instrumentalist) because as a lutanist he had no equal; Zalzal is also credited with the invention of a new type of *‘ūd* called the *‘ūd al-shabbūt*, and with defining the neutral third that was given the name *wusṭa* Zalzal. The supporters of Ibn Djāmi‘ included Mukhāriq (d. ca 845), a freed slave of Hārūn who won high favour in the courts of four caliphs, and ‘Aqīd. The argument between the two rivals represented a confrontation between two tendencies, the Ancients and the Moderns; it became more vehement with the two famous rivals of the next generation, Isḥāq al-Mawṣilī and prince Ibrāhīm ibn al-Mahdī.

Isḥāq is considered the greatest musician of all time and is regarded as the archetype of the perfect, widely cultured musician. In addition to his merit as singer, instrumentalist, composer, theorist and musicographer, he wrote poetry and prose. He was also so well-versed in jurisprudence and philology that Caliph al-Ma’mūn allowed him to appear in his court as an *adīb* (a master of *adab* matters) in the company of writers and scholars. It is said of him that he was outstanding in any assembly of scholars, excelling in entertaining conversation (Bencheikh 124). According to the sources, Isḥāq was very jealous of his art and rarely agreed to disclose its secrets. Due to his powerful influence, his opinion about the music of other artists was usually decisive for their career. The Moroccan man of letters and biographer al-Maqqarī (1591–1632) reports a colourful story that will be discussed in the section on Andalusian music in Chapter 6, according to which Isḥāq's highly gifted pupil had to leave the court, and Baghdad as well, as a result of his master's jealousy. As a typical product of the Baghdad milieu, Isḥāq also wrote as many as 39 works on music, most of which belong to the biographical type; they were dedicated to many famous musicians known up to his time. Unfortunately they have all been lost (Farmer 3: 3–5).

Baghdad-born prince Ibrāhīm ibn al-Mahdī (779–839) was also one of the most accomplished and cultured musicians of his day. Although he belonged to the ruling class, he behaved and dressed like a genuine ‘bohemian’, passing much of his time in the company of poets, musicians and singing-girls. This ‘romantic’ figure became the leader of a modernistic school that attempted to free itself from the bonds of the strict rhythmic and melodic rules laid down by the Ancients. He advocated more artistic freedom and the giving of wider scope to the creative imagination. This was the very ground on which the controversy broke out between him and Isḥāq, who was committed to defending the values of the ancient and classical style. The latter reproached the modernists for having opposed the old school's ideal of simplicity and promulgating a new style marked by a tendency to exuberant or excessive embellishment of the melodic line. Consequently, it was argued, the full significance of the text was blurred. The singer and lutanist 'Allūyah or 'Allawayh, whose grandfather was among the Persian prisoners taken by the Umayyad caliph al-Walīd and freed by him, sided with ibn al-Mahdī although he had been taught music by Isḥāq himself. He is said to have introduced characteristic Persian elements to his music. Another supporter of the modernists, 'Amr ibn Bāna, son of a noted *kātib* (scribe), was also among the former pupils of Isḥāq who was strongly supported by the lutanist Zalzal. The controversy found expression in various forms: challenging competitions were held, there were song tournaments with prizes for the winners and debates took place on aesthetic and technical questions. The argument is the subject of numerous accounts appearing mainly in *Kitāb al-aghānī*.

In a dialogue between Isḥāq and 'Allawayh, the latter informs Isḥāq that his rival, Prince Ibrāhīm ibn al-Mahdī, reproaches him for having neglected to use a device called *taḥrīk al-ghinā'* (embellishing the song while composing). He emphasizes that the beauty of a song consists in its embellishment; the *taḥrīk*, says ibn al-Mahdī, provides the song with many notes. To this allegation Isḥāq replies: 'May we only transmit that we have learned in the same manner that it was taught to us'. In this way Isḥāq expressed his opposition to the excessively lavish embellishment of the melodic line. Another story relates that Isḥāq sent a messenger to taunt his rival ibn al-Mahdī for having pronounced a certain word incorrectly while performing a given song. Immediately guessing the nature of the mission, ibn al-Mahdī said to his guest: 'Tell him you do this (make music) academically while we do it for entertainment and harmless fun'.

This kind of argument took place not only in the caliph's court but in the dwellings of important personages of the ruling class and in the houses of the rich bourgeoisie as well. In the framework of literary sessions, banquets and sumptuous celebrations that brought together poets, scholars and notables, the musician was king; he enhanced the gathering with the finest fruits of his art and participated in the elegant conversation. In many instances, this was the occasion for him to present a first audition of his songs and to teach them to the singing-girls owned by the master of the house (Farmer 100).

The *qayna* (female musician) was an institution in itself, that in some ways dominated the musical scene of the age. As a rule she was a beautiful, gifted slave-girl whose owner endeavoured to provide her with the best education possible with a view to eventually selling her for a very high price. She received her musical training from the most famous musicians of the day; the same held true for all other branches of culture. Hence the accomplished *qayna* could extemporize verses, conduct gracious conversation with guests and gladden their hearts with songs and instrumental music (ʻAmrūchī 109; ʻAllāf 117).

Commerce in female musicians flourished and wealthy people would pay a fortune to acquire one or more of them. The greatest number of these girls was to be found in the caliph's courts. It is said that a hundred of them used to sing and play for the Caliph Hārūn; some of them were freed and gained access to very exalted social status. The prolific writer al-Djāḥiẓ provided a model of an accomplished *qayna* in a treatise dedicated to the singing-girls. He argued with those who adversely criticized possession of these girls and the gatherings with them spent in drinking and listening to music. The female-singers excelled as instrumentalists, particularly on the long-necked lute, the *ṭunbūr*, which was considered effeminate in character. They also distinguished themselves by the rapidity with which they learned and memorized new songs. This might have been the origin of Iṣḥāq's saying: 'Music is like a book that men conceive and women register'. It could also explain the stories according to which musicians subjected to an overwhelming, usually nocturnal, inspiration by *djinns* (supernatural powers) urgently summon their female-singers, to dictate the songs before they vanish from memory.

Many *qaynāt* gained celebrity and were greatly admired for their accomplishments. Among the well-known female singers, mention should be made of ʻUrayb who acquired a tremendous reputation and received the highest praise from Iṣḥāq al-Mawṣilī. Then there was ʻUbayda, surnamed the *ṭunbūrīyya* because of her outstanding artistry on the *ṭunbūr;* Iṣḥāq said: 'In the art of *ṭunbūr* playing, anyone who seeks to go beyond ʻUbayda makes mere noise'. Shāriya was purchased, trained and freed by Ibrāhīm ibn al-Mahdī, and later became his wife. Badhl was admired by Iṣḥāq al-Mawṣilī for her prodigious memory and the fabulous number of songs she retained. Her pupil Danānīr, a gifted poetess and musician who had also been trained by Ibrāhim al-Mawṣilī and his son Isḥāq, was the author of a Book of Songs (Stigelbauer 125).

Finally, brief mention should be made of the class of *ẓarīf* which indicates an elegant, cultivated type of poet and musician who seeks refinement (Bencheikh 124). Although not part of the privileged class, these mostly effeminate individuals of modest extraction were admitted everywhere and admired by all.

4 Islam and Music

The *samāʿ*

The term *samāʿ*, which means both hearing music and the music that is heard, inspired a rich and variegated literature, essentially polemical in character. It deals with the admissibility of music from a legal, theological and mystical point of view, and is therefore concerned with sacred and religious music. In this it contrasts with *ghināʾ*, which is associated with secular art music yet is compatible, to a large extent, with folk music or other simple forms such as the old Bedouin camel song, the *ḥudāʾ*.

In the interminable debate about the *samāʿ*, legalists, theologians, spiritual leaders, custodians of morality in the cities, the *literati* and Ṣūfī leaders all participated. The debate elicited views that varied from complete negation to full admittance of all musical forms and means, even dance. Between these two extremes we can find all possible nuances – some, for instance, tolerate a rudimentary form of cantillation and functional song, but ban all instruments; others permit cantillation and add the frame-drum but without discs, of course forbidding all other instruments and all forms of dance, and so on. The mystic orders, for whom music and dance were an essential part of their spiritual and ecstatic exercises, were seriously concerned with the debate and participated ardently in the polemics. As a result, the controversy touches on a wide range of musical topics sometimes with a view to refuting them and at other times attempting to justify their adoption.

Reference to the sources of law

No legalist or religious authority can prohibit or authorize something *a priori* by personal decision; such an authority is obliged to base his arguments either on direct references in sacred writings, or on analogy. The first and most sacred source in our case is the *Qurʾān*. Both those in favour of music and those opposed had recourse to it, which is perplexing because nothing in the *Qur'ān* concerns music explicitly. Hence, the parties to the dispute address themselves to exegetes who suggest either implicit prohibition or admissibility. Thus, the opponents claim that 'diverting talk' in XXXI, 5 – 'There are some men who buy diverting talk to lead astray from the way of God' – refers to music.

Commentaries vary about the meaning of to 'buy diverting talk' (in some versions called a 'ludicrous story'): for some it meant the acquisition of singing-girls, others interpreted it as giving preference to song and musical instruments rather than to the *Qur'ān*. In turn, those who approve of music claim that verse XXXV, 1 – 'He increases in His creatures that which He wills' – refers to a beautiful voice, a theme discussed at length in the literature about sacred and secular music. In verses XXXIX, 17–18 the lines 'So give good tidings to my servants who listen to *al-qawl* (the spoken word) and follow the fairest of it' are interpreted as referring to singing; incidentally, *al-qawl* is still used in folk music to designate singing of folk poetry.

Recognizing the weakness of these arguments, disputants found stronger support in the authoritative source of the *ḥadīth* (Traditions of the Prophet). By the last year of Muḥammad's life it was already a pious custom, when two Muslims met, for one to ask for news (*ḥadīth*) and the other to respond with a saying of the Prophet or an anecdote about him. After the death of Muḥammad this custom was perpetuated and the term *ḥadīth* continued to be applied to sayings and stories that were no longer new. In the course of time a *ḥadīth* acquired the force of law. The most authoritative collections became models and rules for living; they were compiled by al-Bukhārī (d. 870) and Muslim (d. 874), both collections having been called *al-Ṣaḥīḥ* (The Genuine). Al-Bukhārī, for example, limited the number of traditions he compiled to 7000, chosen from among 600,000 (CHAL 32: 271–278).

Antagonists would cite different *Qur'ān*ic verses in support of their respective theses but, when they had recourse to the *ḥadīth,* opposite conclusions are quite often drawn from the same tradition. Here are two examples connected with the Prophet's wife, 'Ā'isha. As two young girls performed a then-popular song about *Bu'ath* (a famous battle at Medina between two prominent tribes, that took place in approximately 615) in 'Ā'isha's house to the accompaniment of a drum, Abū Bakr (the first caliph) entered and rebuked them for singing. Muḥammad, who sat aside, wrapped in his robe, uncovered his face and said: 'Let them alone'. Another *ḥadīth* referring to the same event says that Abū Bakr rebuked 'Ā'isha and called the singing of the young girls: *mizmār al-shayṭān* (reed-pipe of the satan). Concerning the *mizmār*, a companion of the Prophet, ibn 'Umar, claimed that he had seen Muḥammad plugging his ears when he heard the sound of a *mizmār.* Referring to these Traditions, those favouring music see proof of its admissibility in the fact that Muḥammad listened to the young girls singing and, above all, in his reaction to Abū Bakr's rebuke. Some of those who object more strenuously to music interpret this use of the verb 'singing' as simply raising the voice while reciting a poem; others invoke the folk character of the tune and the festive occasion to which it relates. Another tradition handed down by 'Ā'isha says that Muḥammad declared selling, buying, and teaching the singing-girl (*qayna*), as well as the very concept of the *qayna*, unlawful. The great theologian, jurist and religious reformer Abū Ḥāmid al-Ghazzālī (d. 1111) says that this *ḥadīth* refers only to singing-girls in taverns. Among the Traditions used to defend singing are the following sayings of Muḥammad: 'Allah has not sent a prophet except with a beautiful voice, and Allah listens more intently to a man with a beautiful voice reading the *Qur'ān* than does the master of a singing-girl to her singing'.

In connection with the recurrent reference to the beautiful voice, that of King David the psalmist is often praised. He was endowed with the most beautiful voice ever created by God. When he raised his voice and sang psalms, birds came to rest on his head and listen, domestic animals and wild beasts were drawn together peaceably; they all succumbed to its charm. Seeing that all tamed and untamed animals yielded to the magic of David's singing, *Iblīs* (Satan) summoned his hordes and ordered them to devise something equally powerful. They then invented the reed-pipes and lutes, modelled on David's 70 melodies. David's singing is also invoked in a tradition extolling the most beautiful voice of the angel *Isrāfīl* (Serafil). It is said that when Serafil sings, the inhabitants of the heavens all silence their prayers and praises, the trees bloom and doors tremble, the birds and *houris* sing; this divine chorale is created to delight those who abstained from musical pleasure on earth – but it in turn is overpowered by the voice of David (Poché 226).

The controversy surrounding music alluded to in the foregoing examples covered the entire gamut of themes found in the relevant traditions and in teachings of protagonists of the four great legal schools. In the course of the controversy an ideological system – or systems – evolved that has been the focus of debate in numerous texts. Interestingly, some of the doctrinal views are closely related to those expounded in rabbinical disputations.

The ideological background

When we undertake to discuss the relations between music and a religious doctrine we should consider the fact that the concept of music is integrated into the relevant system of thought. In our case this means that music does not act independently according to its own fundamentals, nor is the musician free to pursue the dictates of his imagination. Religious music is therefore subordinated to or interacts with ideas that are generated by what Max Weber called the theological meaning of man's conceptions of himself and his place in the universe, conceptions which legitimize man's orientation in and to the world and give meaning to his various goals (Parson 212). According to Max Weber, from whom we borrow some basic theoretical ideas, a system is a result of rationalization, and this rationalization comprises normative control or sanction and a conception of motivational commitment which includes both 'belief' and practical commitment – in the sense of readiness to put one's own interests at stake in the service of ideas. In the context of rationalization, Max Weber emphasizes the importance of a sacred written tradition, of sacred books which are subject to continual editing and complex processes of interpretation, and which tend to become the focus of specialized intellectual competence and prestige in the religious field and, on the cultural level, of rationalized systems of religious doctrine.

In light of the above, a look at the meaning and place assigned to music in the normative system of Islam would confront us with conflicting attitudes on the doctrinal level; we would also become aware of obvious conflict and friction between the ideology expounded by prominent religious thinkers and the actual reality that gave birth to the Great Tradition and encouraged it to flourish. Hence, the question on which we should focus our interest is, above all: do the tension, friction and conflict emanate from the concept of music itself, or are they determined by other factors?

As a point of departure let us take the listener's views or feelings regarding music. In all the sources one finds repeated belief in the overwhelming power of music, which exerts an irresistibly strong influence on the listener's soul. Acting as a kind of charm, music produces either sensual pleasure or extreme excitement, and its maximal effect can send the listener into an emotional, even violent paroxysm. As a result of this untamed power, or spontaneous effect, the listener loses control over his reason and behaviour and is consequently governed by his passions. This quasi-somnambulistic state is considered to be in contradiction to the exigencies of rational religious precepts (Shiloah 82: XXI).

One of the earliest treatises prohibiting music is *Dhamm al-malāhī* (The Book of the Censure of Instruments of Diversion) by the theologian and jurist Ibn Abī'l-Dunyā (823–894). It contains a violent condemnation of music, which the author considers a diversion from devotional life; he extends the prohibition against music to all games and pleasures. Multiple variations on this fundamental approach are to be found in the corresponding literature, such as: listening to music is forbidden because it takes one's mind off the devotional life and removes one's thoughts from God; or, a person who deviates from those laws that bring one nearer to God, will find himself ever more remote from Him (Robson 50). The jurist Ibn al-Ḥādjdj (d. 1336) who considered 'knowledge' and 'action' to be inseparable, based his *Madkhal al-*

shar' al-sharīf (Introduction to the Venerable Law) on the principle that an act of worship devoid of true intent cannot accord with the law.

Ibn Djamā'a (d. 1388), who considered music and dance earthly pleasures, claimed that they led the religious man to error and perdition. The theologian and legal consultant ibn Taymiyya (d. 1328) went so far as to state that anyone who practised *samā'* was an infidel and polytheist. The fiercest of these attacks were directed against the Ṣūfīs for whom *samā'* was an essential element in the performance of spiritual exercises, as we shall see later. The *samā'* of the Ṣūfīs, claimed ibn Taymiyya, had an intoxicating effect that excluded all possibility of rational thinking; were it important to religion, the *Qur'ān* would have recommended it. Condemning the practice of shouting during the celebration of *dhikr* (see below), the jurist ibn Bisṭām (d. 1685) concludes that it is better to worship with quiet humility because, he says: 'you are not calling on deaf ears and not invoking a remote God'. The inspirational power the mystics attributed to music presupposes the use of man's inner resources for his spiritual experience rather than dependence on the words of the scriptures which, according to the supporters of the 'nomos' doctrine, should be the only way leading to the true knowledge of God and all He has created. Describing the *samā'* as a source of corruption, many authors ascribe its origin and effect to Satan's evil forces. One of the harshest but most cogent expositions of this theory can be found in *Talbīs Iblīs* (The Devil's Delusion) by the jurisconsult and preacher ibn al-Djawzī (d. 1200). Ibn al-Djawzī claims that music is basically a temptation of the devil who dominates the soul and makes it a slave to passion. Music intoxicates, provoking worldly passions and sensual pleasures usually associated with other indulgences such as drinking to excess and fornication. In his exposition, ibn al-Djawzī also discusses the origin of music as elaborated by various authors who preceded him.

Before proceeding to a discussion about the origin of music, it should be noted that not all theologians were so intransigent. In actual fact not a few adopted a rather more subtly shaded approach in their writings, an approach in some cases reminiscent of that followed by certain mystics. An example is the kind of summary proposed by the traditionalist and jurisconsult Ibn Radjab (d. 1392) in his book *Nuzhat al-asmā' fī mas'alat al-samā'* (Pleasure of the Ears Concerning the Practice of Listening to Music). The author speaks of two categories of music: one discusses it as an amusing pastime, the other as a means for consolidating faith in God and purifying the heart. The singing of any poem that has frivolous content and is intended to stir sensual feelings must be forbidden, even if it is not called *ghinā'* (art or secular song); songs with serious and ascetic contents are harmless. Turning to musical instruments, Ibn Radjab rejects the views of learned people who distinguish between those instruments that cause pleasure and those that do not: he considers all instruments forbidden (Farmer 204; Roychudhury 208).

The origin of music

To a great extent the theory of music's origin, to which chroniclers, legalists and men of letters refer, is based on an interpretation of Jewish exegetic literature dealing with antediluvian stories of creation. Those exegetic sources are to be found mainly in the Midrash, which is a particular genre of rabbinic literature. The Midrash is a sort of anthology, a compilation of homilies consisting of comments deduced from a literal interpretation of scriptural texts. Thus, in commenting on the story ascribing the invention of music to Jubal: '. . . the father of them that play upon the harp and the organ' (Genesis 4:21), the exegetic sources try to resolve the difficulty that arises from confining the invention to the harp and organ; they claim that Jubal invented all the musical instruments in the world and was the first to introduce the art of singing. The proximity of Jubal's human invention to Tubal-Cain's invention of all bronze and iron artifices has given rise to speculation on the association of music with weapons or with metallic sounds, denoting the intrusion of the devil. Another association relates music to depravity, which is said to have been a definitive cause of the flood. The Jewish Midrash says: 'The sons of Cain indulged in amusements and their behaviour was reported to the inhabitants of the mountains, the descendants of Seth. Some of these latter went down to the plain attempting to extract from the sons of Cain their depravity, but alas they themselves were ensnared by beautiful women, music and intoxicating liquors' (Friedlander 200: 158–163).

Drawing upon these exegeses, Muslim sources transferred the invention to Jubal's father Lamech and associated it with the *'ūd,* an instrument of major importance in Arabic music. More or less during the same period, the ninth century, at least six authors included versions of the story ascribing the invention of the *'ūd* to Lamech. All of them used the motif of the relationships between the human body and musical instruments, a motif found in many myths of creation. One of these is reported by al-Mufaḍḍal ibn Salāma (d. 830) in his *Kitāb al-malāhī* (The Book of Musical Instruments) on behalf of his contemporary, the historian Hishām ibn al-Kalbī (d. 819). It tells that Lamech, who lived a long life, had no children until he reached an advanced age. Ten years before he died a boy was born to him, and he was extremely pleased. But the boy died when he was five years old, and Lamech grieved sorely. So he took him and hung him on a tree and said: 'His form will not depart from my eyes until he falls in pieces, or I die.' Then the boy's flesh began to fall from his bones until only the thigh, with the leg, foot and toes, remained. So he took a piece of wood, split it, made it thin, and began to arrange one piece on another. Then he made a sound chest to represent the thigh, a neck to represent the leg, a peg-box the same size as the foot, and pegs (*malāwī*) like toes; and to it he attached strings like the sinews.

Then he began to play on it and weep and lament, until he became blind; and (Lamech) was the first who sang a lament. What he made was called a *'ūd* because it was made from a piece of wood (*'ūd*). This story, with more or fewer details, is reproduced in many later sources (Shiloah 82: II, 400–401).

The reference to Satan's interference and treachery has been pointed out in *Qiṣaṣ al-anbiyā'* (The Stories of Prophets) by both al-Kisā'ī (unknown author) and al-Tha'labī (d. 904). They record the tradition according to which Iblīs (the devil or Satan) inhabits wastelands and unclean places such as ruins and tombs; he recites poetry, his call to prayer (*'adhān*) dwells in the *mazāmīr* (pl. of *mizmār* – reed-pipe), his snares are women and his drinks are intoxicating liquor. These themes are repeated in numerous *ḥadīths* and polemical texts.

In sum, when music is considered a spell inspired by the devil, it calls into question the basic concept of a transcendental divinity with absolute rule over the world and the deeds of men. Acting as an irresistible force, music can be identified with magical powers that oppose religious elements which presumably have an independent capacity to guide man's destiny. These arguments would imply rejection of all music. In fact, the total prohibition involves only art music, which displays man's vanity and primarily furthers interest in mundane, worldly concerns. It does not apply to folk tunes or by extension, to certain forms used in religious music which are not regarded as music *per se* and are not even called music. This is due to the predominance of the text in religious or folk music, wherein the combination of sounds is relegated to a secondary role, or is a device mainly designed to support the words and enhance their meaning.

The best and most efficient of all these forms is one that avoids regularity of rhythmical organization and remains entirely subordinated to the division, fluidity and accents of the text. This form, which we now call cantillation, for present purposes concerns the solemn reading of the *Qur'ān* and the call to prayer (*'adhān)*. Cantillation is or should be much closer to recitation or tensed speech than to song, as strictly understood. It may be ornate and melismatic, but these embellishments should not be independent; they rather emanate from the textual content. This also implies that the reader should look upon himself as bearer and servant of the message contained in the text.

The tadjwīd

In view of the importance of correct and careful solemn recitation of the *Qur'ān*, from the very beginnings of Islam its study and establishing its norms became an urgent task. Under the term *tadjwīd* (embellishment of recitation) that developed as a branch of the koranic sciences, a remarkable system evolved regulating cantillation with respect to the laws of phonetics, correct diction and rendition of the sacred text. As to the musical aspect of the recitation, a *ḥadīth* says that the prophet has recommended reading the *Qur'ān* with melodies of the Arabs from the Najd region in Arabia, avoiding Jewish and Christian melodies. The reference is to the simple pre-Islamic forms of *ḥudā'* and *rakbānī*. With respect to the pause, one of the major traits of koranic cantillation, abū'l-Faḍl al-Rāzī claims that it was inspired by classical poetry's rules of prosody. Thus the recourse to old Arab tunes and classical poetry may suggest a transvaluation, as can be inferred from the statement of ibn al-'Arabī (d. 844): 'The Prophet wanted the *Qur'ān* to become their exclusive passion in replacement of the *rakbānī* that they were accustomed to sing' (Talbi 209).

The *tadjwīd* comprises two basic components: the first, called *taḥqīq,* is of a phonetic nature, that is to say, each consonant is precisely established by giving it its full value. The second is the *tartīl,* which concerns the proper rules of recitation, the flow, force and emphasis. The *taḥqīq* analyses in detail the formation of the diverse consonants in the organs of the phonic apparatus (lungs, nostrils, tongue, lips, etc.) and the way the learned reader should accurately produce corresponding qualities and nuances. To this end, two major factors are of great importance: the degree to which the mouth is opened and the mode of articulation. Thus, each sound is endowed with its proper quality denoting the technical device of its emission and the phonetic nuance heard upon its pronunciation. It is recommended that the pronunciation be without effort or exaggeration. As to the *tartīl,* it concerns the rendition of the text as a whole in a form comprehensible and moving for the faithful. The rendition of the text with adequate rests and pauses, for instance the appropriate alternation of rhythmic flow with the rests and pauses, and well-regulated respiration, is considered a fundamental condition of cantillation. Thus, in observing the rules of the *tadjwīd,* the reader becomes the spokesman and interpreter of the official version of the text as well as of its inherent message. The five essential conditions required from a knowledgeable reader are: the *istirsāl,* prolongation of the sound without the reader letting his voice fall; the *tarkhīm,* softening of a sound without losing the intonation; the *tafkhīm,* amplification of a sound; the *taqdīr al-anfās,* control of respiration; and the *tadjrīd,* perfect command of the transition from a stressed sound to a weak one and vice versa. To this, one should add the beautiful voice frequently referred to in this context. In treating the voice and its multiple qualities, the authors of the *tadjwīd,* and those of the *ghinā'* who followed in their footsteps, propose an impressive classification of nuances including dozens of terms and definitions (Boubakeur 214; Shiloah 345: 91–93).

The melodic line of the cantillation proceeds gradually in ascending and descending phrases interspersed by frequent silences marking the appropriate pauses. It is interesting to note that the *tadjwīd* does not concern itself explicitly with the regulation of the musical parameter as such, because it considers it simply non-existent. It becomes the subject of argument when it exceeds the role assigned to it. This happens when *qirā'a bi'l-alḥān* (recitation with melodies) occurs, and is broadly interpreted by some readers – that is to say, when art singing procedures are applied. The writer and poet ibn 'Abd Rabbih (d. 940), in the section on music of his work *al-'Iqd al-farīd* (The Unique Necklace), tells an anecdote of a man who was arrested by the police because he sang in the mosque compound. A noble man from the Quraishi tribe manages to release him by testifying that he was only reciting the *Qur'ān* in a beautiful manner.

The adoption of art singing becomes more and more widespread, rousing furious attacks on the part of the Andalusian legalist and traditionalist al-Ṭurṭūshī (1126 or 1131) who violently disapproved of borrowing art melodies and procedures in reciting the *Qur'ān*. He maintained that it violated the spirit of the sacred text and distorted the rules of the *tadjwīd*. It should be noted that such excesses were exceptions; throughout the ages, the norms of *tadjwīd* were usually more or less observed (Schneider 206; Pacholczyk 217; Faruqi 219, 228; Nelson 225). (See music examples 1–6 on pages 213–20.)

The 'adhān

The *'adhān* (call to prayer) was instituted by the Prophet himself between 622 and 624. The first muezzin was an Abyssinian *mawla* named Bilāl (d. 641), considered also the first martyr in Islam, having withstood fierce tortures intended to persuade him to abandon Islam.

Originally the call to prayer was a simple announcement in the street or from a roof top. It quickly grew into an ornate, moving chant issuing five times a day from the height of a minaret. Numerous testimonies confirm that several muezzins were employed in a single mosque. In the seventeenth century a guild of muezzins was established in Turkey and it adopted Bilāl as their patron. The call to prayer comprises a sequence of short phrases performed in a chanting tune that varies from country to country. In some places the tune embodies an interesting melodic line shaped like an arch and attaining maximum density at its highest point.

These two forms of cantillation constitute the only compulsory mosque music. In addition there are optional hymns meant to enhance festive occasions, in particular the celebration of the prophet's anniversary. The situation is different with the mystic orders, to whom the following section is devoted. (See music examples 7–9 on pages 221–9.)

The mystic dimension

The first manifestations of mysticism as an organized movement go back to the middle of the second century of Islam (eighth century). The movement assumed different forms in different countries. The divergent tendencies accorded with the spirit – infusing teachings of distinguished theosophists who founded the various schools. Islamic mysticism is known as Ṣūfīsm, a word derived from the Arabic for wool (*ṣūf*) and originally applied to certain ascetics who wore clothes of coarse wool as a sign of penitence and the renunciation of worldliness. The aim of Ṣūfīsm, like that of other mysticisms, is to enter into a closer relationship with God, and to realize a union with the Godhead. To achieve this end, 'they tried to loosen their ties with the flesh and the world, to purge the soul of qualities that had been declared evil or that seemed to them to be concerned only with earthly well-being' (Meier 213: 117).

Little by little the earliest Ṣūfīs' simple piety and gospel of love were transformed into an elaborate mystic doctrine, in which music occupies a prominent role. The concept of music developed by the mystics brings us back from flights of theological speculation to the magical version of the roots of music. The mystics advanced the idea that music is neither monogenetic nor monovalent, although their formulation was different: with regard to its origin, music oscillates between the divine and the satanic, the celestial and the terrestrial. As to its value and nature, these are determined chiefly by the listener's virtues, his degree of mystical cognition of God and His revelation. Indeed, the righteous gnostic is pervaded by keen longing for God when he listens to sweet sounds that impel him to seek the spiritual world. His soul, which originates in the world above, remembers its homeland and yearns to attain the state that would enable it to untie the knots binding it to matter, thereby facilitating mystical union with God. The soul's ascent from its earthly existence to its divine home, which signifies redemption, is symbolized in the mystical imagery of certain Ṣūfī orders by the dance, which they consider to be a manifestation of their infinite, ecstatic love of God. It is said that the dance, uprooting the worshipper's foot from terrestrial mud, transports him upward to the summit of the world (see Chapter 11). In its highest form, listening to music becomes entirely spiritual. The celebrated Andalusian illuminator Muḥyī al-dīn ibn al-'Arabī (1165–1240) who regarded himself as divinely inspired, left Sevilla in 1191 and travelled to Tunisia, Morocco, Egypt, Iraq, Turkey and Arabia. In Mecca, where he stayed for two years, he began to work on his masterpiece, *al-Futuḥāt al-Makkīya* (Meccan Revelations), in which he states that there are two categories of *samā'* – free or soundless and linked to or associated with music. The latter is of three kinds: divine, spiritual, and natural or sensual. The divine emanates from everything, is in everything and is conveyed by everything; those who attain this degree speak to God even when they converse with creatures: they listen to God because He is active in everything they hear. Spiritual audition consists of hearing with a spiritual ear how all things sing the Glory of God, seize and enjoy the significance of this cosmic song. This kind of *samāʿ* helps one to contemplate the universe as if it were an open book. The natural *samāʿ* concerns that which is actually practised by the mystics and others. As regards this *samāʿ*, there are two types of listeners: those who listen with the soul (hearing actual sounds) and those who listen with the mind. Those belonging to the second group hear the glory of God in everything, from everything and as conveyed by everything; independent of music as such, their ecstasy is expressed in a state of insensibility and immobility. Hence spiritually more advanced Ṣūfī participate in what ibn al-ʿArabī terms 'divine audition', while the less advanced, dependent upon music, participate in 'natural audition'. Much later on, the Ottoman Ṣūfī writer al-Uskudārī (d. 1628) also deals with two kinds of *samāʿ* in his *Kashf al-qināʿ ʿan wadjh al-samāʿ* (Removal of the Veil from the Aspect of Listening to Music). He characterizes them as artificial and authentic, subdividing the latter into two categories: natural and spiritual. The natural is that connected with beautiful voices and pleasant melodies (such as actual music); the spiritual is incorporated into the perception of the inner meanings of things, constituting a kind of absolute *samāʿ* reached by Ṣūfī leaders and those who have attained the highest mystical degree; in this case actual music is not needed.

On a more general level, Ṣūfī authorities refer to the question of who should practise *samāʿ*, and they differentiate between the vulgar, the novice and the true gnostic. Some of them believe that *samāʿ* should be prohibited for novices and non-initiates because on them it acts like a poison. Occasionally we find claims of lack of sincerity and recourse to artificial means to attain ecstasy. One of the earliest Ṣūfī authorities, al-Makkī (d. 996), referring to *samāʿ* used in ceremonies, states that the voice is an instrument intended to communicate meaningful ideas; when the listener perceives the meaning of the message without being distracted by the melody, his *samāʿ* is admissible.

Otherwise, when the content expresses physical love, sensual desire or vain frivolities, the *samāʿ* is pure diversion and must be banished. Al-Makkī expresses his dissatisfaction with dance and physical excitation as methods of reaching ecstasy because, he says, in most cases these are manifestations of an artificially induced trance (Ritter 207; Meier 213).

Rituals of the mystics

The mystics developed complex congregational rituals and spiritual exercises designed to send the participants into religious ecstasy (*wadjd*) (Rouget

222: 354–361). The movement was very attractive to all levels of society, but apparently above all to peasants, workers and poor people. They sought to escape from the dullness of everyday life in a heartfelt emotional religion. The most remarkable ritual was the *dhikr* (lit. remembrance) which referred to the koranic injunction: 'To remember God as often as possible'. In mystical practice, or the collective repetition of certain formulae – notably the clause of the Islamic creed, 'There is no God but God' – it marked the collective remembrance of God. The *dhikr* usually included listening to music (*samāʿ*) and occasionally dancing. However, some orders performed only the act of remembrance of God, others only music, while others practised both either separately or simultaneously. By the time the first organized ritual appeared, music and dance already played a prominent role in spiritual exercises leading to ecstasy and mystical union. One part of the ceremony involved cantillation of the *Qur'ān,* the communal recitation of religious writings, the chanting of hymns; the other part involved singing, playing musical instruments and sometimes dancing (Poché 220; Rouget 222: 361–364, 371–374).

The rich literature about the music and dance of the mystics is in part polemical and in part devoted to the rules, fundamentals and structural aspects of the ritual, as well as to its symbolic meaning (Molé 211; Gribets 231). Madjd al-dīn al-Ghazzālī (d. 1121), brother of the famous religious reformer Abū Ḥāmid al-Ghazzālī, was a master of many mystics and his name occurs in the list of initiated authorities of many modern congregations. He wrote an important treatise in defence of *samāʿ* under the ornate title of *Bawāriq al-ilmāʿ fī'l-radd ʿalā man yuḥarrim al-samāʿ* (Lightning Flashes Concerning the Refutation of those who Declare Listening to Music is Forbidden). The largest part of this treatise is dedicated to the legality of music. Two sections are of particular importance: a description of the details constituting a mystical ceremony, and a presentation of the symbolic meaning of the different elements encompassed by the *samāʿ*, for example the role of drum and flute, the role of song and ecstatic dance (Robson 50).

The most spectacular and sophisticated music and dance associated with mystical practices are those accompanying the Mewlevi's *'ayn sherif* in Anatolia (the movement is named after Mawlāna Djalāl al-Dīn al-Rūmī (d. 1273)). In their ceremony music and dance form an indivisible unit, presented by two separate groups: a large ensemble of professional singers and instrumentalists who perform from a gallery, and a large group of dancers in white gowns, black mantles and peaked caps (Ritter 201; Meier 205). The musicians' ensemble comprises numerous flutes, one or two fiddles, lutes and zithers, as well as a group of singers who also beat a variety of drums. The ceremony commences with a recitation of koranic verses and passages from the *Mathnawī* (a poetic work by Djalāl al-Dīn al-Rūmī), then the leading singer performs the *naʿt sharif* (Praise to the Prophet) followed by a series of improvizations on the flute, directly preceding the dancing (see Chapter 11). The music accompanying the ceremony was usually the work of one of the celebrated composers attached to the Mewlevis; it was closely related to Turkish art music, on which it even exerted an influence (see Chapter 7, section on the Ottoman Empire).

In certain marginal groups, the ritual might involve extravagant behaviour such as tearing one's clothing, sitting on hot coals, swallowing glass, entering into an ecstatic trance, exorcism, self-mutilation and the like (Rouget 222: 371–382, 410–428). The canonists considered the very extreme manifestations heretical, and they were condemned by many Ṣūfī authorities. In the main, marginal groups were those that had a very remote relationship to the classical standard. They included, for instance, the Moroccan community of exorcists, the *Ḥamādisha*; the Tunisian *Būrī*; the black brotherhoods *Ghnāwī* in North Africa who placed themselves under the patronage of Bilāl, the Prophet's black muezzin; the northern Moroccan *Ḥaddāwa* who wandered from place to place and imbibed narcotics; the itinerant *Qalandar* dervishes who made no public show of piety, but were only interested in being 'joyful in God'; the *Malāmatīya* in Anatolia who, to combat vanity, perversely cultivated it; and the two Kurdish religious hybrids – the group called *Ahl-i-Ḥaqq* (Men of God or Truth-worshippers) (Mokri 215) and the *Yazīdiyya* sect who did not regard themselves as Muslims and worshipped the Peacock angel (Hassan 379: 179–193).

A concluding note

This general survey of music in Islam is best concluded with the teachings of the great theologian Abū Ḥāmid al-Ghazzālī (1058–1111), religious reformer and mystic. In his authoritative work *Iḥyā' 'ulūm al-dīn* (The Revival of Religious Sciences) he attempts to integrate Ṣūfīsm and orthodoxy. His important chapter dealing with the laws of *samā'* and ecstasy, which became the model for many writers, analyses the mass of controversial opinions; al-Ghazzālī comes to the conclusion that both statutory and analogous evidence indicate the admissibility of music.

A major point in his argumentation is the idea that music and singing are means of evoking what is truly in one's heart; under their influence the heart reveals itself and its contents. This is an elaboration of the pronouncement by the famous mystic authority al-Dārānī (d. ca 820): 'Music does not provoke in the heart that which is not there'. In other words, the nature of music's influence on man very much depends on the basic intentions of the listener and the purpose for which music is used. Nevertheless, al-Ghazzālī clearly defines seven purposes for which music may be used and five cases in which its use is forbidden. Music may be used:

1. To encourage pilgrimage, but only for those for whom pilgrimage is permissible;
2. To incite to battle;
3. To inspire courage on the day of battle;
4. To evoke lamentation and sorrow – the latter being of two kinds: blameworthy and praiseworthy;
5. To arouse joy;
6. To elicit love and longing, in circumstances that permit singing and playing instruments; or
7. To evoke love of God.

Music is prohibited:

1. When produced by women under certain conditions;
2. If the instruments used are expressly prohibited;
3. When the song's contents are not compatible with the spirit and precepts of religion;
4. When the listener is ruled by lust; or
5. If one listens to music for its own sake (Macdonald 39: 219–244).

5 The Science of Music

General background

The treatment of Arabic music theory as a subject of significant intellectual value *per se* began with the process of translation of non-Arab texts, mainly Greek treatises on music. Under Caliph al-Ma'mūn (813–33), the process of accumulating and translating Greek scientific and philosophic books reached its culmination and became a well-organized activity. The Institute of Science – *Bayt al-ḥikma* – created by al-Ma'mūn and established at the huge government-supported library in Baghdad, became a centre of translation into Arabic. Among the most active translators were the Nestorian Christian from al-Ḥīra, Ḥunayn ibn Isḥāq (d. 873); his son Isḥāq (d. 911); and the distinguished mathematician and astrologer Thābit ibn Qurra (a member of the pagan community of Ḥarrān) (d. 901). Consequently, a large corpus of Greek scientific and philosophical writings was thereafter within reach of Arabic-reading scholars. The great impetus given this enterprise and the enthusiasm with which it was received by the ruling class and intelligentsia had practical reasons, such as fortune-telling, safeguarding health, determining time of prayer, the direction of Mecca, and so on; concomitantly, there was marked interest in theoretical and abstract questions.

The revitalization and cultivation of the declining Greek intellectual tradition may be regarded as a continuation of the activities carried on in the important Alexandrian school in Antioch and Ḥarrān as well as in Jundishapur (south-west Iran). The latter had been an active centre of learning in which Greek, Persian, Syriac, Jewish and Indian ideas had intermingled. In the new cultural framework and environment, as A. I. Sabra writes:

> For the first time in history, science became international on a really wide scale; and one language, Arabic, became its vehicle. A large number of scholars belonging to different nations and professing different beliefs collaborated in the process of moulding into this one language materials which had previously existed in Greek, Syriac, Persian and Sanskrit. (Sabra 29: 182–183)

One of the leading ideas found in writings of the time was the claim that one should acknowledge truth and absorb it, from whatever source it comes, always assuming that the borrowed material could and would be improved. Thus, while profoundly respectful of their Greek mentors, the best of the Arab scholars were not slavish followers of their Greek predecessors but regarded them as fallible human beings subject to criticism and correction. The question of their indebtedness to the Greeks was a recurrent subject of lively discussion among Muslim scholars. Under all circumstances, the influence exerted by the translated Greek writings was felt particularly in those branches of learning defined by Muslim scholarship as 'foreign sciences', in contradistinction to 'native sciences'. The latter encompassed the traditional or religious sciences, linguistic sciences including koranic exegesis and criticism, the science of apostolic tradition, jurisprudence, scholastic theology, grammar, lexicography, rhetoric and literature. The 'foreign sciences' comprised philosophy, geometry, astronomy, music, medicine, magic and alchemy. But here too, Muslim scholars did not blindly reproduce everything they received from the Greeks. They expanded, changed, improved, or at least shed new light on every subject, including the theory of music.

Music theory and theoretical writings on music

Arabic music theory is expounded in texts of many forms and types; its material ranges from *musica speculativa* to *musica practica*, from encyclopedism to specialization. In its broadest sense, therefore, it encompasses a wide spectrum of theoretical activity, often offering a vast arena for intellectual pursuits. Due to its multiple connections with other disciplines and cultural areas, Arab treatises on music, like those of antiquity and the Middle Ages, elaborate on a variety of subjects that are interconnected in a very special manner. Because of their interdisciplinary nature, the best contributions are important links in the chain of history of sciences and vital factors in the transmission of knowledge.

It is certain that the appearance of the first Arabic writings on music coincides with and results from newly made acquaintance with translated Greek treatises, a fair many of which were probably known to the earliest generations of Arab music theorists. In this respect, the Baghdadian bibliographer and bookseller Abū'l-Faradj ibn al-Nadīm (d. 995 or 998) provides us with enlightening testimony. His *Kitāb al-fihrist* (Book of the Index to Arabic Books) was designed as a catalogue of all books in Arabic known in his time, whether original or translated. It contains ten discourses (*maqālāt*), the first six dealing with books on Islamic subjects and the last four with non-Islamic subjects. The third section of the third discourse gives the titles of Arabic musical works concerned with biographies of famous musicians, famous collections of songs, instruments and the like; they all belong to the class of Arab native sciences, have an affinity with the oldest form of Muslim historiography and all fall under the literary anecdotal category described in Chapter 3. The first and second sections of the seventh discourse give the titles of books on the theory of music, including 18 treatises translated from the Greek. Among those whose works were translated are Pythagoras, Aristotle, Plato, Aristoxenos, Archimedes, Nicomachous of Gerase, Euclid, Aristides Quantilianus and Themistius. Of the entire list of 104 musical writings mentioned in *Kītab al-fihrist*, only 11 have come down to us, including a few items translated from the Greek. With respect to the lost Greek treatises, traces of them can be found in Arabic writings of earlier and later periods. Many texts included alleged or genuine quotations and references that provide valuable information about ancient Greek theory, as expounded in works the original versions of which have been lost (Farmer 43; Shiloah 76: 201–206).

Although little has remained of the large corpus, the availability of an impressive number of treatises, covering a period extending at least until the close of the first millenium, is highly significant. It also indicates an obvious awareness of the distinction between two basic types of treatises on music: scientific texts reflecting intellectual activity and literary, anecdotal works generally referring to aspects of musical practice and life, including an occasional theoretical contribution. As a matter of fact, these two types have continued to co-exist, either separately or side by side, through the ages.

Scope and development of theoretical writings

The first steps toward shaping the new scientific approach were taken by authors involved in translation. The Christian philosopher and physician Ḥunayn ibn Isḥāq (d. 873) was the most important medium for transmission of ancient Greek science to the Arabs. Ḥunayn, who headed a team of translators, is credited with a tremendous number of translations as well as books he himself wrote on medicine, philosophy, zoology and other themes. He dedicated three chapters of his *Kitāb 'ādāb al-falāsifa* (Book of Aphorisms of the Philosophers) to music. Pursuant to the vogue prevalent among the Greeks, Ḥunayn's chapters on music profess to be records of rare sayings (*nawādir*) uttered by ancient Greek philosophers at festive banquets. According to a certain Ammonius who appears in the incipit of the first chapter as a secondary source, the occasion leading to the compilation of the musical aphorisms was a wedding feast given by King Heraclius for his son. After listening to musicians who enhanced the festivities, the host asked philosophers allegedly present at the celebration to discuss the meaning and value of music. They did so in the form of aphorisms. The 41 sayings refer to the moral and therapeutic effects of music; its spiritual meaning as opposed to its intoxicating influence; cosmological associations of the four strings of the *'ūd*, and so forth. Many of these sayings are ascribed to famous names such as Plato, Aristotle, Alexander, Solon, Euclid and Hermes Trismegistos. A similar work, but on a larger scale, is attributed to a certain Būlos (Paul) and was translated by Ḥunayn's son Isḥāq ibn Ḥunayn.

This genre seems to have been highly esteemed, as two other important contemporary musical sources included a section called *nawādir* with similar aphorisms: the *Risāla fī adjzā' khabariyya fī'l-mūsīqī* by al-Kindī, and the *Rasā'il Ikhwān al-Ṣafā* by the Brethren of Purity (see below). Ḥunayn's work was widely known among medieval Jews through the Hebrew translation rendered by the Andalusian poet Solomom al-Ḥarīzī (1170–1235). Isolated sayings extracted from these texts appear in many writings from the ninth to the nineteenth century.

The three sons of the astrologer Mūsa ibn Shākir, protégés of the Caliph al-Ma'mūn, who became known for their persistent efforts to obtain books from Byzantium and for their generous support of translation activities, wrote a treatise on an automatic hydraulic organ: *al-'Āla allatī tuzammiru bi nafsiha* (The Instrument that Plays by Itself). The wind supply to activate it is obtained by means of compensating water cisterns; this differs little from the automatic wind instrument described by Appolonius of Perga (d. ca 190 BC) whose Greek version was translated into Arabic under the title: *Ṣan'at al-zāmir*. However, the remaining part of the apparatus built by Mūsā's sons is quite novel (Farmer 45: 80–88). Another famous translator from Greek and Syriac into Arabic at the academy *bayt al-ḥikma* was the Christian physician Yuḥanna ibn al-Ba ṭrīq (d. 815). In a pseudo-Aristotelian work he translated reports to the effect that in his advice to Alexander on affairs of government and administration, Aristotle included the recommendation to use a huge organ in wartime to warn fellow-citizens, encourage the army and create fear and disarray within the enemy ranks. It was said that the sound of this remarkable instrument travelled 60 miles, a statement that appears verbatim in the title of the Arabic translation of *Ṣan'at al-urghun al-būqī* (On the Construction of the Flue-pipe Organ) by Muristus. The text describes a large hydraulic organ, more than six metres high, that emits resonant, powerful sounds. Incidentally, this is one of three translated treatises attributed to Muristus (Farmer 45: 88–114).

One of the above-mentioned sons of Banū Shakir was also responsible for introducing the mathematician and astrologer Thābit ibn Qurra (d. 901) as chief astrologer to the court of the Caliph al-Mu'taḍid (892–902). A translator from Greek and Syriac into Arabic and member of the Sabean pagan community of Ḥarrān, he contributed several treatises on music in Arabic and an important one comprising 500 folios in Syriac. All have been lost except one entitled: *Mas'ala fī'l-mūsīqī* (A Musical Problem). The work was written in reply to a question concerning occasional singing in octaves as well as the appropriate accompaniment of a vocal piece on the *'ūd* (Shiloah 67). A similar problem occurs in the pseudo-Aristotelian *Problemata*, fairly well known in medieval Europe through its Latin translation. The 'Problem' in question was raised by the musician and astronomer 'Alī ibn Yaḥya al-Munadjdjim (d. 912) who wrote a *Risāla fī'l-mūsīqī* (Tract on Music) that deals with the differences between 'the masters of Arabian music and the masters of Greek music' (Wright 61; Shawqī 73).

The ethical, cosmological and therapeutic approach

This approach attained pre-eminence with the philosopher and music theorist Ya'qūb ibn Isḥāq al-Kindī (d. 870). The figure of al-Kindī towers over the threshold of Islamic science and philosophy; because of his southern Arabian origin he was called the philosopher of the Arabs. A member of the Arab aristocracy, he established himself as promulgator of the Greek scientific and philosophic tradition. He was the author of at least 265 works covering various branches of knowledge, including music. According to different Arab bibliographical sources, he composed 13 treatises on the science of music in which he took full advantage of newly translated material (Farmer 3: 8–10; Yūsuf 57). Only six treatises have come down to us, but they are fairly representative of his emphasis on the ethical, cosmological and therapeutic approach discussed in this section. Following the Greek model, music is included in the quadrivium – the four mathematical propaedeutic sciences that prepare the student for higher studies of philosophy and for knowledge of the wonders of the creation. The science of harmony in its broadest sense is central for understanding the complex network linking music to all attributes of the universe; it dominates even the technical aspects and the parameters comprising a musical system – whether the theory of sound, intervals, scales and rhythms, or the problems of setting poetry to music and the different kinds of musical composition. The skilled musician must be proficient in the science of harmony in order to adapt his music to any given situation, just as the physician must diagnose his patient's illness before prescribing suitable treatment. The range, volume and timbre of his voice should therefore be in harmony with the predominant feeling and the age of the hearer, as well as with geographical, atmospheric and astrological conditions, days, seasons, elements, winds and humours.

The network of correspondences is explained in reference to the four strings of the *'ūd*, called by al-Kindī the 'instrument of philosophers'. By this he meant the Greek philosophers who allegedly conceived the instrument and its parts as the image of the perfect harmony ruling the universe. In this context quite some numerological speculations are involved. Al-Kindī proceeds in the same spirit when dealing with the harmony of colours and smells and their influence on the human soul (Farmer 106). The differences that affect the music and musical systems of the various ethnic groups and nations populating the world is explained by what we may call an environmental theory. Al-Kindī claims that the multiplicity of music and musical systems reflects the natural differences among human groups in behaviour, tastes, customs and conceptions – differences due to atmospheric and astrological causes. Characteristic examples are to be found in certain culture-bound instruments, in the system of *octoechoes* of the Byzantines, the modal system of the Persians, or the eight rhythmic modes of the Arabs. The technical aspect with which the rhythmic modes are treated also characterizes the exposition of other elements of music, for example intervals, consonances and dissonances, scales, melody types, the setting of poetry to music in song, and the like. Al-Kindī also uses an alphabetical notation by means of which he provides a notated example in two parts for lutanists (Shiloah 71: 203–207).

Al-Sarakhsī (d. 899), one of al-Kindī's most distinguished disciples who also acquired fame as a philosopher, wrote five treatises on music, one of which had the same title as al-Fārābī's monumental work, *Kitāb al-mūsīqī al-kabīr* (The Grand Book on Music). The author of *al-Fihrist* called al-Sarakhsī's book 'the greatest of all the books of its kind'. Alas, all his writings on music have been lost. However, he is frequently cited with veneration by later authors.

The trend represented by al-Kindī reached its zenith in the *Epistle on Music* of the *Ikhwān al-Ṣafā* (the Brethren of Purity), a brotherhood that flourished in Basra in the second half of the tenth century as a society for the pursuit of holiness, purity and truth. They wrote a vast encyclopedic work including 52 tracts and a summary. The tract on music is placed fourth after astronomy, conforming to the order of the quadrivium. The encyclopedia deals with the whole gamut of sciences and philosophy and is meant to initiate the brethren into the basic doctrines. Pursuant to this goal, the tract on music focuses on harmony in its broadest sense, emphasizing the idea that music reflects the harmonious beauty of the universe. Awareness of this supreme beauty should stimulate the reader to seek to transcend material existence, as one who understands the basic laws of musical harmony understands all the secrets of Creation. Musical harmony conceived according to the laws of the well-ordered universe helps man in his attempt to achieve spiritual and philosophical equilibrium. It refines his desires and rouses his courage, propels him toward balanced behaviour, generosity, clemency and renunciation. In short, it acts to create inner harmony among the contradictory forces of man's soul. In the same way, the proper use of music at the right time has a healing influence on the body.

This influence is expressed particularly in the change in composition of the humours; as they are strengthened or weakened they attain an ideal balance. Although this phenomenon is common to all human beings on earth, there are differences among the races and nations. According to the theory of racial differences, which we found in the same context in al-Kindī as well, the distinguishing marks characterizing races and nations are not the result of inheritance, but are caused by climate and by the geographic location of the different groups.

Musical harmony in its most exalted and perfect form is embodied in the heavenly spheres and their music; earthly harmony, including that of the music made by man, is only a pale reflection of the lofty universal harmony. The harmony that governs all celestial and earthly phenomena is expounded numerically. Consequently the *Epistle* is full of arithmetic speculations that overflow into many and varied domains such as calligraphy, language, poetic metre, human corporal structure, the system of the stars and waves, the art of numerology and so forth. The tract elucidates another kind of bond between the celestial bodies and things of this world that has had a considerable effect on the medical dimension of music. It concerns astrology as a whole and places special stress on one of its major aspects: the science of the edicts of heavenly bodies, founded on the general principle that all changes occurring in the sublunary world are intimately linked to the particular nature and movements of the celestial entities. Finally, over and above its strong ideological aspect, the tract contains a valuable theoretical contribution to the study of sound, the science of rhythm and the science of instruments, especially in its discussions of the *'ūd*. It is noteworthy that the dimensions, contents and details of the section on the science of sound serve as an exemplary model of everything written up to that period (Shiloah 75).

The medical dimension

The fervent belief in the therapeutic power of music that we came across in the writings of al-Kindī and the Brethren of Purity can be traced back to a remote past. A biblical instance referred to by medieval authors tells how King David's playing drove away the bad spirit that haunted King Saul: 'And when the minstrel played, the power of the Lord came upon him' (2 Kings 3:15). Frequent references to the method practised by the Pythagoreans, who healed patients with music played on the lyre and aulos, can be found in Greek and Arabic literature as well. Indeed, from the ninth to the sixteenth centuries, many Arabic sources provide details about the doctrine of music therapy. This doctrine incorporated aspects of the theories of medicine and music. Medical theory was indebted chiefly to Aristotle's doctrine according to which physicians established four humours of the human body – blood, yellow bile, black bile and phlegm – analogous with the four cosmic elements (earth, air, fire, water). They also envisaged four qualities of matter – heat, dryness, moisture and cold – consisting of two pairs of opposites. They then ascribed all material existence to various combinations of the four elements and qualities. This doctrine, therefore, could account for climate and temperature as well as for the different temperaments of people: sanguine, choleric, melancholy and phlegmatic (caused by a mixture of the four humours that comprise the body and the four qualities that comprise the climate). All elements of this doctrine and more are developed extensively in the musical writings of al-Kindī and the Brethren in connection with the classical *'ūd* and its four strings (Shiloah 82: I, 199–203).

The association between music and healing procedures was also dealt with by physicians. In his sizeable medical encyclopedia *Miftāḥ al-ṭibb* (The Key to Medicine), Ibn Hindū (d. 1019), one of the earliest Arab authorities on medicine, included a chapter entitled 'Enumeration of those aspects of the sciences the physician must know to be perfect in his profession'. Music is among the sciences referred to. Ibn Hindū acknowledges that in treating certain diseases physicians often have recourse to musical modes which correspond to the condition of the patients and thereby contribute to healing. However, as he says, this does not imply that the physician himself is expected to blow a trumpet or reed-pipe or get up and dance; rather he should use the services of an expert musician, just as he uses the services of other experts, assistants and practitioners (Shiloah 69). Ibn Hindū's more famous contemporary, the great philosopher and physician Ibn Sīnā, Latinized as Avicenna (d. 1037), refuted and rejected as nonsense all theories linking music with astrology and cosmology; but in his monumental *Qānūn fī'l-ṭibb* (Canon on Medicine) we find a special relationship between music and medicine that recurs in Arabic and European texts even as late as the nineteenth century. This relationship combines rhythm, consonances and pulse as chief indicators of good health or illness. A sixteenth-century writer, the blind doctor Dāhūd al-Anṭākī, included in his medical encyclopedia *al-Tadhkira* many of the ideas encountered in the tract on music of the Brethren of Purity, from which he drew extensively. Referring to the doctrine of the Greek scholar (probably Pythagoras) who arranged melodies in accordance with the overall condition of patients' bodies and applied them to astral musical proportions, rhythms and sounds, al-Anṭākī enumerated the various modes and melodies by their characteristics and proper correspondences. More concretely, he introduced medical appellations for the eight rhythmic modes, giving them names that suggested their major effects.

From about the fifteenth century on, the theory of music therapy held a prominent place in literature about music. During this period both medical and musical writings provided detailed tables of correspondences in which the melodic modes under their specific names replace the rhythmic modes of al-Anṭākī and other authors. Thus, according to an anonymous author, the mode *rast* is said to be good for hemiplegy (paralysis of one half the body); the mode *'irāq* helps to cure acute conditions of the humours such as brain diseases, vertigo, pleurisy, suffocation and so forth.

In conclusion, from evidence found in the sources we may assume that musico-therapy belongs more to the musician acting as an auxiliary to the physician, although of course, a physician may also be a musician (Shiloah 82: VI).

The speculative approach

This approach reached its culmination in al-Fārābī's writings on music. A philosopher and musician, Abu Naṣr al-Fārābī (d. 950) wrote on logic, ethics, politics, mathematics, philosophy and music; he became known as the 'second teacher', the first being Aristotle. In Europe, where his works appeared in Latin translation, he was known as Alpharabius Avenassar. His book *Iḥṣā' al-'ulūm* (Classification of Sciences), which enumerates all the known sciences and defines their nature and object, became known in medieval Europe through several different renditions in Latin; it was also translated into Hebrew. One of its chapters includes a comprehensive definition of the theoretical and practical aspects as well as the scope and purpose of the science of music; this chapter influenced Latin music theory of the later Middle Ages (Farmer 42; 'Uthmān 64).

Al-Fārābī's two books on the science of rhythm deal with its governing principles: they define rhythm and its constituents, the different possible arrangements of a succession of beats and the pauses between them, the prime time, basic patterns, their practical combination into modal structure and the various devices permitting change of basic rhythmic patterns (Neubauer 65). However, his *Kitāb al-mūsīqī al-kabīr* (The Grand Book on Music) is foremost among Arabic theoretical treatises in the field, and as such, it exerted remarkable influence on subsequent Arabic music theory. In the preface to the work, al-Fārābī states that he agreed to write it at the request of the vizir Dja'far al-Kirkhī only after he had examined the contents of Greek treatises and found them incomplete, as many lacunae remained with respect to various branches of the art of music. Although he borrowed openly from the Greeks, al-Fārābī shed new light on the borrowed elements and contributed new ideas, while simultaneously basing much of his study on the living music of his time, which as a trained performer he knew well. Later Arab authors, extolling the excellence of his musicianship, cast him in a legendary role; a popular anecdote, attributing to him the invention of the *'ūd*, has been ascribed to several highly authoritative figures.

In the introduction to his monumental work, al-Fārābī emphasizes the necessity of basing theory on musical practice. He points out, however, that the perfect theorist should reason on the basis of his knowledge of all rudiments of the art, from which subsequent material can be deduced in light of the governing scientific principles. Hence the theorist's role is to abstract the essence of knowledge. In addition, he must be capable of discussing erroneous theories, analysing opinions of other authors and correcting their mistakes. Implementing these ideas, al-Fārābī divided his book into two treatises, the second of which is no longer extant. We know from the preface, however, that it comprised the critical analysis of theoretical works written by previous famous theorists explaining 'the value of what each of these theorists has attained in this science, and we have rectified the errors of those who have fallen into fault'.

The extant treatise is divided into sections. In part one al-Fārābī deals with the first principles of musical science, a definition of music, its classification into *musica speculativa* and *musica practica*, musical talent, origin of music and its evolution, musical education and so on. As to the question of origin dealt with in Chapter 4, al-Fārābī proposes a rationalistic theory according to which music was primordially generated by man's natural instinct and inner disposition, to the exclusion of all divine or supernatural powers. Adopting the principle of evolutionary development, he describes how, from a stage determined by instinctive forces, through observation and experience man attained a sophisticated vocal art enhanced by musical instruments, with musical theory subsequently crowning the long developmental process. It is interesting to note that in his learned presentation the peak of the art of music corresponds with the peak of achievement of Islamic civilization.

The second and largest part of this monumental work is divided into three major sections. The first deals with the theory of sound, definition of the note, the different classes and sizes of intervals – accompanied by instructions as to their arithmetic calculations, the consonances, the genres and their various species, their combination into systems and elements of rhythm. The second section includes a description of the following musical instruments: the *'ūd* (short-necked lute), two types of *ṭunbūr* (long-necked lute), flutes and reed instruments, the *rabāb* (fiddle), *ma'āzif* (cithers?) and *ṣunūdj* (open string instruments). The third section is dedicated to musical composition, encompassing melody and its components, the traditional rhythmic modes, vocal melodies and the human voice, ways of setting texts to music, types of embellishment and their relation to emotions (Erlanger 51; Ghattas 62; Hickman 108; Randel 126; Sawa 143; Farmer 235: 386–289).

The subsequent generation of theorists was dominated by the figure of the great philosopher and physician Ibn Sīnā (d. 1037), characterized by his contemporaries as al-Shaikh al-ra'īs (the leading teacher). At the age of 18

Ibn Sīnā claimed to have mastered all the sciences; at the age of 21 he was appointed court physician of the Samanid princes at Bukhara. He was appointed to a ministerial post several times, but became an object of envy and was persecuted by his enemies. His impressive work *Qānūn fī'l-ṭibb* (The Canon on Medicine) was regarded until the seventeenth century as the physicians' Bible; it enjoyed wide circulation by means of its Latin and Hebrew translations, commentaries and abridgements. The Canon includes an important passage on the musical nature of the pulse. Ibn Sīnā's most significant contribution to music theory, however, is to be found in the substantial chapters in his two philosophical works: *Kitāb al-nadjāt* (Book of Delivery) and *Kitāb al-shifā'* (Book of Healing of the Soul). In both cases the science of music is part of the mathematical sciences. The above-mentioned theoretical topics all appear in these two works and are explored from Ibn Sīnā's viewpoint. Of particular interest are the chapters on ornaments and embellishments of melody that elaborate devices used in both melody and rhythm, and the chapter dealing with genres and systems that foreshadows the systematic modal presentation of Ṣafī al-dīn al-Urmayī (Hefni 44; Erlanger III, 52; Farmer 235: 329–332).

Ibn Sīnā's disciple ibn Zayla (d. 1048) abridged the sections on the natural sciences in his master's *Kitāb al-shifā'* and wrote a treatise on music, *Kitāb al-kāfī fī'l mūsīqī* (Book of Sufficiency in Music), in which he quotes long extracts from al-Kindī's theory on rhythm, and includes a whole passage reminiscent of al-Fārābī's writings.

A significant change in music theory occurs in the first part of the thirteenth century with the famous theorist Ṣafī al-dīn al-Urmayi (d. 1294). He was a boon companion and librarian of the last 'Abbāsid caliph al-Mu'taṣim. After the fall of Baghdad (1252) he became official musician of the Mongol conquerors. Ṣafī al-dīn was a distinguished musician and the inventor of two musical instruments. An eminent theorist as well as musician, he achieved a systematization of the general scale and the whole modal system that was probably in practical use long before his time, as can be gathered from rudimentary presentations in earlier works. His two major treatises, the *Kitāb al-adwār* (Book of Cycles) and the *Risāla al-Sharafiyya fī'l nisab al-ta'lifiyya* (The Sharafian Treatise on Musical Proportions) became the authoritative models for subsequent generations; they were widely explicated and commented on. Ṣafī al-dīn based his theory mainly on the music in vogue, thus becoming an ideal junction of the old Persian modal tradition and all the other elements incorporated within the framework of the art of music in Muslim civilization. This may explain the wide acceptance of his works and their lengthy survival throughout an extensive geographical area. Each Eastern theorist in his own way formulated and reformulated the basic principles established by Ṣafī al-dīn. But the majority of treatises written after him differed from their model by singling out local particularities and stylistic features that reflect the practice of each author's milieu (Carra de Vaux 38; Erlanger 51; Shiloah 303: 24–34).

One of the most important later theorists who refer to Ṣafī al-dīn was the music theorist and lutanist 'Abd al-Qādir ibn Ghaybī al-Marāghī (d. 1435). He was chief minstrel of Tīmūr in Samarkand and is usually placed with Ṣafī al-dīn in the front rank of theorists. His five treatises are of the utmost importance because of the information they contain about the practical art of music and, although written in Persian, they exerted an influence over wide areas, particularly, of course, in Persian-speaking regions ('Abd al-Qādir ibn Ghaybī 74, 79; Bardakci 136).

Shortly after the death of Ṣafī al-dīn a new theoretical trend seems to have emerged, based on principles derived from, but not identical with, those of Ṣafī al-dīn's Book of Cycles. This is indicated by al-Qādirī 'Askar al-Ḥalabī (seventeenth century) who refers to the physician and encyclopedist Ibn al-Akfānī (d. 1348) as representing the modern scholars dealing with musical practice. In his encyclopedia *Irshād al-qāṣid ilā asnā'l-maqāṣid* (Guiding the Seeker to the Most Sublime Purposes), Ibn al-Akfānī dedicates a chapter to the science of music. He presents a new classification of the musical modes by reference to those practised by the musicians of his time. An expanded version of the new classification was introduced in the form of a didactic poem by Shams al-dīn al-Dhahabī, who probably lived in the fourteenth century. In his *Risāla fī'l-mūsīqī* (Epistle on Music) Shams al-dīn offers an original contribution – a notational system using a coloured eight-line stave. The names of notes and their equivalent letters are placed between the variously coloured lines, as are the different symbols indicating the initial note, the *finalis* and the direction of the melody. From the early seventeenth century until our own time, a number of European scholars and writers have used this treatise as a sample of Arab musical scholarship and an Arabic notational system (Shiloah 138; 149: 87–90; Farmer 235: 323–326). (See plates 4 and 17 on pages 199 and 212.)

The years following Ṣafī al-dīn's death saw the advent of dozens of important theoretical works in Arabic, Persian and Turkish. Special mention should be made of two most prominent fifteenth-century Ottoman authors: al-Lādhiqī and al-Shirwānī. The former, one of the greatest Arab theorists, and outstanding among his contemporaries in the field, was a favourite of sultan Bayazid II (1481–1512). He dedicated the *Risālat al-fatḥiyya fī'l-mūsīqī* (The Epistle of Victory Concerning the Science of Music) to the sultan, probably in commemoration of the ruler's victory (Erlanger 51: IV, 259–484). Another treatise by al-Lādhiqī is called *Zayn al-alḥān fī 'ilm al-ta'līf wa'l-awzān* (Adorning of Melodies Involving the Science of Composition and Rhythm). Nothing is known about Mawlāna Fatḥ Allah al-Mu'min al-Shirwānī beyond the fact that his *Risāla fī 'ilm al-mūsīqī* (Tract on the Science of Music) was dedicated to the sultan Mehmed, son of

Murad. Among other things, this important treatise includes valuable information about the different kinds of composition known at that time (Shiloah 76: 11–12).

Techniques of scholarship

As we have seen, the study of music in the first centuries of Islam led to the establishment of fundamental patterns and recognized paradigms in scholarship that would be followed by writers in this field until the end of the nineteenth century. The scope of material in the predominant classical paradigm fluctuates between encyclopedism and specialization, and the literary style ranges from anecdotal to theoretical. Many texts that fall within these two extremes combine diverse tendencies and styles, as exemplified by some of the didactic works belonging to the category of theory of practice. These, as we shall see, incorporate cosmological, ethical, therapeutic, speculative, anecdotal and practical aspects. As with most other writings on music, in these texts one usually finds great respect for scholarly and literary authorities, so much so that past authorities were often cited to enhance the prestige of current works. Thus, the works of al-Kindī, al-Sarakhsī, the Brethren of Sincerity, al-Fārābī, ibn Sīnā, Ṣafī al-dīn, as well as several Greek authors, are frequently cited, quoted and even brought into mutual confrontation.

It was perfectly acceptable, for example, to quote lengthy excerpts, to intersperse a quotation with glosses, or even to combine and rearrange several different passages written by the author being quoted. Although the beginning of a quotation was generally indicated by the author's name followed by the verb *qāla* (he said), the end of the quote was rarely marked. Stylistic factors played an important role here. It was considered bad form to interrupt the narrative flow with too many citations and it was assumed that readers would be able to differentiate between the style of the quotation and that of the current author. Sometimes, however, acknowledgement of borrowed material is omitted altogether. As Franz Rosenthal notes, 'The fraudulent omission of the proper acknowledgement of material derived from the works of other authors was no uncommon phenomenon. It is, however, difficult and often impossible to determine where permissible literary usage ends and fraud begins' (Rosenthal 17: 46).

One of the best examples illustrating the aforementioned techniques, the didactic approach and the combination of literary anecdotal material with a highly technical investigation into what might be called the theory of practice, is al-Ḥasan al-kātib's *Kamāl adab al-ghinā'* (Perfection of Musical Knowledge) written in the eleventh century. This is a scholarly text conceived primarily in the spirit of a literary work; information is imparted through the use of brief, well thought-out and eloquently formulated literary sequences. The treatise, which very likely constitutes a summary of the author's teaching experience, comprises 240 pages that include an introduction and 43 chapters. The work contains a general discussion of the virtues of music and of elements pertaining to musical practice and performance. There is also a good deal of theoretical material based, in the main, on al-Fārābī's Grand Book on Music which al-Ḥasan considered a model of scholarly perfection. He quotes other authorities as well, notably al-Kindī and al-Sarakhsī. A keen critical approach is another distinguishing attribute of al-Ḥasan's work. In the last chapter of his treatise, for example, he provides the student with what may be called an analytical bibliography that distinguishes between scholarly works and the writings of *littérateurs* (Shiloah 68; Ghattas 72).

Ibn al-Ṭaḥḥān's fourteenth century work entitled *Ḥāwī al-funūn wa salwat al-maḥzūn* (The Collector of Sciences and Consolation of the Vexed), follows a similar approach, but has a more significant literary character. Many of its 102 tiny chapters discuss the biographies of famous musicians who lived and worked during the first centuries of Islam; it includes important details regarding musical practice and performance, musical instruments and their construction, and a presentation of the modal theory according to the then-new trend.

A cultural phenomenon that enjoyed considerable popularity among medieval Arab scholars was the technique of abridging a basic work in a given area of learning. The main objective of authors of such compendia was didactic. By abridging, they offered educated readers the essentials and made specialized works more accessible to them, while relieving them of the need to peruse lengthy tracts. An author sometimes abridged his own work, as was the case, for instance, with ibn Sīnā who condensed the entire philosophical system contained in his extensive treatise *al-Shifā'* into a small volume, *al-Nadjāt*. In an abridgement the author generally follows the form and content of the original work more or less strictly, while feeling free to add his own glosses – which occasionally grow to considerable dimensions. In the process, such abridgements approach another form commonly practised in medieval scholarship – systematic commentary of an authoritative work, wherein the original work is usually presented phrase by phrase, with the addition of notes and comments. The anonymous gloss on Ṣafī al-dīn's The Book of Cycles is a good illustration of the techniques of systematic commentary. The end result is a work three times the length of the original treatise. The author, a physician who studied music as an indispensable part of his medical training, deplores the general ignorance of musical theory, which prompted him to do his own investigating. He states that his commentary is meant to elucidate Ṣafī al-dīn's complex opus by unravelling its perplexing enigmas and clarifying its obscurities. The original passages in the commentary include a long discussion on musical composition with descriptions of vocal and instrumental forms, and an enumeration of Greek poetical genres related to music (Shiloah 147: 94–95).

Concepts and general characteristics

Our excursion into the field of various types of texts on music has revealed a great deal, but unfortunately it cannot compensate us for the absence of actual sounds that so delighted past generations. From the abundant literature, however, one can glean many hints as to the major characteristics of the practised art, and from them some of its prevailing concepts can be inferred. Alan Merriam was of the opinion that 'Without understanding the concepts held about music, there is no real understanding of music, . . . this is because they underlie the sounds and values associated with them' (Merriam 382: 103). With this statement in mind, we should like to shed further light on some of the prevailing concepts covered so far.

First and foremost, it is essential to understand what music meant to most of its consumers in the lands dominated by Islamic civilization. As noted in a previous chapter, the term music – in its Arabized form *mūsīqī* – was mainly used in a theoretical context; the Arabic term *ghinā'* (cantus) was adopted as the equivalent of art music. There is no doubt that both *mūsīqī* and *ghinā'* and their underlying concepts are applied, in theory and practice, exclusively to the type of sophisticated urban art that developed after the advent of Islam. Consequently, folk and religious music are not considered music and their various forms are given appellations that emphasize their verbal character. The musical component is subordinate and these forms are usually used in contradistinction to the *ghinā'*. Music-making is designated by the verb 'to say': a local style is *lahdja* (dialect); a folk musician is called *qawwāl* (one who says), *shā'er* (poet), *'āsheq* (lover), *beytbig* (the Kurdish bard who performs narrative and didactic songs, *beyt*), *naqqāl* (transmitter), *maddāḥ* (eulogist) and so forth. Cantillation is called reading or reciting, while sacred and religious music as a whole is treated under the general term of *samā'* (audition) which includes music – sometimes embodying a fairly well-developed form – as practised by the mystical orders.

With respect to the manner in which music acts upon the individual, the prevailing perception is that it is an overwhelming power capable of affecting the listener's soul in many different ways. The average person expects to be strongly moved and indeed is easily excited by the sound of music, to the extent of abandoning himself to its domination. Often combined with expressions of sweetness and loving tenderness, music stirs a whole gamut of feelings, from subtle sensual delight to strong emotion described as *ṭarab*. The great faith in the power of music as a sublimating or sensuous agent does not include the obvious quest for what we may call esthetic values. One finds numerous references to artistic devices manifestly targeted towards increasing the beauty and elegance of a musical composition. Such devices include adequate moulding of musical phrases, the proper use of ornaments and vocalizations, the modalities of notes that lend elegance to the melody and render it more pleasing to the ear.

Once the art of music is considered as a creation of human beings, it is perceived as embodying the hubris and evanescent nature of man. It is perceived as irreconcilable with the fundamental moral and theological demands of a religion that proclaims the omnipotence of one God. The sole sovereignty of the transcendental God is challenged the moment music is seen as akin to satanic magic whereby the devil is enabled to control and direct the deeds and wishes of human beings. Considered from the standpoint of its overwhelming power, music indeed has much in common with those magical powers that can effectively 'force' themselves on the individual; religious elements on the other hand, must be 'served' or sought after. In contrast to the forces of magic, religious forces are depicted as able to guide and determine a man's fate. From this standpoint it is easy to understand the religious purists' attitude that considers the powerful effect of music as an intoxicating, misleading agent of the devil. The mystics, in turn, insist on the divine origin of music and its consequent exalting and illuminating impact on the devotee.

In this connection it is interesting to note that the philosophers regarded the sensual and over-excited reaction evoked by music as disrupting the desirable harmony of the soul and social balance. Therefore, unlike the important role played by musical thought in the upbuilding of an educated man, musical praxis never became an integrated part of the official educational system.

In sum, the attitude toward music has always been ambivalent, as expressed in a series of contradictory feelings and concepts: predilection and mistrust; divine–devilish; exalting–disruptive; admissible–prohibited.

In all musical categories, speech and melody are intimately connected, intermingling and complementing each other. Even in the sophisticated art form melody is ideally considered as the best interpreter of the text to which it is set. Speech and melody come closest to one another when the modulating voice is the carrier of both word and music. A major concern of both sacred and secular music is the potential expressiveness of the human voice as a symbol of life, a reflection of the human soul and a medium of communication. A rich palette of timbres enables the musician's voice to interpret the various feelings and meanings contained in the text, whether it is sung or recited. The highest achievement of this potential expressiveness is obtained in the ideal combination of the poetic and melodic, considered by theorists as perfect music; hence the primacy of vocal music that has become a distinguishing mark of Near Eastern music throughout the ages. In that part of the world music-making is essentially individual, based on the skill of individual artists who usually address themselves to an intimate audience. This holds true even when the performance is by a group of musicians, the group generally being small. It comprises a solo singer and three to four instrumentalists who frequently demonstrate their art by performing improvised solo passages.

The audience, never passive, expresses its reaction by frequent applause. Its value judgements are expressed in loud approval or disapproval, demonstrated not by hand-clapping but verbally. Al-Ḥasan al-kātib (eleventh century) devotes a special chapter of his book *Kamāl adab al-ghinā'* (The Perfection of Musical Knowledge) to applause (*zahzaha*) and value judgements (Shiloah 68: 179–182). He distinguishes between two types of spontaneous reaction to a beautiful performance; the one is that of ignorant folk, the other of genuine connoisseurs. The former applaud indiscriminately with the sole aim of satisfying the performer; they do so while using absurd language. The latter express value judgements in their applause, the effect of which al-Ḥasan compares to the brilliancy of a pearl, meaning that if the song contains a pearl, the applause helps display its brilliancy. It also encourages the performer to repeat his achievement, while stimulating his creativeness. Inopportune applause, on the other hand, may mislead the singer, particularly if the musician lacks intelligence, or is highly impressionable. Applause intensifies the artistic communion between the musician and his audience and affects the shaping and development of the musical style. Above all the artist's imaginative power receives immediate stimulation, emphasizing the relatively extensive freedom the musician enjoys. Indeed, the artist is permitted, even encouraged, to improvise spontaneously and gratify his preoccupation with the details comprising a work. In so doing he seems less concerned with a preconceived plan than with allowing the structure to emerge empirically from the details. As in other branches of the arts, one receives many minute observations and images but rarely a full view of the whole process. Cognizant of the fact that, even at its most complex, art music is transmitted orally, we may assume that the *zahzaha* was of particular importance in defining musical style (Sawa 143: 192–200).

The ideal, perfect musician is a singer endowed with a natural disposition for music, one who has solid theoretical knowledge, the faculty of rapidly assimilating all music he hears and retaining it in his memory, who can move his audience and be moved himself. He must possess a beautiful, expressive voice in addition to great creative power evinced in improvisation or the re-creation and embellishment of existing models. Existing models may be transmitted so freely that the borderline between re-creation and the creation of a new composition is blurred – a phenomenon that touches upon another important concept: originality. Indeed, originality does not mean creation *ex nihilo*, but more the expansion or improvement of pre-existing models. Borrowing a beautiful verse or beautiful melody is not disapproved, provided the borrower succeeds in disguising the original in such a way that the adopted material appears convincingly different from its model – a new composition altogether. Alongside the general acceptance of this concept, however, the culture developed criteria for distinguishing between reworking material and plagiarism, the latter being absolutely rejected (Sawa 143: 192–200).

Instruments

Instruments are described in a variety of ways and in almost all known genres used to write about music. Sometimes the approach is anecdotal, sometimes it is of a systematic, scientific nature. A description may embody historic, ethnic, lexicographic, etymological, cosmological, theological, organological or classificatory aspects, and may focus on one or several classes of known instruments.

The earliest works, those going back to the ninth century, refer to instruments by the generic term *malāhī* (pl. of *malha*), or occasionally *'ālāt al-lahw*, linked to the word *lahw* which means 'game, pastime, amusement'. The term is included in the title of eight treatises devoted entirely to *malāhī*, seven of which appeared in the ninth century. Among the oldest works that have come down to us are *Kitāb al-malāhī* by the famous grammarian Mufaḍḍal ibn Salāma (d. ca 905), and *Kitāb al-lahw wa'l-malāhī* by the celebrated geographer ibn Khurradādhbih (d. 911). The first begins by refuting the view that the Arabs did not know the *'ūd* or other *malāhī* and that their language lacked technical terms for the various parts of instruments, and for musical features in general (Robson 49; Farmer 366). In the course of contesting this fallacy the author comments on a large number of terms relating to instruments and music, all gleaned from classical Arabic poetry.

Alongside lexicographic and etymological issues, the author's method of presentation leads him to relate to the important question of the origin of each instrument. The *'ūd*, regarded as the king of instruments, heads the list. In this connection, the author quotes the story attributed to the historian Hishām ibn al- Kalbī (d. 819), according to which the inventor was the biblical figure Lamech. The story telling how Lamech made an *'ūd* in the form of his defunct son's bones is reproduced in Chapter 4.

Ibn Salāma then discusses other biblical inventors of instruments and details of terminology, supporting each comment with references to poetry. He reviews the different names for the *'ūd*: *kirān*, *mizhar*, *barbaṭ* and *muwattar*, and the special names given to the *'ūd's* four strings. He enumerates other stringed instruments and ten different kinds of wind instruments:

mizmār, *zammāra*, *nāy*, *quṣṣāb*, *mushtaq*, *yarā'*, *zanbaq*, and so on. In addition to its lexicographic importance, this work, as well as others of similar nature, is of special musicological interest: all of them provide the scholar with information about many instruments that have since fallen into disuse.

The second treatise, *Kitāb al-malāhī* by ibn Khurradādhbih, also reproduces the story of the invention of the *'ūd* by Lamech and tells of other inventors of musical instruments in biblical times, but the author directs his work toward wider and more universal horizons. His interest indeed centres more on cultural and historical than lexicographic issues. Consequently, he touches on the music and instruments typical of other peoples, in particular those of the Persians, Greeks and Indians; the term *malāhī* has a broader meaning here and becomes the equivalent of 'music' (Shiloah 82: X, 112–116).

These two works are the beginning and end of this category of texts on the *malāhī*. They also mark the introduction of a genre of writings on music already mentioned in these pages: texts that borrow from the anecdotal, edifying *adab* literature which no longer includes the word *malāhī* in its titles. Nevertheless, the term was to appear sporadically for a long time to come, finding its most extreme and protracted use among the religious authorities who opposed music.

The pejorative view of *malāhī*

The theologian and jurist ibn abi'l-Dunyā (d. 894), a contemporary of the two authors cited above, used the term *malāhī* altogether differently, emphasizing its negative association with diversion and entertainment. His work, *Dhamm al-malāhī* (Book of the Censure of Instruments of Diversion), the oldest extant treatise of this kind, is a violent attack on music and musical instruments; he regards them as reprehensible digressions from a life of devoted piety (Robson 50). The same model was followed by the next generation of authors who discussed *samā'*: they thereafter equated *malāhī* with instruments of forbidden diversion.

However, not all of them rejected all instruments; some, after a detailed discussion about the various instruments, differentiated between those that might be tolerated and those that should be banned. Al-Adfuwī (d. 1347), for instance, in his treatise *al-Imtā' bi aḥkām al-samā'* (The Benefit of the Laws of Listening to Music), identified the concept *malāhī* mainly with the stringed instruments that are closely linked to art-form music; he tolerated the *daff* (frame-drum), the *yarā'* and the *shabbāba* (flutes).

The flute occupies a prominent place among the mystics, to whom it symbolizes the human windpipe. A charming legend depicting the divine origin of the flute recounts that before Adam was expelled from the Garden of

Eden, a secret was delivered to him. Soon after his expulsion, the secret he was forbidden to divulge weighed on him, causing him painful torment. Coming to his aid, the archangel Gabriel advised him to throw the secret into a well; he did so and was relieved. The secret penetrated the reeds that grew around the well and imbued them with the divine substance; it was from these reeds that the first flute was manufactured. In an anonymous Ṣūfī treatise the seven holes of the *nāy* (flute) were compared to the seven heavens and seven planets.

In the overall schema of literature on *samā'* there are other points of view about the term and concept of *malāhī*. Al-Nābulusī (d. 1731) in his *'Īḍāḥ al-dalālāt fī samā' al-'ālāt* (Clarification of Proofs Concerning Listening to Musical Instruments) suggests that the word *lahw*, by which one describes the instruments (*malāhī* or *'ālāt al-lahw*), does not necessarily indicate that musical instruments are invariably used for purposes of entertainment. This qualification and the implied prohibition are relevant when the desired end is merely amusement, but they are no longer valid when the issue is the spiritual elevation of the Ṣūfī.

The cosmological approach

A network of astrological, cosmological, therapeutic, and ethical correspondences is explained by al-Kindī, Ḥunayn ibn Isḥāq and Ikhwān al-Ṣafā in reference to the four strings of the *'ūd*, which they called the 'instrument of philosophers'. By this they meant the Greek philosophers, who allegedly conceived of the *'ūd* and its parts in the image of the perfect harmony ruling the universe. In addition to a special tract on the *'ūd*, al-Kindī wrote a work entitled *Kitāb al-muṣawwitāt al-watariyya min dhāt al-watar al-wāḥid ilā dhāt al-'asharat awtār* (Book of Sounds Made by Instruments Having One to Ten Strings). In this work al-Kindī undertakes to explain why there is such a great variety of instruments and music. His fundamental assumption is that the instruments help create harmony between the soul and the universe; consequently, each society has instruments that reflect its nature, and each instrument is purported to express the specific beliefs and characteristics of the society to which it belongs. Thus, he claims that the *kinkala* – a one-stringed instrument – is characteristic of the Indians; a two-stringed instrument, of the Khorasanians, etc. In their Epistle on Music, Ikhwān al-Ṣafā developed many similar ideas, but also devoted a special section to the making and tuning of instruments. This section begins with a list of 17 instruments, although the only one it describes at length and in detail is the *'ūd*. The list includes a few Greek and Byzantine instruments: *urghan* (organ), *armūnikī* (panpipes), *salbāb* or *salbāk* (*sambyke* or *sambuca*); the Persian *djank* (harp), and 13 others (Shiloah 82: III,

32). A contemporary encyclopedic work *Mafātīḥ al-ʿulūm* (Keys of Sciences) by Aḥmad al-Khwārizmī, contains a section listing the names of 20 different instruments, with indications of their respective origins; 11 of the names appear in both sources. In addition to the three Greek and Byzantine instruments, al-Khwārizmī included the *lūr* (lyre), the *qiṭāra* (cithara) as well as the Chinese mouth organ *mustaq* or *mushtaq* also mentioned in other ancient sources (Farmer 54: 2–3).

Musical apparatuses and automatons

In connection with such 'foreign' instruments, mention should be made of treatises, both translated and original, devoted to pneumatic and hydraulic apparatuses and organs. Among the treatises translated from the Greek, mention should be made of the following: *Fī ʿamal al-bankāmāt* (On the Construction of Clepsydras) attributed to Archimedes (d. 212 BC), which describes an instrument with pipes made to whistle by means of hydraulic pressure, and an automatic wind instrument that plays four times a day; *Ṣanʿat al-zāmir* (On the Construction of the Wind Instrument Automaton) by Appolonius of Perga (d. ca 190 BC), an elaborate example of a water-operated automaton, consisting of the figure of a man playing a reed pipe – (Farmer 45: 80–88); *Madjmūʿ ʾālāt wa-ḥiyal* (Collection of Apparatuses and Machines) by Ayrun (Heron of Alexandria fl. AD 62), which describes several pneumatic and hydraulic automatons. Among them is one activated by water; it has birds perched on rocks or trees that produce different sounds by means of whistles placed in their beaks (Farmer 45: 114–118). Three other treatises are ascribed to the author Muristus whose identity is obscure. They are: *Ṣanʿat al-urghun al-būqī* (On the Construction of the Flue-pipe Organ), a hydraulic organ, more than six metres high, with a powerful, resonant sound said to 'travel sixty miles'. This may be the same instrument mentioned by Yuḥanna ibn Baṭrīq (d. 815) in his pseudo-Aristotelian translated work *Kitāb al-siyāsa fī tadbīr al-riyāsa* (The Book of Administration): (See Chapter V) (Farmer 45: 119–138).

The three sons of the astrologer Mūsa ibn Shākir (fl. ninth century) were among the scientists installed by Caliph al-Maʿmūn in *Bayt al-ḥikma* (House of Wisdom). Their works include translations from the Greek and original texts on geometry, astronomy and mechanics. Among the latter is *al-ʾĀla allatī tuzammiru bi nafsiha* (The Instrument That Plays by Itself), a treatise on an automatic hydraulic organ. The wind supply to activate it is obtained by means of compensating water cisterns; in this it differs little from the automatic wind instrument described by Appolonius. However, the remaining part of the apparatus built by Mūsā's sons is quite novel (Farmer 45: 88–114; Cara de Vaux 365).

One of the most important Arabic works on automatons is *Kitāb fī ma'rifat al-ḥiyal al-handasiyya* (The Book of Knowledge of Ingenious Mechanical Devices) by Badī' al-zamān al-Djazarī(twelfth to thirteenth century); several musical automatons are described in it. One of them depicts two drummers, two trumpeters and a cymbalist who play every hour on the hour up to six. Another portrays a drinking session. On a balcony are four slave-girls, one with a flute at her lips, another with a frame drum slung around her neck. Above this balcony is a platform where a dancer holding batons in both hands stands on a ball. Another drinking party takes place in a boat floating on a pond. On the poop deck opposite the king is a platform with a flute-player, a harpist and two frame-drummers. These and many other automatons are depicted in illustrations that adorn the text (Wiedemann 364).

The classificatory approach

In writings of a speculative nature, the approach and treatment are considerably different. Endeavouring to evaluate and classify musical instruments in his Grand Book on Music, al-Fārābī offers two explanations. The first, included in the introduction, concerns the question of origin and function. Al-Fārābī argues that instruments were invented to accompany and enrich vocal music which had already undergone a long process of development, and he maintains that instruments are inferior in quality to the voice. In the hierarchy suggested by al-Fārābī, the string and wind instruments are at the highest level, followed by drums and percussions, with dance at the end of the list. Among the melodic instruments, the *rabāb* (fiddle) and the winds were given priority over all the others because of their ability to sustain sounds, implying that they are closest to the voice (Erlanger 51: I, 20–23). The second explanation appears in two long sections devoted to the study of instruments proper. To test the theoretical elements, al-Fārābī here considers the instruments empirically. The *'ūd* enjoys first and highest place; it is followed by the long-necked lutes, winds, *rabāb* and harps (Erlanger 51: I, 165–215).

In his *Kitāb al-shifā'*, Avicenne classified instruments as follows: fretted and plucked (short- and long-necked lutes); board zither and open string (types of lyre and harp); other instruments such as the *urghanun* (organ) and one that is struck with sticks – *ṣandj djīni* (xylophone?) (Erlanger 51: II, 233–234). Ibn Ghaybī, in his *Djāmi' al-alḥān* (Compiler of Melodies), established three major classes: chordophones or stringed instruments offering an impressive list of 25 different instruments, many of which are no longer known; aerophones or winds numbering 12, including the *urghanun* (organ) and three idiophones or percussions; the drums are not mentioned.

In his monumental bibliographical work *Kashf al-ẓunūn 'ann asāmī al-kutub wa'l-funūn* (Clarification of Conjectures about the Names of Books and Sciences), the Turkish encyclopedist Ḥadjdjī Khalīfa (d. 1657) includes a section 'On the science of musical instruments'. He grouped the instruments in three classes: drums, wind instruments, and strings.

Finally, an interesting anonymous treatise called *Kashf al-ghumūm wa'l-kurab fī sharḥ 'ālāt al-ṭarab* (The Unveiling of Grief and Sorrow in Commenting on Instruments of Music) should not be overlooked. This lengthy treatise, devoted entirely to instruments, contains separate chapters on the organ, *'ūd*, *djank* (harp), *sanṭīr* or *sanṭūr* and *qānūn* (two types of trapezoidal zither, the first being struck, the second plucked), three kinds of drums, *shabbāba* (flute), *rabāb* and *kamandje* (fiddles), *shu'abiyya* (pan-pipes) and different ensembles, the largest of which comprises seven musicians (four drummers and three flautists). The work also includes eight beautiful coloured miniatures illustrating the above-mentioned instruments and the ensemble.

A glance at the multiple sources reveals a bewildering number of instruments designated by name and specific characteristics, many being of widely divergent origin including, to mention only a few, the Bible, the Greeks, the Indians, and so on. They number 138, not including the pneumatic, hydraulic and mechanical automatons. By family affiliation the 138 instruments subdivide as follows: idiophones 10; membranophones 18; aerophones 48 and chordophones 62. Many of these instruments, of course, have fallen into disuse.

6 Decentralization and Advent of Local Styles

On the face of it, the 'Abbāsid caliphate (750–1258) was the longest dynasty. Soon after the brilliant reign of Hārūn al-Rashīd, however, the extensive empire was beset by a process of disintegration, accompanied by territorial and political fragmentation of the caliphate. Independent dynasties arose in various parts of the empire and assumed effective control over their territories. Although most of them continued to recognize the supremacy of the 'Abbāsid caliphs, some nevertheless undermined the caliphate's hegemony. From that time on, in effect, three major groups of non-Arab converts to Islam began to share dominion over the empire and contributed to its expansion; they were the Persians, Turks and Berbers.

General background

The Persians

In the East the Persian and Persianized dynasties (Ṭāhirids, Saffārites and Sāmānids), while ruling as vassals of Baghdad, encouraged a revival of separate culture and literature, thereby generating a sense of Persian cultural identity within Islam. During the ninth and tenth centuries, Persian became the dominant language in Iran and in the Central Asian sphere of Iranian cultural influence. Together with others, Persians also played a prominent role in one of the most striking movements in Arab cultural history and literature – the *Shu'ūbiyya,* which in diverse forms extended from Spain and the Maghrib to remote parts of Central Asia (Mottahedeh 30).

The *Shu'ūbiyya* emerged during the time of the Umayyads as an expression of dissatisfaction on the part of various subject races suffering from the inequality and discriminatory status imposed upon non-Arab people by the dominating élite of Arab extraction. But the movement erupted most vehemently during the time of the early 'Abbāsids, when it became a vociferous response to Arabian aristocracy's boastful claims that it was the noblest of all races and spoke the purest, richest language in the world. Asserting that the Arabs were surpassed by other nations in virtues and abilities, the bolder spirits among the *Shu'ūbī*s adduced proof of the absurdity of Arab claims, arguing that the latter were altogether inferior to the Persians, Greeks, Indians and others. Thus, for instance, certain *Shu'ūbī*s refuted the generally recognized excellence of the Arabs in rhetoric and oratory, claiming that they distracted their listeners' thoughts and obviously failed to grasp the essentials of the art of rhetoric. Commenting favourably on the poems written and set to music by the *Shu'ūbīs* H. T. Norris writes: 'The better and more accomplished singer was the one who dispensed with the rhythmic beat sustained by an instrument when he sang his air'. This statement probably refers to the much appreciated form of singing that emphasizes long and expressive unaccompanied vocal improvisation. In the same spirit, Norris goes on to make the following astonishing statement: 'The Shu'ūbīs scorned the Arabs for their rhythmic deficiency, although Arabs, they suggested, tried hard to hide this defect in metre and rhyme when they contended with their opponents' (CHAL 35: 31–47).

In the main, the *Shu'ūbiyya* aspirations were rather of a socio-cultural than a political or even religious nature; those aspirations were indeed defended by social and cultural arguments. Examining the ethnic pride inherent in the *Shu'ūbiyya* movement, the eminent scholar I. Goldziher contended that the cultural conflicts were caused by the assimilation into the very diverse Islamic ethnic community (Goldziher 25). The motivations of the *Shu'ūbīs* and their opponents were analysed differently by the distinguished orientalist H. Gibb (Gibb 24), who believed that some *Shu'ūbīs* wanted to remould the political and social institutions of the Islamic empire and the inner spirit of Islamic culture on the model of Sassanian institutions and values. This was probably the case at that time in Persia, where being *Shu'ūbī* meant endeavouring to re-establish Persian as the literary language, while confining the use of Arabic to the theological sciences.

The Turks

The second element, the Turks, made themselves felt by the second half of the ninth century when, as military commanders, they assumed control over the caliphs in Baghdad, dethroning them at will. Their influence became decisive in the eleventh century when masses of their tribes led by the Seljuqs – named after their first chieftain Seljuq – occupied North India and most of the Iranian plateau, defeated the emperor of Byzantium and spread into the plateau of Anatolia. Seljuq's grandson Tughril beg, after taking the caliphate seat of Baghdad in 1055, was invested by Caliph al-Qā'im with his own sultanate, or temporal authority, thereby marking the inception of a separate political institution – the universal sultanate. Once firmly in control of the caliphal territories, the Seljuqs, who had embraced *Sunnī* Islam, came under the powerful influence of High Islamic traditions in government, politics and culture and identified their interests with those of the urban élites. In this capacity, they claimed authority over the whole of *Sunnī Islam*, while recognizing and co-existing with the caliphate. Tughril, and his nephew Alp Arslan who succeeded him, led a sustained confrontation with the Fātimid's dissident Shī'ī caliphate in hope of assuming control over their territories and regaining them for the orthodoxy. On the northern front, the Seljuqs achieved a resounding victory in 1071 against the large army commanded by the Byzantine emperor Romanus Diogenes at the battle of Manzikert near lake Van. As a result, Anatolia was now open to permanent Turkish settlement.

The defeat of the emperor of Byzantium provoked the First Crusade, in response to the Byzantine government's appeal to the pope. The First Crusaders, under Godfrey of Bouillon, conquered Jerusalem on 15 July 1099. The Crusaders' arrival in the East was to have several effects, which we shall return to later.

The Berbers

In 909 Arabs and Berbers of Kabylie established a dynasty of Shī'ī rulers in Tunisia who denied the rights of the 'Abbāside caliphs; they established the Fāṭimid caliphate, claiming descent from the children of Fāṭima, the prophet's daughter. They conquered large areas of North Africa, Egypt, Syria and parts of Arabia. In 969 they moved their capital from al-Mahdia in Tunisia to Cairo; the actual name of the city is derived from Miṣr al-Qāhira, a town established in 970 by the first Fāṭimid caliph al-Mu'izz. The claim of the Fāṭimid caliph to universal sovereignty was soon confronted with reality: Fāṭimid power proved too weak to overthrow the 'Abbāsid caliphate of Baghdad. Nevertheless, for about a century, under the caliphs al-'Azīz, al-Ḥākim, al-Ẓāhir and al-Mustanṣir, Egypt played the role of a major Mediterranean power; for some two centuries, Cairo was the scene of brilliant intellectual development and of a splendid court renowned for military pageantry. Intellectual and religious life was concentrated in the great Mosque al-Azhar, the building of which was begun in the reign of al-'Azīz and completed by his successor al-Ḥākim.

Music at the court of the Fāṭimids

Music was passionately cultivated by almost all the Fāṭimid caliphs. They spent fabulous sums on musicians, singing-girls, dancers and banquets. The Caliph al-Mustanṣir (1036–94), for instance, tolerated pictures of dancing-girls in his vizier's dwelling, even though possession of such paintings transgressed the precepts of Islam. The caliph himself indulged in drinking wine and feasting to the accompaniment of music in a special pavilion he had constructed in imitation of the *zamzam* building and well at Mecca. He is also said to have given a gift to a favourite singing-girl – an estate near the Nile known as *arḍ al- ṭabbāla* (the land of the female drummer). However, the most vivid musical pictures contained in accounts of this glorious period described the military bands adorned with colourful banners and insignia that augmented the splendid pomp of royal ceremonial processions and festivals. Even the various classes of officers and court officials were entitled to have their own lavish ceremonials – *mawākibs.* Contemporary eye-witnesses, such as the traveller Nasir-i Khusraw who visited Cairo during al-Mustanṣir's reign, confirm these accounts (Nasir-i-Khusraw 14: 128, 137).

According to the historian ibn Khaldūn, the *'āla* (outfit) under the Fāṭimids was composed of 500 banners and 500 trumpets (Rosenthal 63: II, 48–49). The Egyptian historian ibn Taghrī Birdī (1409–1470) wrote a ten-volume history of Egypt from its conquest by the Arabs in 641 to 1469, called *al-Nudjūm al-ẓāhira* (The Resplendent Stars). Numerous passages of this tremendous work refer to music and its function in relation to many aspects of culture; it also includes comments on famous musicians. In describing the celebration of the new year by the Fāṭimids in 975, shortly after their capital was moved to Cairo, he reports that 50 *naqqārāt* (kettle-drums) and 50 *kūsāt* (cylindrical drums) players all mounted on mules, participated in the grand procession. As the caliph approached the city gate, a golden horn with a curved head emitted marvellous sounds, and other horns replied. Following the caliph through the gate was a vast ensemble of *ṭubūl* (drums), *ṣunūdj* (cymbals) and *ṣafāfīr* (whistles) 'making the world hum'. A similar celebration was held on the occasion of the sacrificial feast *'īd al-aḍḥa.*

Ibn Taghrī Birdī also informs us that in the year 978 the 'Abbāsid Caliph al-Ṭā'ī (974–991) was the first to have the *ṭablkhane* (military and ceremonial band) play in front of his palace three times a day. The *ṭablkhane,* which was elevated to great prominence and attained its largest size under the Fāṭimids, played a significant role as a symbol of prestige and mark of royalty in all territories under Islam. Its major functions, as described repeatedly by ibn Taghrī Birdī in his book, were to accompany feasts, play at the sultan's coronation, announce good news such as the sultan's recovery from an illness or his reaching maturity. Led by the emir's *ṭablkhane* these bands participated in battle, as for example in the battle against the French Crusaders that took place on Egyptian soil in 1250; they also took part in victory parades and the like (Farmer 95: 206–208).

Incidentally, the end of Crusader presence in that region coincided with the fall of the Fāṭimid caliphate; both powers were defeated by a Seljuq Kurdish officer – Saladin. Initially sent to help the Fāṭimids against the Crusaders, Saladin overthrew them in 1171, restored their territories to *Sunnī* allegiance and established the new dynasty of the Ayyūbides.

The foregoing description of the role of music in Egypt is only one of many examples demonstrating that the fragmentation of political power into many independent dynasties was not detrimental to cultural development. On the contrary, the decentralization and proliferation of ruling centres offered increased support and patronage for learning and culture, as can be confirmed by a few other examples of famous scholars and writers on music with whom we have already made acquaintance. The great philosopher and music theorist al-Fārābī, al-Iṣfahānī, the author of the Book of Songs, and the historian al-Mas'ūdī, all flourished under the reign and patronage of the Ḥamdānids in Syria; the philosopher, physician and music theorist Avicenne was patronized by the Sāmānids in Central Asia; the theologian and religious reformer abū Ḥāmid al-Ghazzālī who had a considerable impact on Ṣūfīsm, taught at the *Niẓāmīya,* the most famous of the *Madrasahs* (theological schools) created by the Seljuqs.

The third element of non-Arab converts to Islam – the Berbers, who as we have seen, began to share dominion over the empire and to contribute to its expansion, became particularly prominent in North Africa, the Saharan and sub-Saharan areas and in the Iberian Peninsula. The conquest of the Iberian Peninsula by the Muslim armies, their long-standing presence there, as well as their cultural achievements, will be treated in the following section. At this point, however, it is interesting to conclude this general background survey with an intriguing fact that pursuant to the establishment of a branch of the Umayyad dynasty in Spain by an Umayyad prince who escaped the massacre of his kin in the East, and, more particularly, with 'Abd al-Raḥmān the third who proclaimed himself caliph in 929, three caliphs were in power at the same time: one in Baghdad, one in Cairo and one in Cordoba.

The Andalusian musical tradition

In the year 711 the Berber officer Ṭāriq, at the head of 7000 warriors, crossed the straits of Gibraltar and established a foothold on Spanish soil. Thereafter, assisted by Ibero-natives, the Muslim armies swept through vast territories, encountering resistance in only a few towns. The victorious march was halted in 732 with the defeat of Muslim conquerors at the gates of Poitiers (France). Together with the 'clients' of his house, in 755 the Umayyad prince 'Abd al-Raḥmān landed on Spanish soil; in May 756 he established his residence at Cordoba where he founded the brilliant

Marwānid kingdom and was recognized as emir. The Umayyad rule lasted from 756–976. ʻAbd al-Raḥmān the third, who proclaimed himself caliph in 929, raised Muslim power in the Peninsula to its ultimate heights.

Under the Umayyads *al-Andalus* (the Arab name for Spain) knew its most flourishing period, but this came to an end with the fall of the caliphate and the establishment of the petty states (*mulūk al- ṭawā'if*), coinciding with the first steps of the *Reconquista*. 'The *ṭā'ifa* (singular of *ṭawā'if*),' writes E. García-Gómez, 'may be likened to the republics of Italian Renaissance, wearing a turban, but lacking a purse, and moreover inclined to betray one another at any moment' (García-Gómez 31: 232). The deteriorating situation brought to the scene the *Almoravids*, who were summoned from North Africa. Their domination between 1091 and 1145 hardly improved matters; the period was also marked by the growing success of the *Reconquista*. In 1145 the *Almoravids* were replaced by another North African movement, the *Almohads*, who emphasized the unique values of Muslim tradition as the norm of life. At the end of their reign in 1269, the Christians were already masters of almost all Spanish territories, with the exception of the Nāṣarite kingdom of Granada which resisted for two and a half centuries more.

The fall of this last stronghold in 1492 marked the end of eight centuries of Muslim domination. During that period the Iberian Peninsula was the scene of one of the most fascinating examples of cultural interchange. Indeed, a multitude of human groups, different in race, religion and social class, interacted and intermingled until they finally moulded a new type of Andalusian individual with a unique cultural style. This variegated society was compounded of a minority of Arabs of pure extraction, a majority of neo-Muslim Hispano-Christians converted to Islam, numerous Berbers, Negroes and freed slaves from Eastern and Western Europe, Mozarabs – that is to say Christians who refused to convert to Islam and perpetuated their unique rites and music – and, in addition, Jews.

The Jews had been in Spain uninterruptedly for many centuries starting with biblical times, and relatively many came there after the destruction of the second Temple of Jerusalem in 70 AD. As a component of the heteroclite Andalusian society, they interacted with all the other entities to create a social and cultural symbiosis. Within this framework, music occupied a prominent place. The Jews also contributed to the development of various branches of knowledge and the arts and were active as councillors, ambassadors and agents , promoting contacts between *al-Andalus,* Europe and the Orient. Until the fifteenth century they also functioned as court-musicians in Muslim and Christian territories. However, despite their profound involvement in the consolidation of the new Andalusian culture, they became extremely eager to demonstrate their own cultural identity. Under the patronage of Jewish notables and statesmen such as Ḥisdāy ibn Shaprūṭ in

Cordoba and Shmuel ha-nagīd in Granada, artists working in the Hebrew language created refined liturgical and secular poetry and songs, while scholars devoted themselves to the study of Hebrew and other fields of Jewish learning, including the science of music (Shiloah 265).

It should be noted that in the process of crystallizing the Andalusian culture the Arab minority vigorously pressed its influence in ways that would ensure the hegemony of Arab language and values. Under the first Umayyad rulers, singers were imported from the East. The prolific Tunisian writer Aḥmad al-Tīfāshī (1184–1253), in his newly discovered manuscript on Andalusian music, reports in the name of a local expert that 'The songs of the people of Andalus were, in ancient times, either in the style of the Christians, or in the style of the Arab camel drivers (*ḥudā'*) . . . until the establishment of the Umayyad dynasty' (Liu 81: 42). According to the same author, a significant change came about due to the great Baghdadian musician 'Alī ibn Nāfī', nicknamed Ziryāb, who arrived at the Cordoban court of 'Abd al-Raḥmān II in 822 and 'introduced previously unheard [innovations], and his style was systematically adopted, while all others were forgotten' (Liu 81: 42). This concise but significant statement became a highly colourful and detailed story under the pen of a later Maghreban author, the *litérateur* and biographer al-Maqarrī (1591–1632).

Al-Maqarrī's story as it appeared in his work *Nafḥ al-ṭīb* . . . in turn became the basis and point of departure for all subsequent writers on Andalusian music who often reproduced his work with additional elaboration. Al-Maqarrī described Ziryāb as a highly gifted and inspired innovator who, soon after arriving at the court of 'Abd al-Raḥmān the second, became chief court musician and was charged with improving and raising the level of all musical activities. Due to his highly refined taste, this artist, still in his early thirties, came to be regarded as an authority on such matters as fashion, hair-do, perfumes, culinary art and the like. In the realm of music he was credited with improving the strings of the *'ūd*, increasing their number from four to five and replacing the plectrum with an eagle's feather. In addition, he was considered the inventor of the performing sequence *nashīd-basīṭ-ahzādj* (vocal improvisation, metrical slow movement and rapid rhythmic finale, respectively), as well as of the sophisticated compound form: the *nūba,* along with its related modal concept and arrangement. This gifted musician, who had a phenomenal memory, was also a distinguished educator said to have conceived a special educational method. He pioneered the institutionalization of musical education, his school having been widely known and respected. As a result, by the time he died in 857, art music in al-Andalus had reached its peak and on the whole had divested itself of the bonds of Oriental models. Yet, although well on its way to shaping a splendid local art, the Oriental Great Tradition continued to be this music's guiding spirit.

Unlike Al-Maqarrī who depicted Ziryāb as a cultural hero and the innovator of the Andalusian style *in toto*, al-Tīfāshī presents us with a more balanced and dynamic image of those developments. Thus, for instance, extolling the remarkable contribution to the fusion of styles in Andalusian music of the great philosopher and 'most illustrious music expert' ibn Bādjdja known in the West as Avempace (d. 1139), al-Tīfāshī writes: 'After having secluded himself for a few years to work with skilled singing-girl slaves, he improved the *istihāla* and *'amal* (two musical forms) by mixing the songs of the Christians and those of the East' (Liu 81: 42). This key statement alludes to a process that starts in the ninth century with Ziryāb, culminates with ibn Bādjdja in the twelfth century and continues on after him with improvements by other great musicians whose names are cited by al-Tīfāshī: ibn Jūdī, ibn al-Ḥammāra, and 'the seal of this art' abū'l-Ḥusayn al-Ḥāsib al-Mursi (Liu 81: 42).

It is interesting that the intermediaries in ibn Bādjdja's enterprise were singing-girl slaves who obviously played an important role in all Andalusian musical activities. Seville was the major centre in which gifted singing-girls were trained and given a comprehensive general education in addition to music. Among those girls were white Christians taken as slaves. They were called *rūmiyya* and in poetry were often likened to doves on the summit of trees. When put up for sale, the qualifications expected of a singing-girl included elegant handwriting, excellent memory, mastery of the Arabic language, expert performance on various instruments, proficiency as a dancer and in shadow play. Such a consummate artist was sold for a very high price.

Curiously enough, the suite form *nūba,* which Al-Maqarrī claims was invented by Ziryāb, is not expressly mentioned in al-Tīfāshī's treatise. Might it then have been in the process of elaboration? The idea of this form may even have existed during Ziryāb's time or before. Indeed J. Pacholszik, in an unpublished lecture, suggests the existence of an earlier hypothetical source – a suite in the Eastern tradition – which would mean that Ziryāb might have been only a transmitter and modifier rather than a creator. In any event, the Andalusian *nūba* as it survived in the North African centres took considerable advantage of the new poetic strophic genres, *muwashshaḥ* and *zadjal,* that flourished during the tenth and eleventh centuries.

The new poetic genres

The eminent Spanish scholar E. García-Gómez writes : 'The *muwashshaḥ* is undoubtedly the most original product of the Umayyad culture, rising far above the provincial level of its other achievements' (García-Gómez 31: 229). Indeed, the *muwashshaḥ* in classical Arabic and *zadjal* in the vernacular constitute a common denominator of sorts whereby the different groups could take advantage of the remarkable local innovation.

The inventor of the *muwashshaḥ* is said to have been the blind poet Muqaddam ibn Mu'āfa (end of the ninth or beginning of the tenth century). As to when the *zadjal* was created and by whom, we do not yet know definitively. In any event the *zadjal* reached its peak with the outstanding poet Abū Bakr Muḥammad ibn Quzmān who died in Cordoba in 1160. It is said that ibn Quzmān, known to his contemporaries as the prince of *zadjal,* at first used the classical forms and language but, realizing his inability to compete with the great poets of his time, he decided to shift to the vernacular and popular forms. Knowing the Romance dialect well, ibn Quzmān interspersed his compositions with Romance words and phrases. His exciting *chansons* with their characteristic and admirably musical metres were enthusiastically received by both the élite and the common folk.

The *muwashshaḥ* derives its name from *wishāḥ* – a belt ornamented with pearls and rubies; the *zadjal* means elevation of the voice and singing. In both genres the fundamental unit is the strophe, and (*bayt* or *djuz'*). The perfect form (*tāmm*) of the *muwashshaḥ* begins with one or two lines (prelude) called *madhhab, ghuṣn* or *maṭla'* with a rhyme scheme: AB or ABAB. Then come the two parts of the strophe: (a) *dawr* or *simṭ* which includes a varying number of hemistiches sometimes with the same rhymes as the prelude; the rhymes of the *dawr* vary from strophe to strophe, and (b) *qufl* which maintains the same rhyme all the time and is exactly like the prelude with respect to number of lines and rhymes; it is a sort of refrain and in songs may repeat the line of the prelude identically. A *muwashshaḥ* of five to six strophes can have the following rhyme scheme:

--------A   ---------B or ABAB   ---------c   --------c
--------c   or cdcdcd ---------A   ---------B   or ABAB etc.

The structure of the *zadjal,* which usually includes more strophes than the *muwashshaḥ,* is as follows: AA bbbA cccA or A bbbA cccA. A most striking feature of the *muwashshaḥ* is the use of concluding verses in Romance called *khardja* (clausula, exit). Some writers maintain that, in part, it may have been borrowed from a popular lyric and in part was composed by the poet to be incorporated into the *muwashshaḥ.*

The bilingualism or trilingualism expressed in the *khardjas* represents a confluence of three literary traditions and the elaboration of different linguistic permutations – Arabic/Romance, Hebrew/Romance and Arabic/Hebrew – within a single artistic tradition. A plebian tendency and the influence of bilingualism found fullest expression in the zadjal, wherein, incidentally, there is no *khardja.* The discovery in 1948 by Samuel M. Stern of this surprising unit at the end of Hebrew and later at the end of Arabic poems, gave rise to a heated argument between Romanists and Arabists that we shall refer to when treating the Arabian influence (Stern 241). It is generally accepted that the two genres were closely linked to music. Commenting on a definition in Aristotle's *Poetics,* the famous Andalusian philosopher ibn Rushd, Averroes (d. 1198), writes in his *Talkhīṣ*:

> The imitation in poetry that is sung pertains to three things: the harmony of notes (melody), the rhythmic component (rhythm) and the imitation itself (words). Each of these three can exist by itself, like the melody that is heard in wind instruments; the rhythm in dance; and the imitation in verbal articulation, that is to say, the non-rhythmic suggestive part of poetic discourse. It is also possible for all three to be used together as in the case of the genres in vogue in our locality known as *muwashshaḥ* and *zadjal* that characterise the poems created in this language (Arabic) by the people of the Peninsula.

Due to the intimate association of these strophic genres with music they gained considerable popularity, not only in Spain, but also in North Africa and major Near Eastern centres where they continue to thrive both in art and folk music.

The zambras and leilas

These two key terms refer to major musical activity in Andalusia – the nocturnal music and dance entertainment sessions that were held in palaces and private homes, sessions frequently referred to by ibn Quzmān in his *zadjal* poems. The term *leila* corresponds to the Arab *layla* (night – sing. of *layālī*) while *zambra* derives from the Arabic *samar* or *musāmara* which means nocturnal conversation and depicts a 'literary' genre most typical of Bedouin life. Similar to the *zambra,* we find the term *samra* in Yemen and elsewhere designating a nocturnal entertainment session which includes songs, dances and instrumental music (Lambert 418: 129–134, 193–197).

In his *ḥadīqat al-afrāḥ*, the author al-Shirwānī tells the story of a writer who visited Malaga in 1016 and could not sleep at night because of the noise emanating from a *zambra* being held in a neighbouring house. At a certain point he is fascinated by a musical piece, goes out and observes the happening which he describes as follows: in the middle of a vast dwelling there was a big garden in the centre of which 20 guests were seated in a row, wine goblets and fruit within reach. Young girls holding lutes (*'ūd* and *ṭunbūr*), cithar (*mi'zaf*), an oboe-like instrument (*mizmār*) and timbrels, stood aside without playing. A female musician was seated alongside them, her lute in her lap: the eyes of the entire audience were on her, their ears attuned to her songs that she accompanied with her instrument. The female ensemble described by this eyewitness was called *sitāra;* they played with the soloist and also accompanied the female dancer. In these typically Iberian entertainment sessions male musicians also took part.

In addition to *zadjal* poems, many sources describing the *zambra* emphasized the prominent role played in this session by the instrument known as *būq*. Al-Tīfāshī describes it as 'the noblest instrument among them, and the one producing the greatest pleasure in dancing and singing' (Liu 81: 43); and the historian ibn Khaldūn evaluates it as 'one of the best instruments of its time' (Rosenthal 63: II, 396). The *būq* usually designates a horn, yet in the context of Andalusian music it might have corresponded to a double reed instrument similar to the shawm. It may be possible to resolve this difficulty by reference to the *albogon* depicted in a miniature of the Alfonsino codex E1 of the *Cantigas de Santa Maria* (see below, p. 80). The miniature of *Cantiga* 300 shows an instrument with a bell made of a big horn, a conical tube made of wood and pierced fingerholes, and a double reed surrounded by a circular disk on which the lips of the player rest (Alvarez 261: 83–84). This unusual instrument was favoured in both folk and art music. It is said that Emir Muḥammad the first had at his service a number of *būq* virtuosi, and that he himself excelled in playing a golden ebony *būq*, set with precious stones.

Finally, it should be noted that the *zambra* and *leilas* were so deeply rooted in Andalusian customs that they continued to exist for more than 70 years after the fall of the last stronghold in Granada, mainly among the *Mudjeras* (Muslims living under Christian rule) and *Moriscos* (Moors converted to Christianity) (Manzano 260: 17, 29).

Arabian influence on medieval European music

The question of the Arabian influence on Medieval European music has been heatedly debated among scholars of our time. The discussion involves an era when Islamic culture was most widespread and had tangible as well as intellectual contact with Latin Christendom. During the high Middle Ages these contacts were established by way of the Crusaders in the Holy Land and the Muslims who occupied the Iberian Peninsula and Sicily.

The Crusaders

For two centuries the Crusaders were in direct contact with the Muslims, yet Muslim influence seems to have been insignificant. The sporadic interest that was echoed in their contemporary accounts and literary writings such as the cyclic poems, was confined to the Saracen military bands and their overwhelming effect. Those bands combined different types of drums, trumpets, horns, shawms and cymbals; they were used ceremonially to mark rank and prestige, as well as to exhort warriors in battle and for tactical purposes. From the many colourful descriptions in Christian chronicles one can infer the formidable effect produced by those bands on the Crusader troops. The French chronicler Joinville wrote in his description of the siege of

Damietta in Egypt (1249): 'The noise they made with their kettledrums and trumpets was terrible to hear' (Bowles 247: 17). In the numerous reports on those bands and the tumultuous sound they produced, the instruments' names appear in latinized form: the French *nacaires* or English nakers for *naqqārāt*(kettledrum); *tabor* for *ṭabl* (cylindrical drum); *anafil* for *al-nafīr* (trumpet). As to the latter, the term *fanfare*, still in use in the context of military bands, may have been derived from *al-nafīr*. The question is, of course, the extent to which this contact influenced European music. Available evidence indicates that the long exposure of Christian forces to this martial music led to the importation, adaptation and improvement of Islamic prototypes (Farmer 237).

Sicily

The Muslim conquest of Sicily began when the armies of the North African Aghlabid dynasty succeeded in establishing a firm foothold on the island by taking Palermo in 831. After a long period of disunity and unrest among the conquerors, the second half of the tenth century and beginning of the eleventh were marked by the spread and consolidation of Arab civilization in the island. In 1060 the Normans, under Count Roger de Hauteville, put an end to Muslim rule. However, the new ruler adopted the Arab administrative system as well as basic elements of Islamic culture in intellectual life and the arts. His successors, Roger II (d. 1154) and Frederik II of Hohenstaufen (d. 1250) followed in his footsteps and were ardent Arabophiles. Nevertheless, one should not overlook the ambivalent attitude of the Normans that expressed itself in their persecution of Muslims and vehement liquidation of an Arab communal presence in Sicily.

Sympathy for Arab and Muslim culture manifested itself in the encouragement and support the rulers gave Arab scholars and artists. Thus, for example, it was at the court of Roger II that the Arab geographer Idrīsī wrote his famous description of the world. As a result, the scholars, particularly Jews – who as linguists and translators encouraged the transmission of Arab sciences to the Occident – and the many musicians and court dancers who enhanced the banquets of the aristocracy ensured the survival, at least for a time, of fundamental aspects of Arabic music in Sicily (Burnett 263). A chronicler describing a reception in honour of the Earl of Cornwall, who was on his way back to England after the crusade, referred to the strange music and bizarre instruments that 'the Englishman had never before seen or heard', as well as to 'acrobatic dances of lovely Saracen girls' (Bowles 247: 21–22).

Further evidence of the artistic influence is to be found in the richly carved and painted ceiling of the Capella Palatina in Palermo, founded in 1140. A number of Near Eastern artists were summoned by the monarch to contribute to the realization of the monumental edifice. The painted ceiling, representing themes and techniques typical of Near Eastern paintings, includes the pictures of a variety of instrumentalists and dancers; the instrument depicted most frequently is the *'ūd* (lute) (Villard 18; Granit 33).

Spain

The other and much more important conduit through which Muslim culture and music reached the West was Spain. Indeed, in the twelfth century the Latin world began to absorb oriental lore; many pioneers of the new learning turned to Spain when seeking knowledge in mathematics, astronomy, astrology, medicine and philosophy. Many important Greek scientific texts were preserved in Arabic translation, becoming part of the body of Arab scientific knowledge. Although the Arabs did not alter the foundations of Greek science, they made several important contributions within its framework.

The rich literature dealing with the influence of Hispano-Arabic music on European song was marked by controversial views on many issues such as the nature and origin of Andalusian music, and the part played in its development by the different components of Andalusian society. The debate over the two poetic genres discussed above, the *muwashshaḥ* and *zadjal*, was intense and heated. In 1912 the eminent Spanish scholar J. Ribera y Tarrago (1858–1934), who wrote on historical, literary and musical themes, launched this debate in a lecture on the outstanding composer of *zadjal,* the poet ibn Quzmān. He contended that the two genres born in Muslim Spain in imitation of already-existing Romance-language lyrics had exerted considerable influence on the lyrics of the Troubadours in Provence and the rest of Europe as well. He considered ibn Quzmān's collection of poems the key to his advanced thesis. His conclusions evoked furious polemics (Ribera 232). After Samuel Stern's discovery in 1948 of the final verses (*khardja*) in Romance (Stern 241), Ribera's disciple E. García-Gómez offered further support to the thesis that the source of inspiration had been earlier, already existing Spanish poetry. He considered the invention of the two above-mentioned genres an '. . . enterprise of folklorists who undoubtedly were aristocratic Arabs, but amateurs when it came to popular folk arts' (García-Gómez 243: 122).

Ribera y Tarrago launched the same debate in connection with the famous musical work the *Cantigas de Santa Maria*. This collection of 413 songs about the Virgin Mary was accumulated between about 1250 and 1280 under the direction of King Alfonso and was illustrated with illuminated miniatures. There is disagreement as to whether the king limited his participation to supervision or actually wrote some of the words and music himself. The 41 miniatures included in the Alfonsine codices reflect the musical cosmopolitanism of Alfonso's court. They depict musicians of all three faiths as well as 44 different Spanish and Arab instruments.

In a solemn lecture delivered in 1921 at the Royal Spanish Academy on the occasion of the 700th anniversary of the birth of the enlightened Spanish king Alfonso el Sabio (the wise), Ribera extolled Alfonso's breadth of mind, tolerance and keen interest in cultural matters. He then went on to suggest that the king had naturally addressed himself to the best and most flourishing music of his time, that is to say, the music of the defeated Arab subjects, and had set to it the texts of the famous *Cantigas de Santa Maria*. Ribera also argued not only that the rhyme scheme of most of these cantigas corresponds to that of the *zadjal,* but also that the whole work in its original form was performed by famous professional musicians of the three faiths according to the norms and performing practice of Andalusian music then in vogue. At a later date Ribera, among the first to precipitate the debate about Hispano-Arab influence, addressed himself to this thesis in two other publications. One of those who took exception to the idea of Arabian musical influence on the cantigas was the eminent Spanish scholar Higinio Angles (Ribera 238). Angles made a monumental study (1943–1964) of Alfonso's *Cantigas de Santa Maria* and publicized the entire corpus of 413 melodies which he transcribed in modern notation, identifying ten distinct musical genres such as *virelai, rondeau, sequence* and *lai.* Concerning Arab influence, Angles maintained that the lack of Arabic-notated documents hampered such an investigation. He contended that Spain had had indigenous music long before the Arabs arrived and that this tradition was never supplanted by the Arabic musical idiom (Katz 259).

One of the strong supporters of Ribera's thesis was the celebrated expert on Arab music, Henry George Farmer, who gave special impetus to the entire question of Arab influence. In 1925 he published a pamphlet called 'Clues to the Arabian influence on Musical Theory' (Farmer 233), in which he took issue with the view that there was less Arab influence on music than on other Western European cultural manifestations. Among the clues attesting to Arab influence on music, Farmer pointed to the instruments that were adopted by the West, first via the military at the time of the crusaders, and later through other contacts and in connection with other musical forms. Among the instruments borrowed by the West and cited as clues are the lute (*al-'ūd*); the *rebec* (*rabāb)*; the guitar (*qīṭār*); *adufe* (*al-daff*) and *pandore* (*al-bandair*). Another important subject to which Farmer paid particular attention concerned the origin and characteristics of the Andalusian strophic genres *muwashshaḥ* and *zadjal,* their link to later Roman musical forms and lyrics, as well as their affinities with the *Cantigas de Santa Maria*. Thus we find him a fervent champion of the thesis stressing unequivocally that 'many of the song forms and dance forms of the minstrelsy of Medieval Europe can be traced to the Arabs' (Farmer 233: 62).

It is in the realm of music theory and musical thought that the most convincing traces are discernible. However, when published, Farmer's far-reaching arguments about the primordial achievement of the Arabs in general music theory and their innovation of compositional procedures such as the organum, notational system, rhythmic modes and so forth, met with both enthusiasm and criticism. In the case of his chief opponent, Kathleen Schlesinger, the issue was publicly debated in the *Musical Standard* (Schlesinger 234), which led Farmer to write his book *Historical Facts for the Arabian Musical Influence* (Farmer 235). It is true that in the realm of musical thought and music theory, the influence should have been perceptible, yet its traces here were rather meagre, unlike the obvious Arab influence on medicine, mathematics, physics, astronomy, astrology and philosophy.

With the exception of the Latin translations of al-Fārābī's book *Iḥṣā' al-'ulūm* (Classification of Sciences) which includes a chapter defining the division and objectives of the science of music, there are no extant Latin translations or compilations from the Arabic to help us (Farmer 42). Nevertheless, al-Fārābī, the great Arab philosopher and music theorist, has often been extolled along with Boethius and Ptolemy as one of the great authorities on the science of music. It is noteworthy, however, that the masterpiece *The Grand Book on Music* and other important musical treatises of his are not found among the many Arabic works that have been translated into Latin.

In more than a few studies on the influence of Arab music the prevailing tendency has been to emphasize the unilateral nature of that influence – usually justified by the cultural superiority of the disseminators. Furthermore, no attempt has been made to single out the distinctive traits that underlie the Andalusian style's particular confluence of diverse stylistic features; nor have studies been conducted to show how the musical system of the recipient culture responded to the influence, or how Arabian music impinged on it.

In view of the foregoing, it appears likely that the question of the influence that naturally accrues from contact between two different cultures can best be considered from the standpoint of the nature and degree of impact on the music. For present purposes, therefore, it is pertinent to ascertain whether musical influence remained on the level of borrowed ideas and random superficial elements, or left significant imprints. We may assume that borrowing certain musical elements from another culture does not necessarily imply adopting its music; general and philosophical ideas cross cultural boundaries much more easily than do stylistic, creative and sentient components. This is particularly true in the case of music, which is an emotional language laden with culturally bound symbolic codes; hence it is understood, felt and appreciated by those who are entirely integrated within a given culture. Thus, for instance, the Arabs who borrowed extensively from

Greek theoretical writings on music and incorporated much of their content and methodology into their own system remained quite indifferent to Greek music and its practice. While the Arabs' indebtedness to Greek science and philosophy is recognized, one does not find traces of such indebtedness in their rich literary and dramatic output.

During recent decades a few scholars who ardently posited Arabian influence reached far-fetched conclusions with regard to all the above fields. They point to the compound form, the *nūba*, as the predecessor of and model for the European suite; with no supporting evidence, they claim that the instruments borrowed by the Europeans brought their characteristic music across the borders with them. An Arab example quite close to our own time belies this view. In the second half of the nineteenth century, under the impact of European influence, musicians from various Near Eastern centres replaced the traditional *rabāb* (a fiddle usually played on the knee) by the European violin. This instrument was immediately incorporated into the traditional ensemble to fulfil a role identical with that of the *rabāb*. It brought no violin music with it and, moreover, to fit the new environment it underwent a change in intonation and in the technique by which it is played; in North Africa the violin is even played on the knee as the *rabāb* was in its time. This seems to confirm that the partial or total adoption of another musical language implies radical transformation and transvaluation of the musical style and behaviour in the recipient culture.

Survival of Andalusian music in the Maghrib

It is almost certain that the numerous musicians included among the Hispano-Arab exiles who took refuge in the Maghrib brought the flourishing Andalusian art with them and endeavoured to transplant it in their new environment. We may also assume that the imported art was not unknown and might have been cultivated in major Maghrib centres even before the last Muslim left Spanish soil.

There is evidence that the sophisticated Andalusian compound art music form, the *nūba,* was most highly esteemed among the people of the Maghrib. In cultivating it they even perpetuated certain local Spanish styles and schools. According to Alexis Chottin, the French scholar and expert on Moroccan music, the school of Sevilla found its continuation in Tunis; that of Cordoba in Tlemcen; and the schools of Valencia and Granada were perpetuated in Fez (Morocco) (Chottin 159: 93–94) .

It should be borne in mind that Spanish musicians used a system of 24 *nūbāt* (pl. of *nūba*), alleged to correspond to 24 modal scales and to possess a whole range of cosmological affinities. Among the rare documents describing this system is a poem by ibn al-Khaṭīb al-Salmānī from Granada (fl. 1294) whose authorship is not yet definitively ascertained. The poem deals with the classification of 24 Andalusian modes into four principals and their branches, as well as their affiliation to humours, elements and natures. The poem was published by Farmer in his *An Old Moorish Tutor* (Farmer 47). Did that complex, flourishing tradition survive in its entirety? The first Western scholar who addressed this question was the Spaniard Raphael Mitjana (Mitjana 92). In an article published in 1906 he claimed, with no supporting evidence, that when in 1492 the last Arabs left Spain and took refuge in the Maghrib, a famous musician named al-Ḥā'ik devotedly collected the traditional *nūbāt*; to make them more accessible, he reduced their number from 24 to 11. Alexis Chottin in his *Corpus de la musique marocaine* (Chottin 155: 98–101), agreed that the anthology of 11 *nūbāt* was compiled by al-Ḥā'ik, but not before 1792. C. Brockelmann, in his authoritative German *History of Arabic Literature* (Brockelmann 16: SII, 709), contended that the work was completed in 1717. Since the discovery of new manuscripts and related collections of *nūbāt* ascribed to al-Ḥā'ik, it has become clear that the various questions concerning the transplanting of the Spanish tradition call for serious re- examination. Indeed, one of the later collections ascribed to al-Ḥā'ik (Leiden Or. 14100) as well as a treatise by 'Abd al-Raḥmān al-Fāsī (d. 1685) include lists of 24 *nūbāt* (Shiloah 76: 108–109). Hence, it is conceivable that the material was newly organized or simplified at some time near the beginning of the eighteenth century.

Be that as it may, it is evident that the ramified Andalusian *nūba* has been decisive in Maghreban art music and was eventually considered by its practitioners as the distinguishing mark of that music. The safeguarding and local enrichment of it has not been limited only to propagators of urban art music. To some extent, it also owes its preservation to religious movements and mystical Muslim brotherhoods. In Lybia, for example, the repertory of Andalusian *nūba* form, known as *ma'lūf,* could survive only thanks to the '*Isāwiyya* confraternity; the musical repertory of the *Qādiriyya* brotherhood in Tunisia comprised 13 complete *nūbāt.* When they assigned the term *ma'lūf* to the Andalusian art tradition, the Tunisians began to distinguish between its serious religious aspect – *ma'lūf al-djad* – as opposed to its profane aspect (Guettat 185: 179–180). In the same spirit, Jewish communities in North Africa, particularly in Morocco, adopted the model of the *nūba* for singing *Baqqashot* (supplications) – post-midnight ceremonial singing on Friday nights in winter. This custom originated in Safed (Palestine) under the influence of the Kabbalistic school that flourished there during the sixteenth century. The mystics of this school and their followers attributed great importance to singing from midnight on.

Several different names designate local compositional sequences of a basic compound form that corresponds to and perpetuates the structure and ideals of the Andalusian *nūba*. It is known variously as-*ṣan'a*, *'āla*, *gharnāṭī*, *ma'lūf*, and *mūsīqā andalusiyya*. Of course, like all living traditions, those of the Maghrib absorbed influences emanating from the immediate milieu in which each tradition emerged. This compound art music form will be discussed further in Chapter 10.

Arab and Islamic music in sub-Saharan Africa

North African Arab and Berber elements that played a significant role in establishing and elaborating the Andalusian style and later ensured its survival outside the Iberian Peninsula were also quite active in the long process of Islamization of African societies south of the Sahara. The Islamization of black African societies, however, acquired certain previously unknown aspects. It was not only that the contact involved strong, well-anchored pagan tribal beliefs, customs and outlooks, usually accompanied by distinct functional musical idioms; there was also something very special about the way by which Islam reached those societies. Traders, not warriors, carried the new elements across the Sahara. Arab military conquerors of North Africa in the second half of the eighth century stopped on the fringes of the Sahara and, from centres established in oases at the northern gates, traders began to penetrate into the sudanic belt of West Africa. As trade developed, they established towns in the southern Sahara, opened new routes and created commercial centres which became arteries and foci for the spread of Islam among black peoples. At the same time they engaged in slave trade to North Africa that later gave rise to the establishment of large communities in various Maghreban centres. There they formed religious confraternities of their own and distinguished themselves as musicians and dancers (see Chapter 11).

According to N. Levzion, there were three successive stages in the Islamization of West Africa: first the growth of a Muslim community under a non-Muslim king; then the adoption of Islam as the court religion; finally, the rise of Islamic militancy, entailing the imposition of Islamic law and conversion of the common people. It was the second stage that was most typical of West Africa until the eighteenth century (Levzion 34).

In the Eastern Horn (Ethiopia and Somalia), where geographical proximity had created long-standing relations between Arabia and Ethiopia, the eighth century saw the establishment of the first Muslim settlements. By the ninth century there were Muslim communities all along the trade routes to the interior. While in Ethiopia the Muslims were unable to proselytize among the Christians, farther southward their influence resulted in the emergence of Muslim political units. The most important of these were the twelfth-century sultanate of Ifat and that of Mogadishu – which in the thirteenth century was the major coastal town.

Early settlements of migrants from Persia and Arabia on the East African coast go back to the sixth and seventh centuries; Afro-Arabic interaction over the centuries stimulated the growth of a new civilization, known as Swahīlī, from the Arabic Sawāhila (people of the coast). Islam reached this area and West Africa at about the same time, but while in West Africa the faith penetrated inland, in East Africa it remained confined to the coastal areas, manifesting itself only through individual conversion.

The impact of Islamic and Arabic cultures undoubtedly had a far-reaching influence on many cultures of these areas, but the nature of this influence varied; it was more effective in Northern Sudan and Mauritania, while in most other places it underwent varying degrees of modification. Referring to the cultural dynamics in the sub-Saharan area, N. Levzion argues that the Islamization of Africa was greatly aided by the Africanization of Islam. Even in the case of Arabic, the language of Islam, although most Muslims can recite from the *Qur'ān,* their knowledge of Arabic is very limited. Only scholars have acquired a good command of the language and have produced works in various fields of Islamic sciences. In order to win adherents, he adds, Islam had to adopt the this-worldly orientation of African religions. Furthermore, Islamic ideas were interpreted in traditional terms and Muslim festivals were transformed to such an extent that their original Islamic features were hardly recognizable. Essentially, therefore, rites of passage combine Islamic and traditional ceremonies (Levzion 34: 355–356).

Dealing with the effect of Islamic and Arabic cultures on the musical traditions of African societies, the African musicologist Kwabena Nketia argues that in most parts of sub-Saharan Africa the musical traditions underwent various degrees of adjustment and, according to him, 'the adjustments were not as radical as it is generally supposed'. He adds: 'It appears that African converts did not have to abandon their traditional music completely, even when they learned Islamic cantillation or became familiar with Arabic music' (Kwabena 250: 10). The latter remark contrasts sharply with any expectation one might have had that the influence would be apparent above all in the *Qur'ān* recitation and the *'adhān* – the call to prayer – because they are both performed in Arabic. To explain this seeming incongruity, one should remember that, due to the importance of correct, careful, solemn recitation of the *Qur'ān* known as *tadjwīd,* a remarkable system evolved regulating cantillation with respect to the laws of phonetics and precise rendition of the sacred text. Although they tried to adhere to the rules of the *tadjwīd,* few African readers managed to acquaint themselves with the characteristics governing voice quality, intonation, pitch, vocabulary, pronunciation and stresses; their reading remained coloured by residual elements of African vocal style. If that is the case with *Qur'ān* reading, it is interesting to examine what occurred with other forms of Islamic religious music, namely the music accompanying festive occasions such as the *mawlid* – the celebration of the Prophet's birthday – and the rituals of mystic brotherhoods.

Scholars who have explored these forms of Islamic ceremonial music point to the existence of many local styles that vary according to place and social class. They also are distinguished by a pronounced African stamp. The use of indigenous resources in musical practice is referred to by J. S. Trimingham who observes: 'the musical aptitude of the African, characterized by the chant, highly developed rhythm and antiphony, has found expression in the recitals of religious poems in Arabic and vernaculars at *dhikr* gatherings' (Trimingham 22: 125). Arthur Simon, who investigated the ceremonial music of brotherhoods in Sudan and Nubia, comes to the conclusion, in view of the predominant African elements, that the music he analysed presents an example of the Africanization of Islamic elements. And he adds: 'Influences might go back to the religious practices of Islam like that of the brotherhoods, but, as we can see, its range of influence upon secular music and its tonal structure is limited' (Simon 255: 18). Indeed, in the realm of secular music, it is generally acknowledged that the influence of Arabian music is even less pervasive, with the Sudanic area revealing the greatest increment in Arabic and Oriental instruments such as the (oboe-like) *ghaita,* the long-tubed trumpet and a number of bowed string instruments. In relation to these and other borrowed instruments, K. Nketia says: 'Generally speaking, the different types of Arabic instruments have simply furnished models for the manufacturing of local equivalences. It follows that certain instruments, like the one-stringed fiddle, occur in different sizes, forms and timbres' (Kwabena 250: 10).

An interesting case is that of Mauritania which, culturally speaking, forms a bridge linking the Arab–Berber region of North Africa and the 'land of the Blacks'. Formerly Berber-speaking, it was the homeland of the *Almoravid* dynasty which invaded and conquered the Maghrib in the first half of the tenth century and later ruled in Spain between 1091 and 1145; it was converted to Arabic speech in the fourteenth century. Arabic-speaking peoples in the north constitute 80 per cent of the population and are called the 'Moors'; they refer to themselves as *bīḍān,* 'whites', to distinguish themselves from the negro inhabitants of the south who speak various African languages.

On the whole, the 'Moors' cultivate poetry sung in Arabic and to a lesser extent in vernacular languages. Their classical music is founded on four 'modes', each of which can be expressed either in the 'white' or 'black' style, or the intermediate 'spotted' style. There is a professional class of musicians called griots who, like their counterparts among the Wolof society of Senegal and Gambia, sang praises and were genealogists. In both cases their 'art' reflects an admixture of Negro and Muslim cultures (Guignard 174: 103–110; 155–168; 178–180).

7 From Constantinople to Kashmir

The Ottoman dynasty

A momentous event took place a few decades before the departure of the last Muslims from Spain: on 29 May 1453, Constantinople was captured by Sultan Mehmed II, known as 'the conqueror'. The city became the capital of the Ottoman empire and the cultural centre of Islam. Sultan Osman (1258–1326) founded the Ottoman dynasty; after defeating a Byzantine army he opened the way to the extraordinary expansion of the Ottomans. His followers pressed the attack against a retreating Byzantium, and in 1357 they crossed the Dardanelles to Europe, establishing vassal dynasties in the Balkans. At a later phase, Sultan Bayazid I eliminated those dynasties and created a centralized state. Thus, after the fall of Constantinople, the Balkans were fully integrated into the empire all the way to the Danube. Ottoman conquests reached their peak in the sixteenth century under the reign of Süleyman (1520–1566), known in the West as the Magnificent. His predecessors having gained control of large parts of the Balkans, Süleyman defeated Hungary, one of Europe's major powers, at the battle of Mohacs in 1526 and surged north to the gates of Vienna. Under his reign the empire extended from the borders of Austria and southern Russia to the bounds of India, the Arabian peninsula, Syria, Egypt and large parts of North Africa. Control over these vast territories and conquered nations was secured by creating an interwoven central and provincial administrative system that rested on highly trained civil servants who belonged to the privileged military class. The most famous members of this class, which was on an exalted social level, were the Janissary élite corps; originally they were drawn from prisoners of war and subsequently from among slaves procured in various ways, including those taken as a levy of Christian youths. Following a selection process, the best of the male children were given training that prepared them for the highest military and administrative positions in the empire.

One of their most celebrated representatives, Lutfi Pasha, was elevated by Süleyman to the grand vizierate.

Intellectual and artistic activity

The continual din of warfare accompanied by the high prestige of the military class throughout Ottoman history did not silence the muses or in any way hamper the striving for intellectual achievement. Indeed, by the sixteenth century the term Ottoman had acquired a cultural connotation that gradually found expression in distinct traits which in the course of time made their mark on most cultural fields.

During Süleyman's reign – the golden age of the empire – contacts with Europe were intensified as diplomatic and commercial relations expanded. Although Venice established a permanent diplomatic mission in Istanbul toward the end of the fifteenth century, the treaties concluded in 1543 between Süleyman and the 'King of Christians', François I of France, were the most significant factor in increasing opportunities for deeper and more meaningful cultural interaction. It is noteworthy that on the occasion of the treaty signing, François I sent Süleyman an orchestra as a sign of friendship; guest performances by the newly arrived musicians seem to have inspired the creation of two new rhythms: *frenkcin* (12\4) and *frengi feri* (14\4). The French embassy – as well as other embassies, although to a lesser extent – became an attractive centre for scientists and artists who were invited to record their observations on various aspects of Turkish life and culture, including music. These early European accounts on music give us valuable hints as to performance practice, instruments, military bands and ceremonies of mystical fraternities.

Desiring to display their empire in the best possible light, Ottoman sovereigns awarded special privileges to purveyors of the arts and to culture in general; they extended their favour and support to poets, musicians, painters, *littérateurs* and historians. Ottoman literature, which placed special emphasis on poetry and history, was written in Arabic script and used Arabic, Persian and Turkish grammatical elements. One of the greatest Turkish poets was al-Baqi, a protégé of Süleyman. The sultans had a predilection for history and particularly encouraged chronicles portraying the Ottomans as the forceful and successful arm of Islam.

The sixteenth and early seventeenth centuries represent the most prolific period of Ottoman painting. The workshops of the saray created an original art which gradually freed itself of the Persian influence that was still perceptible during the fifteenth century. In the course of time the court artists also included some European painters and architects. Just around that time Turkish artists developed a Turkish style of calligraphic art; calligraphy occupied an important place due to the sacred character of Arabic script, which was considered the instrument for transmission of God's words.

The music

In the capital and other major centres of the Ottoman empire, an art music flourished that was essentially rooted in basic concepts of the Great Musical Tradition. However, in the course of time, it developed characteristics of its own that had their source in the Turkish temperament, the specific nature of their folk musical traditions and centuries of acculturation with subjected countries. In time, the distinctive style exerted influence on the entire region dominated by the Ottomans, while the separate folk traditions survived and continued to flourish, occasionally interacting with art music.

Numerous early European accounts reflect the salient particularities of Ottoman music by reference to four major features: Instruments, Janissary or *Mehter* music, female dancing and dancers, and the whirling dervishes. As to instruments, the detailed observations made in 1553 by the Frenchman, Pierre Belon, are of particular interest. Belon points to the excellency of the Turks in making bow and lute-strings out of intestines which 'are much more common there than in Europe'. Belon explains this as being due to the fact that the Turks had a great variety of lutes and 'many people know how to play one kind or another, which is not the case in France or in Italy'. He also mentions a variety of flutes or air instruments including the *miskal* (panpipes), which were in great vogue at that time (Belon 140). While Belon emphasized the wonderful sweetness of the *miskal's* sound, the Italian traveller Pietro Della Valle, who described it in 1614 as an instrument made of 14 or 15 canes over which the player runs his lips forward and back, argues that: 'the sweetness of its sound does not equal the long flute of the dervishes' (de la Valle 145).

The Mehter or Janissary band

This band won particular attention on the part of Europeans. In his *De La Republique des Turcs*, the orientalist Guillaume Postel who was sent as scientific attaché to Constantinople by François I, wrote: 'The first and most common diversions are big tambourins without snares and small ones of brass, hautsbois which play the same as they do in war, and so strangely that to the nations on our side it is necessary to stop one's ears or leave, otherwise the sound is only really good for a (military) campaign' (Postel 142). A year later, in 1551, the Italian Antonio Menavino described the Grand Turks' ensemble of 150 trumpeters and other musicians: 15 trumpeters were stationed on a tower next to the Saray, and 15 in another part of the city. The *Mehter* that comprised '*trombette*, *pifferri*, and *tamburi*' played at two o'clock in the morning and then an hour before dawn. Another part of them went to war with the Gran Turco. 'They have drums so big that a camel cannot carry more than one, and seems to make all the land around it tremble' (Menavino 141).

In its fully developed form the well-organized Janissary band which had as its patron Hadjdji Bektash, founder of the Bektashi religious order, comprised giant kettledrums: *kos* in pairs of various sizes mounted on camels; bass drums: *davul*; small timpani: *naqqārāt*; cymbals: *zīl*; oboe-like instruments: *zurna* reinforced by trumpets: *boru* and the *çevgan* or Turkish crescent, known as a 'Jingling Johnnie', 'chapeau chinois' or 'Schellenbaum', which when shaken up and down produced faint jingling sounds. Their leader, the *Mehter bachi*, played a *zurna*. The *Mehter* performed a special kind of musical repertory; it differed from that played previously by bands throughout the Muslim world, known as *ṭablkhane*. It also differed from Turkish art music. Their music, which in the course of time Europeans began to identify with Turkish music as a whole, was much in vogue in eighteenth-century Europe. Augustus II of Poland (d. 1735) was presented with a band by the sultan, and Central European princes had authentic *Mehter* bands performing in their courts. Musical instruments were adopted by European military bands, some of them, like the bass drum called in German *Türkishe Trommel*, finding their way to symphony orchestras. Many composers wrote *alla turca* passages or compositions, and the 'Turkish March' became an exotic piece. Turkomania encompassed many operas, ballets, musical compositions, and plays, and involved such famous composers as Gluck, Mozart and Beethoven (Signell 248).

The abolishment of the Janissary corps and their bands by Mahmud II in 1826 presaged the reform movement in Turkey called *tanzimat*, which opened the doors to Europe. The following year the sultan invited Giuseppe Donizetti, brother of the famous composer Gaetano Donizetti, to form and train a Western-type band that would play Western music. He also established a symphony orchestra and ballet troupe and sent the first Turkish missions consisting of 158 students to several European countries. One of the participants in such a mission had returned to Istanbul after studying the piano in Paris. The *Revue et Gazette musicale de Paris* (1839), reports that the Sultan, a great music-lover who was an admirer of Rossini and Meyerbeer, invited all his courtesans as well as a number of French guests to celebrate an exceptional event: in a sumptuously decorated hall the young Turkish artist gave a piano recital for the distinguished audience, and the program included piano variations and a sonata by Beethoven (RGMP 89).

The Mewlevis

The Mewlevi Order that established itself as early as the thirteenth century in Konya, the capital of the Seljuqs, manifested certain unique characteristics in their music as well as their ritual. The following excerpt is from an account of the Order's whirling dance written in approximately 1630 by Henry Blount, one of the many Europeans who described this particular ritual. After the sermon and the reading of *Qur'ānic* verses,

> The Dervises bowing with profoundest reverence to their superior, begin their usual dance, turning round with (such) swiftness that their faces can scarce be seen . . . when the musick ceases they all stop in an instant, not at all disordered with the circular motion, to which they have been accustomed from their infancy. . . . This custom they observe with great devotion in imitation of their founder Mevaluna (sic)'; (Blount 146)

Blount is referring here to Mevlana Djalāl al-dīn al-Rūmī (d. 1273), the founder of the Mewlevi Order (Random 221).

The order developed highly regulated ritual ceremonies in which music, dance and instrumental accompaniment acquired an importance and a degree of sophistication unparalleled in Muslim lands. This implied well-trained professional musicians and dancers, as well as a growing need for composed music. Thus for many centuries certain orders, the Mewlevi in particular, became catalysts for the promotion and expansion of art music. Indeed, many well-known early composers, some of whose works have survived, were connected with and sometimes adherents of the Order of the whirling dervishes and supplied it with their music. As a matter of fact, the title *dede* (dervish) was appended to the name of many of them, such as: Yusuf dede (d. 1669); Mustafa dede (d. 1683); the famous flute player Nayi Osman dede (d. 1732) who is said to have written contemporary compositions using an alphabetic notation of sorts; 'Abdül-Bâki dede (d. 1820) who in response to an imperial commission wrote an important treatise on musical practice, *Tedkīk-ve-tahkīk* (Research and Studies), and created a system for alphabetic notation; Ismail dede (d. 1845) and Zekâi dede (d. 1897).

More important is the fact that a number of these composers worked in two different spheres: in the monasteries and the Sultan's palaces. Hafiz Post (d. 1693), a favourite musician of Mehmed IV, is said to have composed 1200 works including many secular compositions. Another musician favoured by the same sultan, Buhurîzade Mustafa Itrî (d. 1712) was regarded as the outstanding master; he composed more than 1000 works and set to music the *na't* (hymn of praise) that is still performed today as the ceremony of the whirling dervishes begins. Mustafa efendi (d. 1786), the head muezzin for Sultan Ahmed III, gained fame as a composer in the *lâle devri* or Tulip Era (1718–30), a most fruitful period for the arts, named after the gorgeous tulip gardens on the shores of the Bosphorus. It was in those imperial gardens that the court musicians were first exposed to the folk poet-musicians *âshik* who influenced their endeavours to give their own compositions a stronger Turkish or folk flavour (see Chapter 12). Their search for a synthesis of classical and folk music was particularly apparent in the compositions of Eyyûbi Bekir Ağa (d. 1730).

Art music enjoyed a golden age under Selim III (1789–1807) who had many musicians serving in his saray. The sultan, himself a fine musician, elevated the most famous musician of the time, Ismail dede (d. 1845), to the highest rank. It should be noted that other composers and musicians, who had no connection with music of religious orders – including non-Muslims – also acquired prominence. Zaharya efendi (first half of the eighteenth century), a Christian-Orthodox, composed numerous secular art songs, in addition to hymns for Greek mass; the Armenian Nikiğos (nineteenth century) and the Jewish *ṭanbūr* player, Tanburî Isḥaq (d. 1815) are among the more celebrated of those composers. They and many others are still remembered not by virtue of their life stories, but thanks to compositions that have survived them, first through oral transmission and, for approximately the last 200 years, through various forms of notation.

We owe our first knowledge of those musical works to Albert Bobovsky (1610–1675), a Pole from Lwov who as a youth was taken prisoner by the Tatars and sold as a slave to the Turks. He received a sound education in the saray's school, and after being freed and converting to Islam, he assumed the name of 'Ali Beg or 'Ali Ukfî. For 18 years he served as chief drogman (translator) and musician at the court of sultan Mehmed IV. He left us a collection of songs, their texts transcribed in Arabic and Latin characters and their airs in Western notation, with the name of the *maqām* for each melody. This is an invaluable collection for anyone seeking knowledge of seventeenth century Ottoman music (Behar 322, 324a). He also wrote a manual containing dialogues in French and Turkish. Somewhat later a Moldavian prince, Demetre Cantemir (1673–1723), arrived in Istanbul, first as a hostage and then as a diplomat representing his father who ruled Moldavia. As a musician Cantemir became a famous virtuoso on the long-necked lute, the *ṭanbūr*, and a highly regarded composer of *ilm-ül musiki*; he left us a collection of 366 compositions for which he used a special notational system that he himself invented (Popesco-Judet 170; Alexandru 178a; Behar 324a). Some of his pieces appear in the French essay written in Istanbul by Charles Fonton in 1750, in which he compares Turkish and European music (Neubauer 77, 78; Behar 80; Shiloah 414). Cantemir's notational system is described in his theoretical treatise *Kitab-i ilm-i muziki* (Treatise on Musical Science). After a sojourn of 22 years in Istanbul, he returned to Moldavia in 1710; in 1714 he was elected to the Berlin Academy. It is important to mention, however, that the first notation used by Turkish musicians was the letter-like notation based on the Armenian ecclesiastical system that the church musician Hampartzum Limoncuyan introduced in 1810, in response to a commission by Sultan Selim III (Seidel 295). Western notation came into use after 1880. Hundreds of musical works composed before and during the nineteenth century are extant today as a result of transcriptions made by Raouf Yeqta, the twentieth-century composer and musicologist (Yeqta 152; Behar 324a).

The Iranian state

In earlier chapters we have shown the significant part played by Persians in the flowering of Muslim culture as a whole and in the crystallization of the Great Musical Tradition in particular. With the decline in power of the caliphate, the Persians re-emerged on the political scene and endeavoured to foster their distinctive national identity through reviving Persian as a written language. A series of independent dynasties arose in Persia and adjacent territories: the Ṭāhirids (820–73); Sāmānids (874–999) and Būwayhids (932–1055). After the invasion of the Mongols who devastated the lands of Islam and destroyed the Baghdad caliphate in 1258, Persia became the centre of a Mongol dynasty established by Hulagu. After a long period during which Persia was ruled by successors of the Mongol conquerors and a number of Turkish dynasties, the Safavid dynasty emerged and, at the beginning of the sixteenth century, established an Iranian national state. This dynasty had its origin in a Ṣūfī order – the Safawiyya – whose centre of activity was in the town of Ardabil in Azarbayjan. Considered as the founders of modern Iran and using Iranian as the official language, the Safavids promulgated Shiism as their state religion; following the Arab conquest Shiism had been one of the main factors in the preservation of Persia's identity. The height of Safavid power was attained under Shah 'Abbās I (1588–1629) who distinguished himself by his religious tolerance, by increasing Persian diplomatic and commercial relations with the West, and by the impetus he gave to the extraordinary renaissance of Persian culture.

The arts and classical music

When he made Isfahan his capital in 1598, Shah 'Abbās I grouped a number of architectural masterpieces round a piazza seven times the size of San Marco in Venice. This remarkable architectural achievement, which also demonstrates consummate perfection in the use made of polychrome and mosaic tiles to coat the basic structures, was only one facet of the marvellous flowering of the arts: carpet-weaving, textiles, metalwork, music and painting. Brilliant colour and design distinguished the painting and miniatures that are outstanding attributes of the art of the book in which Persia excelled. Manuscripts were gloriously embellished by illuminations and ornamental figures. Miniatures depicted scenes of great epics such as the *Shah-Name* (Book of Kings) written by the famous poet Firdawsi in the eleventh century. Among the many illustrated versions of this book, the best is the one commissioned by Shah Ismā'īl; it contains over 250 miniatures. Musical scenes, dancing and instruments are frequently depicted in the miniatures; a typical setting, for instance, is a garden party with refreshments of wine and fruit, and musicians singing to the accompaniment of various instruments. This juncture of poetry, painting and music on the pages of books was more than just an artifice; it reflected a high practical level of linkage among the different arts which drew upon common esthetic and communicative resources.

The intimate bond between sophisticated musical forms and poetry is a case in point and is not hard to understand: on the whole, Persians consider music incomplete if poetry is missing. The special expressive traits characterizing Persian music – a sense of melancholy pessimism, longing, pervasive sadness and solemnity – were due to the union on a spiritual level of musical components with highly refined, often mystical poetic texts. Indeed, the texts for traditional art music are most frequently mystic poems by great Persian poets such as Djalāl al-dīn al-Rūmī, with whom we became acquainted in connection with the Mewlevi order, Rudaki, Sa'adi and Ḥafez. It was Ḥafez who established the symbolism of the mystic (lover) in search of the Beloved (God), expressed in the imagery of the nightingale bemoaning the cruel indifference of the beautiful rose whose sharp thorns keep the sorrowful lover at bay. It is significant that Islamic mysticism, or Ṣūfīsm, has been called the supreme manifestation of the Persian mind.

The contentment and state of meditative fascination that sound and rhythm create in the heart of the listener are brought about by an intimate musical discourse, particularly in the case of unmeasured pieces. These are outstanding for their high technical level of sophisticated sonorities and their luxuriant ornamentation. Although much of Persian music is unmeasured, a traditional performance contains both unmeasured and measured compositions. Aside from the rhythmic pieces, even the so-called free melodies are almost always subjected to a subtle rhythm; in both cases, the rhythmic elements are borrowed from poetry. A good performer is expected to be proficient in the science of poetic metres; he must see to it that the song preserves, and does not conflict with, each particular metre of the text.

Persian classical music was able to develop and maintain its intimate sophisticated character due to the fact that essentially it was practised by a small élite group of initiates performing in restricted or closed circles of connoisseurs. Many of those musicians belonged to a class of professional amateurs; this class emerged and probably became increasingly important as a result of religious disapprobation of art music that hampered official sponsorship and encouragement.

At an earlier period of the Iranian state one finds rare texts devoted to art music such as the anonymous treatise *Bahjat al-ruh* (Gladness of the Soul), probably dating from the beginning of the seventeenth century (Zonis 177: 209–212). It deals among other things with the question of how the skilled musician should adapt his programme to the audience and to many other extra-musical elements by using the musical mode suitable to each situation. Enumerating the modes then in vogue, the author refers to an old theoretical system unlike that which emerged during the nineteenth century. Chevalier Jean Chardin, a French Huguenot jeweller who travelled in Persia in 1711, wrote a book, one of several contemporary European accounts, that shows penetrating insight into the instruments and dances involved. In his chapter on music, he describes the general characteristics of Persian music, aspects of its performance practice, its notational system or tablatures, and modes. About the modes he writes: 'The names of the forty-eight different modes are town-names because, they say, these different modes are much used in and unique to the towns' (Harrison 122: 132). In his description of all musical instruments then in use, he makes the following interesting remark about the string instruments: 'You will observe that the strings of their instruments are not gut, as ours are, because it is a contamination by their law to touch dead parts of the animals; their instruments' strings are either of twisted raw silk or of spun brass' (Harrison 122: 132). From the religious standpoint this statement conflicts with evidence brought by Belon in 1553, whom we cited above; he praised the Turks as excelling in producing bow and lute-strings from intestines (Belon 140). This discrepancy, of course, might have stemmed from a divergent *Shīʿī* interpretation or may be a residue of Zoroastrian beliefs. On a separate plate Chardin also supplied a notated example of 'a little Persian tune'. Under the title *chanson Persane*, the famous encyclopedist, author and composer Jean-Jacques Rousseau used Chardin's tune in the entry 'Musique' of his *Dictionnaire de la musique*; it appears there as one of the four pieces illustrating non-European music. (Rousseau 83: B14)

The complex modal system that seemed 'much fuss and confusion' to Chardin was clearly classified under the Qajars. By the end of the eighteenth century, after a period of decline and civil war, the Qajars established a dynasty that ruled Iran until the *coup d'état* of Riza Khan in 1921. By the beginning of the nineteenth century, a change occurred in the official attitude toward music. Persian writers began to discuss music and to report on the activities of musicians at the royal court. The second half of that century was marked by a major event: Naser ed-din Shah (1848–1896) formally introduced Western music into Persia. In 1858 he imported a French music master to train his *corps de musique*. Another notable event was the enterprise undertaken by the famous musician Murzah Abdullah (d. 1917) who collected and classified all melodies that formed the basis of classical Persian music. This work, known as the *radif*, includes the entire repertory of *gushehs*, the smaller elements that constitute the *dastghah* mode, arranged in order and numbered by mode (see below).

Ceremonial music

Royal ceremonial music held a special fascination for European travellers to

Iran during the seventeenth, eighteenth and nineteenth centuries. The traveller Olearius (1603–1671), in describing the instruments constituting the band that played 'loud musick', drew particular attention to a 'kind of instrument called *karrenai*' which is a long trumpet, the *karna*. The four trumpets that take part in the ensemble are of brass, 'being above eight feet in length, and at the extremity, about two feet in diameter'. Another traveller, Jean Chardin, wrote about how difficult it was to handle the instrument: 'The player of this instrument has trouble holding it up and he bends under the weight' (Harrison 122: 132). With respect to its sound, described as 'dreadful howling' by Olearius (Harrison 122: 63–64), Chardin wrote: '. . . is rough and dull when solo, but it does well enough when mingled with other instruments, when it serves as bass' (Harrison 122: 132).

Because it symbolized royalty, ceremonial music was played from an elevated gallery or tower and was known as Persian tower music. Much like the *ṭablkhaneh*, the Persian *nagharah khaneh* (the house of kettledrums) is a military band comprising kettledrums, double- headed drums, long trumpets, horns and shawms. The band played every evening at sundown and at midnight in the capital and in any other city that had a royal or princely governor. Appointed by the king, the musicians were called *naqqaratchi*.

The Zurkhaneh music

Zurkhaneh (house of strength) is the name given to octagonal mirrored rooms in which groups of men did strenuous physical exercise under the guidance of a *Morshed* (mentor). While conducting the exercises the mentor sang hymns of praise to God or recited epic poetry such as Firdawsi's *Shah-Nameh* (Book of Kings) to the accompaniment of virtuoso drumming. These colourful traditional exercises must originally have been associated with heroic rites. Referring to them, the traveller Chardin wrote that 'Wrestling is the exercise of people of the lowest order'; in his account he describes the scene:

> They are naked except for knee-breeches made of very close-fitting leather which is oiled and greasy, and a cloth around the waist (that) is also greasy and oiled. This is so that the opponent has less grip and cannot take hold by the clothes . . . a little drum which is played continuously during the wrestling to enliven it, gives the signal. They begin by declaring a thousand vainglorious boasts; then they mutually promise a fair fight and shake hands . . . (Harrison 122: 129)

It is interesting that Chardin does not mention the mentor's hymns and epic poetry, sung to compositions based in part on the modal concept, elaborated in the *radif,* which contains the foundation of Persian art music. Furthermore, the *morshed's* specific rhythmic style became the model imitated by players of the main percussion instrument – the *zarb*.

Religious music

Unlike the low profile that characterized secular art music during the time of the Safavids, a sophisticated kind of music practised by the Ṣūfī orders played an important part in their ceremonies. The singing of highly refined verses by famous mystic poets was enhanced by the accompaniment of the *setar* and *tar* (two long-necked lutes), the *kamanche* (fiddle), the *ney* (flute) and the *daff* (frame-drum). In some cases one instrument would play alone, for the purpose of intensifying a meditative state of mind. In view of their affinity, it may be assumed that the systems of art music were considerably influenced by Ṣūfī music. The influence was manifested in the seriousness, pervasive sadness and devotional quality that characterize Persian art music. Not all Ṣūfī music is akin to art music; certain traditions focused on folk music, while others, such as that of *Ahl-i-Haqq* which differs somewhat from classical music, are kept secret (Mokri 215). Different levels of prestige prevailing among the several folk Dervish orders gave rise to subtle distinctions in singing style.

The ta'ziye and the rouze-khani

Hossein, son of the second Caliph 'Alī and grandson of the prophet, was martyred in the battle of Kerbela on the tenth of *muḥarram* 680. This event gave rise to one of the most fascinating developments in Persian religious music: annual commemorations called *ta'ziye* (condolences) take place during the first ten days of the month of *muḥarram*. The ceremonial mourning dates from the period of Būyīd rule (932–1055) and has profoundly affected the development of music and poetry in Iran over the past millennium. A *ta'ziye* is a kind of religious drama or passion that re-enacts the martyrdom of Hossein and his followers. Actors participate in the various passions, impersonating Hossein and other martyrs; they sing and chant dolefully, employing a rich gamut of vocal intonations, including moaning and wailing. Each of the drama's characters sings in a specific *dastghah* (a major system of Persian art music); certain *dastghah* are used traditionally for heroes and others for villains. A solo voice, duet, or even choir, may do the singing. Instrumental passages – interludes, postludes – are played by drums, long trumpets (*karna*) and cymbals.

Numerous religious processions are held on the ninth and tenth days of *muḥarram*. The martyrs are mourned in chants and recitations, marchers often flagellating themselves with special chains. Sometimes they beat their chests rhythmically, representing the passion of Hossein (Rossi 210).

Performances of *ta'ziye* involve the participation of a *Rouze-khvan*, one who recites verses relating the events that surrounded the deaths of Hossein and other martyrs. At the beginning of the seventeenth century, Hossein

Vaezi Kashefi wrote a book called Rouze of the Martyrs which was recited from the height of the minbar (pulpit); the reading of this book was called *Rouze-khvani* and the *Molla* – lector or cantor – was known as *Rouze-khvan*. Subsequently, the term *Rouze-khvani* was applied to the reading of any book of this kind. The *ta'ziye*, a true play that under the Qajars achieved its highest form as sacred drama, with many actor-singers and lavish performances, begins and ends with the *Rouze-khvani* declamations.

The *ta'ziye* was extremely effective in safeguarding traditional art music due to the exceptional vocal and musical qualities required of the *ta'ziye-khvan*.

The Mughul dynasty

Periodic Muslim invasions of India began as early as 711, but the first Islamic dynasty was established there by the Turkish Ghaznavids (998–1030) who formed an administration on Iranian lines and adopted Persian as the court language. The outstanding example of Persian cultural transplantation, however, is that of the Mughul empire, which derives its name from the Arabic and Persian form of the word Mongol. The dynasty that ruled large parts of India from the early sixteenth to the mid-eighteenth century was founded by Babur (reigned 1526–30), a descendant of Tīmūr (Tamerlane) and Genghis Khan. His grandson Akbar (reigned 1556–1605) emerges as the key figure in the story of the Mughuls; he distinguished himself as a commander, administrator, and patron of the arts. Due to his religious tolerance he contributed to the integration of Muslims and Hindus into a united Indian state. The arts all flourished during his reign, with Persian style as the basis for an evolving synthesis of Persian and indigenous features; such a building as the famous *Taj Mahal* epitomizes this synthesis. Other manifestations of it are found in the art of miniatures, culminating in the sumptuous illuminations of *Hamza-nama* with no fewer than 1004 illustrated pages, executed mainly by local artists under the supervision of two painters summoned by Akbar from Persia. Then, of course, there is the music that was often performed by Persian musicians. Akbar introduced the custom of making ceremonial public appearances in the morning, either at a window or on a balcony; a large drum was beaten to announce his coming. According to a court chronicler, Akbar had several musicians in his retinue. The same chronicler also gives an extensive account of the *nagarah khaneh* that was conceived and played following the Persian model. In his reception hall Akbar dispensed justice and received ambassadors, scholars, poets and musicians. On festive occasions, particularly on *nawruz* – the first day of the Iranian calendar's new year – talented people including musicians exhibited their skills in a brilliantly decorated hall. In the eighteenth century women played an active part in politics, patronized poets, men of letters, and musicians (Rizvi, S. A. 'Muslim India' in 31: 301–320).

Persian influence could still be traced in the language, such as the names of certain instruments: *tambura* and *sitār* (long-necked lutes), *surnāy* (shawm), *nafari* (trumpet) and *tabla* (drum), or the names of forms and styles: *gazal, tarana* and the like. On the other hand, it is much more difficult to discern vestiges of this influence in the music itself.

Central Asia

The long and complex political and cultural development that characterizes the history of this region since the inception of Muslim incursions early in the eighth century, necessitates an approach that perceives of Central Asia in its broadest sense. Consequently, the Islamicized area we are concerned with would encompass the vast geographical space comprising present-day ex-soviet Central Asian Republics: Uzbekistan, Tajikistan, Turkmenia, Kirghizia and Kazakhtan, as well as the Republic of Azarbayjan and the Persian province of that name, Daghestan, Afghanistan, Singiang and Kashmir in South Asia.

Less than a century after the first Muslim conquests, this region saw the advent of an important local dynasty, that of the Iranian Sāmānīds (875–1020), who established an enlightened Muslim regime in Transoxania with Samarkand, Bukhara, Ferghana, Shash and Herat as its main centres. The Sāmānīds attained the peak of their power in the first half of the tenth century when they controlled extensive territories, including the flourishing Khwarizm province in the fertile area of the upper Oxus. Situated on the fringe of the steppes, this province soon became the target for invasions by the Turks who began to infiltrate from the north; their growing influence on the language and culture finally led to attenuation of the region's original Iranian character, culminating in complete Turkization. Khwarizm and other parts of Transoxania thus became bastions of Muslim orthodoxy and Sunnism, and a launching-pad for the mystical dervishes who devoted themselves to missionary activities among the pagan Turks of the steppes.

The Turks, a collective designation covering a number of related peoples possessing kindred languages and sharing basic shamanistic religious practices, in the sixth century AD formed a vast nomad empire stretching from the frontiers of China to the borders of Persia and Byzantium. Persian kings of the Sassanian dynasty built long walls to protect themselves from incursions of the nomads. The conversion to Islam of the Ghuzz, or Oghuz tribe, and its entry into the history of this region and other Muslim lands as well, had far-reaching consequences. In 977, while serving under the Sāmānīds, the slave general Sebuktigin founded the dynasty of Ghaznavids in the city of Ghazna (Afghanistan). His successor, the crude Sultan Maḥmūd, extended the dynasty's domination from western Iran to the Ganges valley in India.

The advent of another Oghuz clan, the Seljuqs, named after its progenitor Seljuq, was a turning point in the history of the whole Muslim empire as these people were destined to rule the entire Near East. In 1040, they defeated the Ghaznavids and established supremacy in Iran. In 1071, they defeated the Byzantians, occupied much of Anatolia and paved the way for their descendants, the Ottomans, who established the largest and most enduring empire.

The invasion in the thirteenth century of the heathen Mongol armies headed by Genghiz Khan left ruin and devastation throughout the Muslim lands. Nevertheless, they were later converted to Islam, as a result of which several new Islamic states of marked Turko-Mongol character arose in the Middle East and Central Asia. The most celebrated of these were the Il-Khānid and Tīmūrid empires and the Khanates of the Golden Horde and Chaghatay in the Eurasian steppes. Some positive developments resulted from the Mongol arrival in the lands of Islam. Among them were economic prosperity stemming from the uninterrupted flow of trade between Western Europe and the far East, religious tolerance, and the significant addition of a new dimension to the entire cultural area of Central Asia (Bartold 20).

The last Turkish power to enter the region was that of the Uzbeks in 1500. They made Samarkand their capital but later moved it to Bukhara. Samarkand, Bukhara, Ghazna, Khwarizm, Herat, Merv, Tibriz, Urmiya, Ardabil and Maragha were all flourishing sites of sophisticated culture, were renowned producers of jewels, silks, rugs, tiles and metalwork, and served as international trade centres. This was particularly true of the cities situated along the famous silk route linking China and the Mediterranean. Most of the rulers encouraged and supported a galaxy of *literati*, poets, theologians, scholars and musicians, some of whom moved to the centre of the caliphate and acquired far-flung fame. Suffice it to mention the names of only a few: Al-Bīrūnī (973–1048), a native of Khwarizm, one of the greatest and most original scholars of Medieval Islam, revised the calendar, determined latitudes and longitudes, and did pioneering work in empirical physics. Al-Bīrūnī travelled extensively through conquered India, learned Sanskrit and produced his comprehensive *Ta'rīkh al-Hind* (History of India), just one of the 180 scientific works he wrote. His contemporary, the great philosopher and physician Ibn Sīnā, known as Avicenna in the West, at the age of 21 was appointed court physician to the Sāmānid princes and subsequently wrote his great work *al-Qānūn fī'l-ṭibb* (The Canon on Medicine). The mathematician Abū 'Abdallah Muḥammad al-Khwārizmī (d. 977) dedicated his encyclopedic volume *Mafātīḥ al-'ulūm* (The Keys of Sciences) to a Sāmānid vizir; the book includes one of the earliest chapters ever written on the science of music (Farmer 54). The three sections comprising this chapter deal with a description of 22 instruments, the elements of music, rhythm and the rhythmic modes. In the realm of music theory, two names usually head the list of theorists: Ṣafī al-dīn al-Urmawī who became the official musician of the Mongol conquerors, and 'Abd-l' Qādir ibn Ghaybī al-Marāghī, a native of Azarbayjan who toward the end of the fourteenth century served in Samarkand as chief minstrel to Timur (Tamerlane). Unlike Ṣafī al-dīn who wrote in Arabic, as did all the other authors we have mentioned, Ibn Ghaybī wrote in Persian. It should be noted in this respect that in Bukhara and other Transoxanian cities, neo-Persian literature and poetry flourished and reached their zenith with the works of the great Persian poets Rudaki and Firdawsi.

The music

Viewed against the background of the political and cultural history of the region, it becomes clear that in various ways and with different degrees of intensity, the diverse musical traditions combined autochthonous elements and borrowings from adjacent cultures with features transferred from the Great Musical Tradition of the Near East. That tradition, for example, was the source of the basic modal concept and much of the terminology, including names of instruments – *rabāb*, *dūtār*, *setār*, *chartār*, *naghara*, *daira* – and of the musical modes – *rast*, *dūgah*, *bayāt* and *ḥidjāz*. It should be remembered, however, that the kinship with the Great Musical Tradition which reached its height during the first centuries of Islam when political and cultural contacts were most intense, concerns mainly urban classical music; the folk traditions were always distinguished by relatively homogeneous styles reflecting their original indigenous elements. In later periods, the cultural emanation from the centre diminished, leaving fertile ground for the evolution of local styles. When seeking aspects characteristic of urban music, the numerous determinants received or adopted from the centre should be taken into account, as should the unique features derived from other musical traditions; they too are attributes of the synthesis eventually achieved. Central Asia was the crossroads at which East and West exchanged not only wares, but musical instruments and stylistic elements as well. The proximity of Indian, Chinese and Persian borders and the contact with their music left traces, some stronger and some weaker, on the musical traditions of the Turkmens, Tajiks, Uzbeks and Kirghiz. They in turn were probably active in transmitting musical elements borrowed from Muslim lands to China and India (Slobin 182).

Attempting to characterize the eclectic aspect of Bukharian classical music, a fifteenth-century historian described it as Persian in style, Arabic in melodic substance, Turkish in performance practice and Mongol in vocal techniques. The link connecting the bulk of classical music styles of the region with each other and with the Great Tradition seems to rest in the concept and application of the *maqām*, particularly in the sense of a large, cyclic, vocal and instrumental composition with contrasting parts that include various levels of improvisation. This link is at least implied by the common use of the term *maqām*, or slightly modified forms: *maqom* in Uzbekistan and Tajikistan and *mughām* or *muqām* in Azarbayjan. It should be remembered that the different regional maqamic traditions developed distinctive stylistic traits indicative of varying degrees of affiliation to the Great Tradition. Uzbekistani and Tajikistani classical music are closely related. Both refer to the corpus of *shashmaqom* (six *maqām*) compositions which was codified in its present form in the eighteenth century. A different style characterized the Khwarismian *maqām* tradition; it is founded on seven *maqāmāt* and contains elements characteristic of classical Ottoman music. The Azarbayjani *muqam* tradition was strongly influenced by Iranian, Turkish and Arab features, while in performance its style drew upon elements from Kurdish and folk art of the region. It contains 12 principal and ten secondary modes (See Chapter 9).

The *maqām* concept or system conducts the observer along a path leading as far as Kashmir in India where Islamization was introduced by Ṣūfī missionaries. There the *maqām* tradition of classical music combined local developments related to Indian music with a strong Persian component, due mainly to the presence of Khorasanian musicians at the court of Zaynu'l-'Ābidīn (1420–1470), and perhaps somewhat influenced by Ṣūfī music (Qureshi-Burckhardt 193; Powers 319; Pacholcyzk 302 and 321).

8 The Advent of Recent Trends

The innovations and transformations characteristic of most present-day musical traditions germinated in the nineteenth century and were closely aligned with events then taking place in the entire Islamic world. At the close of the eighteenth century, power relationships were changing and large areas of Islam were subjected to occupation by European colonial armies: the French rose to dominance in North Africa, the British in India and parts of the Middle East, the Dutch in South East Asia, and the Russians in the Caucasus, Transcaucasia and Central Asia. It might seem reasonable to expect to find a significant European imprint resulting from the intimate contact between subjugated local populations and Europe's conquering forces.

Europe, however, seems to have influenced the peoples of these areas less by way of military conquest than by way of ideas, procedures and methods. This pertained particularly to the impact on members of the ruling classes and educated élite in Turkey, Iran, Egypt and Central Asia. Sultan Selim III and his cousin Mahmud II in Turkey, Shah Nasr ed-Din in Iran and Muḥammad 'Alī in Egypt, each in his own time and place, became convinced of the necessity of 'reform'. To them 'reform' meant emulating what they considered to be the only worthy models: those Western institutions that were the foundation stones of European superiority. They believed that by employing the same methods, the Muslim world could flourish and recoup its strength. In general, reforms were initiated in the military sphere, pursuant to the conviction that survival depended on rapid adoption of European military techniques. The first ruler who tried to introduce changes in the armed forces was sultan Selim III, but reform was not actually begun until he was succeeded by his cousin, Mahmud II, who abolished the strong Janissary corps. At the same time an Albanian officer in the Ottoman force sent to Egypt to dislodge the Napoleonic army managed to have himself recognized by the Sultan as governor of the province, where he created a European-style army and navy. The same pattern was followed in 1858 by Nasr ed-Din Shah in Iran.

As time passed, the realization grew that for reform to be truly effective, it had to be more profound than the mere introduction of new military techniques and administrative methods. Thereupon, European influence was ushered into the intellectual, educational and artistic spheres. New literary genres, largely inspired by the French classics, found fertile soil on which to flourish. A massive translation enterprise was instituted, encompassing comedies and dramas as well as other literary works. A thriving theatre with staged dramatic productions – a form almost unknown until then – was a highly important innovation. Prestigious leaders enthusiastically encouraged sweeping changes in literary life, which simultaneously increased the momentum behind a revival of Arabic literature. This revival found expression in vast publication enterprises undertaken in Lebanon and Egypt. In the Russian empire and the Central Asian Khanates under Russian protection, a vigorous movement initiated the reform of Muslim education. Among the most famous educated Muslims who became intimately associated with European ideas were the Caucasian playwright Mirza Fatḥ ʻAlī Akhundzada (1812–78) and the Bukharan writer Aḥmad Makhdūm Donish (1827–97). A group of Bokharan modernizers who adopted the Arabic title *djadīd* (innovators) began to function actively toward the end of the nineteenth century. The term *djadīd* (new) as against *qadīm* (old) was usually adopted in reference to the antagonism between old and new styles in music.

Modernization and Westernization of music

In discussing concepts of modernization and Westernization of music, we must relate the aspirations for reform discussed above to the question of how they applied to and corroborated with the changes evolving in the various musical traditions. At first, as might be expected, Western music made inroads via the military bands that were now becoming an integral part of the fighting forces being reorganized in accordance with European models. These bands were drilled by European composers and musicians summoned by the rulers to instruct local musicians in the handling of European instruments and to acquaint them with the basics of Western music. The Europeans were also in charge of providing suitable musical material and conducting performances. With the growing receptivity to European influence in various cultural spheres, Western music acquired prominence in public performances and education. Young talents began to study composition or piano-playing with European musicians invited to the respective countries. Some young people went abroad to study, as was the case with the Turkish pianist who upon his return home from Paris performed Beethoven's works at court (RGMP 89).

Sa'īd, the European-educated fourth son of Muḥammad 'Alī, became the ruler of Egypt in 1854 and two years later granted Count Ferdinand Lesseps the concession to build the Suez canal. The canal was completed under his successor, Ismā'īl, who adopted the ancient Persian title of *khedive* (ruler). On 17 November 1869, Ismā'īl presided over a brilliant celebration in honour of the opening of the canal. As part of the festivities he planned to inaugurate a new opera house in Cairo, and chose a scenario by the French Egyptologist Auguste Mariette as eminently suitable for the grand opera that would enhance the occasion. The scene of the action was ancient Egypt – pyramids, sphinx and obelisks designed to link the old with the new and excite the curiosity and imagination of multitudes of tourists. Realization of the grandiose project was consigned to the famous Italian composer Giuseppe Verdi.

The performance of Verdi's masterpiece *Aida* in Cairo on 24 December 1871 was the first opera ever performed in this region; it signified a true juncture of the ascendant modern world and ancient civilizations, a tangible meeting of East and West. With respect to the music, on the whole the score bears few traces of old Egyptian music, nor does Verdi seem to have tried hard to reproduce it; colourful passages interspersed here and there are reminiscent of devices used to characterize 'orientalism in music'.

This historic performance was undoubtedly a landmark event in the chronicles of music, but it was much more significant than just a first instance of Western penetration into the musical world of the East. Performances of operas, ballet, and works from the standard European repertory by European composers, or compositions by local musicians educated in Europe, became part of musical life in Istanbul, Tehran, Tashkent, Baku and other major centres. However, the new breezes from the West did not blow away all vestiges of traditional forms of music-making or eradicate attempts to modernize old forms. As a matter of fact, despite its impact, virtually no radical westernization of music occurred: there was no total changeover. On the whole, the crossing of lines was relatively marginal. Its major effect was apparent in the search for valid amalgams or syntheses that could combine the native heritage with features inspired by models of Western music. Leiylâ Hanim (1850–1936), one of the rare Turkish women-composers who won a serious reputation, was among the first to strive for such a synthesis. Almost all of the 200 songs she composed were influenced by Western music.

In the second half of the nineteenth century most older musical traditions were being conspicuously changed; the tendency was toward reform of what protagonists of modernization considered the heavy, slow, somewhat monotonous character of classical music. They believed that the introduction of a more dynamic spirit would align their music more closely with the modern world's rapid march of progress. Consequently, musical compositions became lighter in character; the focus turned to simple texts and short rhythmic pieces with a leaning toward folk or popular tunes. In a way this tendency, expressed primarily through growing recourse to simplified metric structure, led to the impoverishment of improvisational and non-metric pieces. In Iran, the repertory embracing such light songs was known by the general term *motrebi*, implying a contrast with the classical way of making music. During the second half of the nineteenth century some highly talented musicians in Turkey had already undertaken to create lighter and more gracious genres, and made frequent use of foreign forms such as the Balkan *longa* and *syrtos* dances. Among those who excelled in the new genres were the Turkish composers: *santurî* Ethem efendi (1855–1936) who incorporated the Roumanian *longa* in his dance suites; Ş̱evki Bey, a principal protagonist of new rhythms inspired by folk elements; and *tanburî* Cemil Bey, considered the last eminent representative of classical music who was, nevertheless, a great admirer of popular music. Turkish works in light genres were transmitted to other major Near Eastern centres and were very favourably received by their musicians. They can still be heard along with other musical forms of Western origin such as the polka, 'monologue' and 'dialogue'.

The increased emphasis on composed music led to further deviations from established norms and ideals of classical music. This was characterized by a growing separation between composers and interpreters and a loss of intimacy due to considerable ramification of the performing ensembles. The great orchestras of the West made an overwhelming impression and inspired the introduction of large musical bodies in place of the small, intimate ensembles of four or five instrumentalists that traditionally accompanied a vocalist. These new groups were comprised of random combinations of traditional and Western instruments including, for example, guitars, accordions, banjos, double basses, bongos and a violin section that became the heart of the orchestra. The introduction of new instruments and new techniques of playing altered the forms of interaction between a singer and the traditional instruments, eventually even leading to changes in structure and size of the instruments themselves. The need to play together in large ensembles shifted emphasis from displays of individual virtuosity and personal creativity to collective discipline; hence the growing stress on rhythmic pieces rather than improvisational and non-metric ones.

The concept of a concert performed on stage by a large ensemble created a barrier between musicians and audience and changed the intimate relationship that had previously prevailed. These new conditions, and the ardent desire to keep pace with technological progress, led to electronic means of amplification. This in turn led to the appearance of a new type of singer who no longer relied on the power and versatile nuances of the voice. Although on the whole the vocalist's role remained predominant even in the new composed genres, the role of the instruments changed. Unlike their function in the traditional ensemble wherein the instruments accompanied a vocalist and played solo passages as well, a new feature emerged: independent instrumental music came into being and, circumstances having changed, it could be performed publicly by a single instrumentalist or by several playing in concert (Racy 395; Shiloah-Cohen 407).

The growing institutionalization of musical life, also manifested in state support, prompted the establishment of educational institutions wherein traditional music is taught by Western methods; the studies are based on fixed models of notated music, rather than on oral transmission which implies using individual models as a basis. Education of this type necessarily leads to standardization, and the same holds true for the vast enterprise that is considered one of the principal achievements of Western music: transcribing traditional material in Western notation.

Under the impact of these changes and others – such as the introduction of time limits for radio and television concerts or phonograph recordings – the major central art forms of the long-standing Great Tradition, with its local ramifications, began to give way to new musical styles with conflicting norms. These styles arrange themselves along a continuum stretching between two extremes: the *qadīm* (old), most closely akin to the ideals of the Great Tradition, and those compositions that have totally adopted Western music. Among the syntheses characterizing the different types of music found between the two extremes, is the 'mainstream' style dominant at present. A confluence of divergent stylistic elements, it has its origins in the Great Tradition, the diverse regional little traditions, ethnic and linguistic groups, and light and classical Western music. Closer to the other extreme are the attempts to create a synthesis of local traditions based on European compositional models.

Analysing cultural influences impinging on the world of Islam, the eminent scholar E. G. von Grunebaum explains the difference between influences received during the early 'Abbāsid period and those characterizing the nineteenth and twentieth centuries as a function of the power relationship between receiver and diffuser. He considers this variable as 'the most important in the transmission of influence' (Grunebaum 21: 95). Regarding the early period he contends that

> The sense of the Muslims of being masters in their own house was in no way weakened by the knowledge that they were taking over the best the others had to offer; on the contrary, it merely strengthened their belief in the potentialities of their aspirations . . . The complexion of Westernisation during the last 150 years is totally different. It was the inadequacy of their power which first induced in some of the Muslim elites a readiness to reform (Grunebaum 21: 95–96).

As far as art and literature are concerned, von Grunebaum argued that 'Western ideas effected a transvaluation of traditional forms and norms of self-expression . . . foreign patterns supplanted rather than supplemented the inherited kinds' (Grunebaum 21: 96).

9 Scales, Modes and Rhythms

The elements of music

Most treatises written after the inception of the science of music in the ninth century were avowedly concerned with two major components:

1. Application of the science of music to the definition, nature, and classes of the musical notes, and the way they are combined in intervals, genres and systems, as well as in melodies or melody types;
2. The science as it pertains to principles of rhythm and how its elements are combined to form specific organized patterns.

The musical notes are examined, according to Ibn Sīnā, 'in respect to *ittifāq* (consonance) and *ikhtilāf* (dissonance)' (Erlanger 51: II, 110). Some theorists tend to emphasize the component of melody in their definitions. In his *Iḥṣā' al-'ulūm* (Classification of Sciences), al-Fārābī writes:

> And as for the science of music it comprises, in short, the investigation of the various kinds of melodies *(alḥān),* what they are composed of, what they are composed for, how they are composed, and what forms they must necessarily assume so that the performance of them becomes more impressive and effective. (Farmer 42: 13–14)

According to Ikhwān al-Ṣafā:

> The *ghinā'* (music) is composed of harmonious melodies, melody is composed of well-ordered notes, notes are measured sounds, sound is a shock produced in the air following a collision of bodies against each other. (Shiloah 82: 17)

Accordingly, like most theorists of subsequent generations, the Ikhwān proceed with a substantial exposition of the science of sound and the definition of musical notes, in one of the best examples of everything that had been written until that time. After defining the manner of producing sound in general and how it is captured by the sense of hearing, they go on to a systematic, detailed classification of all sounds that exist in nature or are manmade, and ultimately arrive at the sounds that serve as the basis of musical composition (Shiloah 82: II, 9, 18–21).

Acoustical considerations associated with principles governing the production of sound and its perception by the aural faculty usually lead to the first condition determining the essence of a musical note – the *bu'd* (interval). Of the various intervals, a specific place was assigned to the three perfect consonances called respectively: *al-bu'd al-ladhī bi'l-kull* (octave); *al-bu'd al-ladhī bi'l-khams* (fifth); and *al-bu'd al-ladhī bi'l-arba'* (fourth). The earliest theorists classified all intervals within three main categories: large (the double octave – the framework of the general scale, the octave plus a fifth, the octave plus a fourth and the octave); medium (fifth and fourth); or small (the tone and smaller steps called intervals of modulation, or melodic intervals – *al-ab'ād al-laḥniyya.* In his systematic theory, Ṣafī al-dīn al-Urmawī (d. 1292) combined the first two categories.

All calculations and demonstrations of intervals were based on the division of a monochord or referred to the strings of the classical *'ūd.* This *'ūd* had four or five strings called in ascending order: *al-bamm* (the lowest), *al-mathlath, al-mathna*, *al-zīr*, and *al-ḥādd* (the highest); different sections of the strings are sounded to obtain different notes. The frets (*dasātīn*, pl. of *dastān*) are usually fixed at a fourth of the length of each string. There are four frets, in keeping with the four fingers used to shorten the strings when playing; the interval thus obtained on each string is the fourth, which corresponds to the Arabic melodic system. The usual frets as well as the notes corresponding to them bear the names of the fingers: the *sabāba* (index – interval of the tone 9/8); the *wusṭa* (middle finger – minor third, variable); the *binṣir* (ring finger – major third 81/64); and the *khinṣir* (little finger – a fourth 4/3). With the *muṭlaq* (note of the open string), each string has five basic sounds. The strings of the *'ūd* used in theoretical demonstrations are stretched in such a way that the second, if open, produces a note identical with that rendered by the first string stopped at the level of the little finger fret, and so on. Thus the same succession of intervals is produced on all four or five strings. If we arbitrarily assign the pitch G to the note of the first open string we obtain a succession G–C on the first string; C–F on the second; F–B flat on the third and B flat–E flat on the fourth. For example, one thus finds the octave of the 'index' of the first string at the level of the 'ring finger' of the third string, and so on.

This early 'solfegio' system indicates certain important features comprising the basic concept of tetrachordal organization, by which Arab theorists usually describe the octave as the sum of two conjunct tetrachords plus an interval of tone or a combination of a tetrachord plus a pentachord. The tetrachord *(djins,* pl. *adjnās,* borrowed from the Greek *genus*) was of three basic classes: *qawī* (diatonic), *lawnī* (chromatic), and *rāsim* (enharmonic). The various kinds of intervalic distribution within each general type of tetrachord are called *anwāʿ* (s. *nawʿ*), meaning species. In the framework of a tetrachord, the first degree, the major third and the fourth are fixed; as many as seven mobile degrees (some semitones, thirds and steps larger than a semitone but smaller than a tone) were placed between the *muṭlaq* and the *binṣir* or the first degree and the major third; this brings the total number of degrees in an octave to 24. The definition of the mobile degrees was a controversial subject among theorists. The following breakdown illustrates the way al-Fārābī described the ten degrees dividing a fourth in his *Kitāb al-mūsīqī al-kabīr*.

1. *muṭlaq*: note of the open string.
2. *mudjannab*: diatonic minor second equal to the proportion 256/243.
3. *mudjannab furs*: Persian minor second = 162/149.
4. *mudjannab Zalzal*: the neutral minor second.
5. *sabāba* (index): interval of a tone = 9/8.
6. *wusṭa* (middle finger): diatonic minor third = 32/27.
7. *wusṭa furs* (middle finger): Persian minor third = 81/68.
8. *wusṭa Zalzal* (middle finger): the neutral third established by Zalzal = 27/22.
9. *binṣir* (ring finger): major third = 81/64.
10. *khinṣir* (little finger): a fourth = 4/3. (Erlanger 51: I, 172)

Ṣafī al-dīn al-Urmawī, attempting to systematize the theory of music, contributed to the correction and definition of the mobile degrees in the general scale. His calculations, based on various divisions of the monochord, led him to establish three subdivisions within every 9/8 tone (204 cents) equalling two *limmas* (90 cents each) and a *comma* (34 cents). His tetrachord therefore included eight degrees, his octave 18. Each degree was designated by a letter of the *abudjed* or *abdjed* – alphabet. The Arabs sometimes use the letters of the alphabet to express numbers; in this case, the numerical value of the letters accords with the more ancient order of the Hebrew and Aramaic alphabets. The letters are arranged in eight mnemotechnical words of which the first is *abdjed*, corresponding to the first four letters of the Hebrew alphabet: *alef, bet, gimel, dalet.* It should be noted that the same alphabetical system was used much earlier by al-Kindī (d. 870) to identify the notes and their positions on a five-stringed lute. The following table illustrates Ṣafī al-dīn's division into octaves in accordance with alphabetical notation:

A	B	G	D	H	W	Z	Ḥ	Ṭ	Y	YA	YB	YG	YD	YH	YW	YZ	YḤ
g	a♭	a𝄳	a♮	b♭	b𝄳	b♮	c	d♭	d𝄳	d♮	e♭	e𝄳	e♮	f	g♭	f♯	g

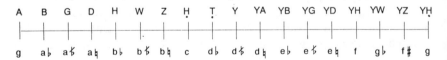

In Chapter 18 of his book *Kitāb al-adwār, Ṣafī al-dīn*, while dealing with the *'ūd* and its accordatura, provides a drawing displaying the five strings and the levels on which the 36 pitches are to be produced, the pitches designated by the *abdjed* – letters. For fuller comprehension of the system, an exact copy of the drawing as found in a manuscript of the Bibliothéque Nationale in Paris (Ar. 2865, fol. 11a) is reproduced on p. 114.

Based on the above division of the octave, Ṣafī al-dīn classified all the intervals within two main categories: large (octave, double octave, fifth, fourth, octave plus fifth, octave plus fourth), and small (the tone and smaller steps). These latter were designated by T (for a tone), J (a large semitone equal to *limma* + *comma* or three quarters of a tone), and B (*limma*).

Taking into account certain established rules such as the inadmissibility of three successive limmas, Ṣafī al-dīn found seven ways of dividing the fourth, or seven tetrachord species (e.g. TTB, TBT, BTT . . .), and 12 for the fifth, or pentachord species (e.g. TTBT, TBTT, TJJT . . .). A scale can be constituted by combining either similar or different genera (*adjnās*, pl. of *djins*) (Erlanger 51: II, 294–308). Through combinations and permutations of tetrachords and pentachords, with the tetrachord invariably placed below, 84 octave scales *(adwār,* pl. of *dawr*) are derived, represented by the letters corresponding to their respective degrees. The first octave scale, for instance, is: a d z ḥ ya yd yh yḥ which is simply the major scale: g a b c d e f g. This was the foundation of Ṣafī al-dīn's modal exposition and it became the chief and most popular model for subsequent generations (Erlanger 51: III, 308–311).

The modal concept

In Arabic literature one finds references to a pre-Islamic Sassanian organization of a modal system. Dealing with the multiplicity of existing musical systems, in his *Risāla fī'l-luḥūn wa'l-anghām* (Treatise on the Melodies and the Notes) al-Kindī refers to the Persian *ṭurūq* (modes) and the Byzantine *Octoechos* (Farmer 268). A few decades later, in his *Murūdj al-dhahab*, al-Mas'ūdī provides a list of the same modes. Both sources extol the excellence of the Persian modes. The first serious information on Arabic art music, however, is transmitted by al-Iṣfahānī in his *Kitāb al-aghānī* (Book of Songs). The modal theory described there is attributed to the great musician Isḥāq al-Mawṣilī (d. 850) whose system became known as the theory of *aṣābi'* (fingers) and *madjārī* (courses) because it is related to the frets of the *'ūd* and the corresponding fingers used to produce notes. The relevant string is given in the indications that introduce the songs, together with the finger corresponding to the main degree of the modal scale; the course (*madjra*) then designates one of the three kinds of thirds, the major, minor, or neutral (which may first have been introduced by Zalzal, Isḥāq al-Mawṣilī's uncle

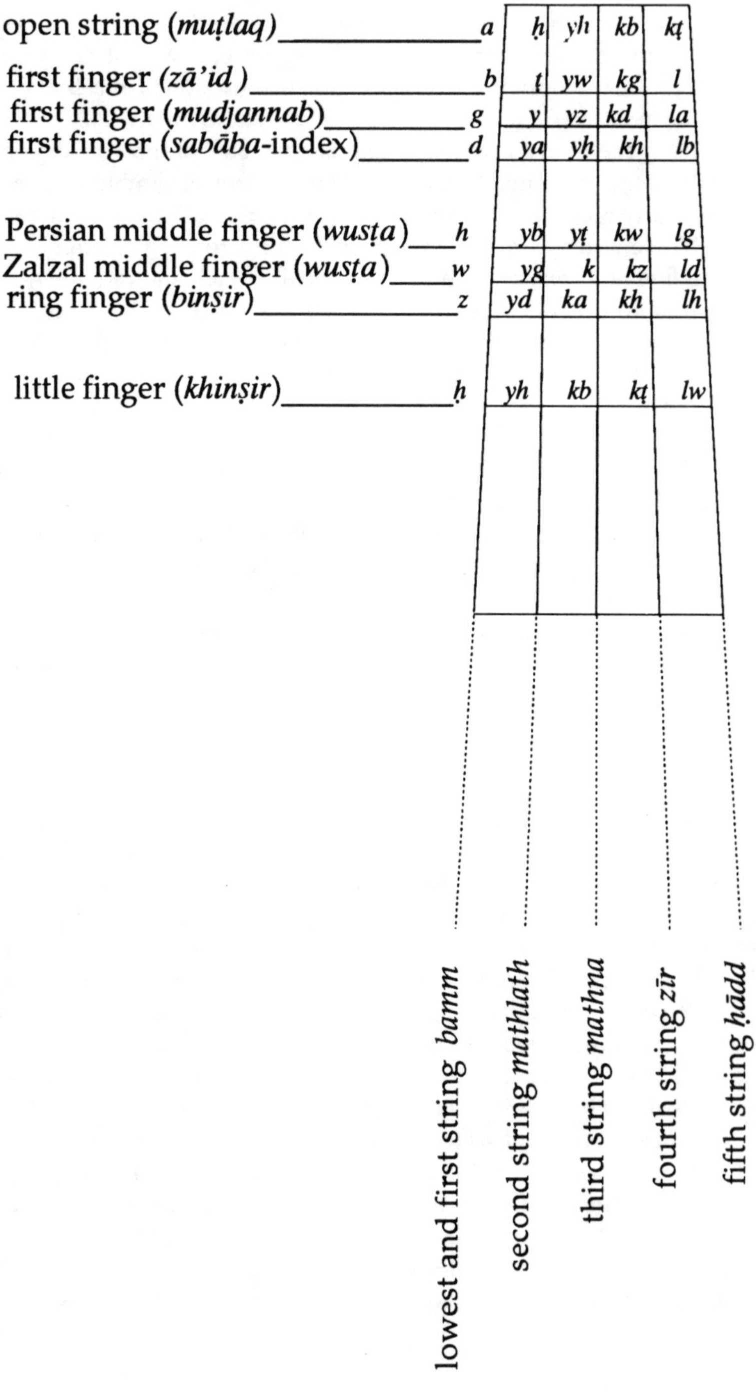
open string (*muṭlaq*) a ḥ yh kb kṭ
first finger (*zā'id*) b ṭ yw kg l
first finger (*mudjannab*) g y yz kd la
first finger (*sabāba*-index) d ya yḥ kh lb
Persian middle finger (*wusṭa*) h yb yṭ kw lg
Zalzal middle finger (*wusṭa*) w yg k kz ld
ring finger (*binṣir*) z yd ka kḥ lh
little finger (*khinṣir*) ḥ yh kb kṭ lw
lowest and first string *bamm*
second string *mathlath*
third string *mathna*
fourth string *zīr*
fifth string *ḥādd*

and teacher). Occasionally the name of a corresponding rhythmic mode is added. Heading the text of a song, therefore, an indication may appear such as *muṭlaq al-mathna fī madjra al-wusṭa* (note of the third open string by the course of the middle finger) which corresponds to f g a-flat b-flat or f g a (neutral third) b-flat. Such an indication of the modal pattern served as an *aide memoire*, providing the performer with necessary information about the modal scale. This system allowed for 12 fundamental modes which in later times were given fanciful names (Shiloah 82: IX, 30).

Ṣafī al-dīn's modal theory departed from the 84 octave scales (*adwār*) only some of which, by his own testimony, were accepted in practice. Among these are the 12 cycles to which 'the practitioners of the musical art gave the name of *shudūd* (s. *shadd*)', later called *dastghah*, *maqām*, *laḥn*, and *naghma*. These 12 modal scales, probably already implying specific patterns, melodic types, and other characteristics besides intervallic structures, Ṣafī al-dīn identified by proper names as follows: *'ushshāq*, *nawā*, *abūsalīk*, *rast*, *'irāq*, *iṣfahān*, *zīrafkand*, *buzurk*, *zangula*, *rahāwī*, *ḥusaynī*, *ḥidjāzī*. The scale type for each shadd refers to a corresponding cycle in the list of 84 *adwār*. Thus, for instance, the corresponding cycle of the third *shadd abūsalīk* is number 27 represented by the letters: a b h ḥ ṭ yb yh yḥ (e.g. g a-flat b-flat c d-flat e-flat f g) (Erlanger 51: III, 376–385). In addition to these 12 *shudūd*, there were six secondary modes called *awāzāt* (s. *awāz*), which were also given proper names: *shahnāz*, *māya*, *salmak*, *nawrūz*, *kardāniya*, *kuwasht*. These 12 plus six modes became the central corpus of the system (Erlanger 51: III, 386–394).

In addition, according to Ṣafī al-dīn, other modes were used in practice that were not specifically named, but were designated by the general term *murakkabāt* (s. *murakkab*) – compound modes that derived from the principals. Such derivations are potentially inherent in one of the basic principles of the entire system, wherein a whole range or scale is conceived as the sum of several smaller elements; this also permits mobility and permutation of these elements within the framework of the resulting extended range. The process, then, is a kind of mosaic composed of multiple combinations derived from relatively minimal elements.

Later on, new classifications were established in various centres; pursuant to the same spirit, they were based on similar principles but emphasized local approaches and traditions. In the Turco-Arabic world the new classification that emerged had 12 *shudūd*, called *maqāmāt* or *alḥān* or *anghām*, that were divided into four *uṣūl* (principals): *rast*, *'irāq*, *iṣfahān*, *zīrāfkand* (there are other variations) and eight *furū'* (branches). The latter are treated as derivations: two branches for each principal. Eleven of the 12 terms in Ṣafī al-dīn's nomenclature were maintained, yet one finds authors differing as to what belongs to the principals and what belongs to the branches. There is one exception, however: everyone gives absolute primacy to the *rast* and it is designated as the first, central, most complete source of all the *maqāmāt*. As to the *awāzāt*, they retain Ṣafī al-dīn's nomenclature but are now considered derivatives of the 12 *maqāmāt*. The compound modes, now called *shawādhāt*, *shu'ab*, or *tarākīb*, vary in number according to the different sources. This line of thought evoked the tendency that prevails in the Turco-Arabic world to constantly multiply the abstract 'scale types' (Shiloah 82: IX).

Recent trends

In the nineteenth century attempts were made to divide the octave differently. The system of dividing the scale for Arabic music into equidistant quarter tones is ascribed to the Syro-Lebanese music theorist and mathematician Mikha'īl Mashāqa (1800–1888). However, it was established earlier by Mashāqa's mentor, the Syrian mathematician and music theorist Muḥammad ibn Ḥusayn 'Aṭṭārzade (1764–1828) in his unpublished treatise: Rannat al-awtār . . .(The Sounds of Strings . . .). 'Aṭṭārzade's division of the general scale of two octaves into 48 pitches, with the corresponding nomenclature, is shown in the following table:

yeka (sol 1)	*nīm ḥuṣār* (sol 𝄲)
nīm ḥiṣār (sol ♯)	*ḥuṣār* (la 𝄳)
ḥiṣār (la bemol)	*tīk ḥuṣār* (la 𝄳)
tīk ḥiṣār (La 𝄳)	*ḥusaynī* (la 2)
'ushayrān (la 1)	*nīm 'adjam* (la 𝄲)
nīm 'adjam (la 𝄲)	*'adjam* (si ♭)
'adjam (si bemol)	*awdj* (si 𝄳)
'irāq (si 𝄳)	*nahaft* (si)
kawasht (si)	*tīk nahaft* (si 𝄲)
tīk kawasht (si 𝄲)	*māhūr* (do)
rast (do)	*nīm shahnāz* (do 𝄲)
nīm zarkula (do 𝄲)	*shahnāz* (re ♭)
zarkula (do ♯)	*tīk shahnāz* (re 𝄳)
tīk zarkula (re 𝄳)	*muḥayyar* (re)
dūkah (re)	*nīm sunbula* (re 𝄲)
nīm kurdī (re 𝄲)	*sunbula* (mi ♭)
sīkah (mi 𝄳)	*buzurk* (mi ♭)
abūsalīk (mi)	*djawāb abūsalīk* (mi)
tīk abūsalīk (mi 𝄲)	*djawāb tīk abūsalīk* (mi 𝄲)
djaharkah (fa)	*māhurān* (fa)
nīm ḥidjāz (fa 𝄲)	*djawāb nīm ḥidjāz* (fa 𝄲)
ḥidjāz (fa 𝄲)	*djawāb ḥidjāz* (fa 𝄲)
tīk ḥidjāz (sol 𝄳)	*djawāb tīk ḥidjāz* (sol ♭)
nawā (sol 2)	*ramal tūtī* (sol 3)

It is noteworthy that in the second octave the names of the same principal degrees of the scale vary and the terminology used by 'Aṭṭārzade to designate them consists of ordinal numerals, e.g. *yegah*, *dūgah* (first, second and so on) as well as some names that correspond to the ancient names of *maqāmāt*, *awāzāt* and *shu'ab*, e.g. *rast*, *'irāq*. The terms *nīm* and *tīk* indicate respectively a quarter below and a quarter above the altered degree. In Turkish music we find the same division into 48 pitches including the use of *nīm* and *tīk* or *dīk*, although there are slight variations in the names of some principal pitches (Erlanger 51: V, 3–30).

This new conception introduced the possibility of transposing modes to any scale degree; it became widespread in Arabic music through the version published by Mashāqa in his *Risāla al-Shihābiyya* and the earliest English translation of it that appeared in 1849 (Smith 37; Collangettes 91: 412–414).

In Turco-Arabic tradition, there is a perceptible tendency to subsume the various structural categories within the main *maqāmāt*. Following the lead of past theorists, the old categories of *awāzāt*, *murakkabāt* and *shu'ab* seem to have found their place as subordinate elements used to amplify and enrich the principal *maqāmāt*. They were introduced as substructures either in the middle, at secondary centres or at the extremities of the scale of one or another *maqām*. In this fashion they were assimilated by their new environment and either lost their independent existence or gave birth to new maqamic combinations. Modern theorists classify all modal scales according to their point of departure, which coincides with the degrees of the central *maqām*.

The division of the two octaves into 48 pitches received particular attention at the first International Congress on Arabic music held in Cairo in 1932 (Racy 48). Attended by famous Near-Eastern and Western composers and musicologists, the Congress rejected the system, mainly because it was unfamiliar to the practitioners whose microtones vary from player to player. On the other hand, in the course of the Congress, the existence of a large number of *maqāmāt* as a body of scalar patterns was confirmed. Indeed, over a hundred different modal scales were identified and were later analysed in Volume 5 of Erlanger's *La musique arabe*. Erlanger, one of the initiators of the Congress, also provided in his book a definition of the *maqām* based on 'the teaching of the modern masters'; it involves five essential elements:

1. the ambitus or range of the modal scale
2. the constituent genera of the scale (*adjnās*)
3. the point of departure (*mabda'*)
4. the momentary or secondary stopping points (*al-marākiz*)
5. the final point of repose or tonic (*al-qarār*) (Erlanger 51: V, 100–101)

As can be seen, this definition, like many others in earlier theoretical writings, emphasizes the tonal category but ignores another essential aspect of the Turco-Arabic *maqām,* the 'melodic type'.

The dastghah system and the radif in Persian music

Present-day Persian art music is organized into 12 systems called *dastghah* (lit: apparatus or scheme); seven are principals and five, considered subsidiary and designated by the term *avaz*, are related to the principal *dastghah* by their scales. A *dastghah* is distinguished by a musical scheme having its own scale and its own hierarchy of degrees. As such, it is somewhat related to the early categorization established by Ṣafī al-dīn. In addition to the scalar patterns of the 12 *dastghahs*, each one has its own repertory of traditional melodies used by the musician as the basis for composition, improvisation and performance. The traditional melody types appropriate to each *dastghah* are in the form of small pieces called *gusheh* (corner), usually confined to a five- or four-note compass. Until the present century, they were transmitted orally; the versions generally practised today are based on a nineteenth-century tradition transmitted by Mirza Abdullah, who allocated a specific number of *gushehs* to each *dastghah* – usually between 20 and 50. The entire repertory of *gushehs* contained in the 12 *dastghahs* is called *radif* (row or order); the total number of pieces in Ma'rufi's *radif* is 470 (Ma'rufi 275; Barkechli 276). According to Bruno Nettl, 'row' and 'order' connote a large and comprehensive corpus arranged in a particular sequence, emphasizing the concepts of unity and order (Nettl 308: 4).

At a performance, these short pieces are presented in a given order which corresponds to the increasing range of the *dastghah,* moving from its lowest to highest tetrachord – which may rise to the second octave – and back to the finalis of the *dastghah*. The *gusheh* prescribes the tetrachord genre, the notes of the tetrachord that are stressed and certain cadential patterns. Furthermore, the *radif* contains the order in which to play the *gushehs* and the way to progress from one *gusheh* to the next. For the performer, however, the *gusheh* is no more than a melodic formula or genetic material for his improvisations. 'Broadly speaking,' writes Ella Zonis, 'improvisation in Persian music consists of a series of decisions: how many *gushehs* of that *dastghah* to play, the order in which to play them, the way of progressing from one *gusheh* to the next and the manner of performing each one' (Zonis 177: 99–100). In order to comply with the concepts of order and unity, and to produce a coherent development, the *gushehs* should be chosen according to their affinities. In a single *dastghah* most of the *gushehs* end with the same conclusion (*forud*), which may either be somewhat varied or exactly the same. A major portion of the *radif* consists of unmeasured pieces, although a close examination shows that they undergo a subtle rhythmic organization which stems, particularly in the vocal parts, from the metrical structures and accents of the poems that have been set to music. The most important genre of measured pieces is the *chahr mizrab* (four beats), characterized by rapid tempo, recurring ostinato and a virtuoso rendition by the instrument accompanying the singer.

To conclude, the *dastghah* system as embodied in the *radif* tradition can be said to represent an amalgam of both *maqām* principles, the 'melodic type' and the 'cyclic genre', the latter genre being the major characteristic of the Central Asian *maqom.*

The Central Asian shashmaqom

In Central Asia (mainly Uzbekistan and Tajikistan), as well as in Azarbayjan and Khwarizm, a local modal system evolved. Although certain aspects of this system are affiliated with the Persian and Turco-Arab traditions, it has its own distinguishing traits. The *shashmaqom* (six *maqāmāt*) of the Central Asian classical style that reached its height in the court music of the kingdom of Bukhara, was codified in its present form during the eighteenth century. Five of the six *maqoms* have Persian names but are also found in the Turco-Arabic maqamic nomenclature: *buzruk*, *rast*, *nava*, *dugah*, *segah*; the sixth, *iraq*, is exclusive to the Turco-Arabic tradition; three of them, *rast, nava* and *segah*, are names of Persian *dastghahs.* This and the other maqamic traditions of the region such as the system of seven Khorizmian *maqāmāt*, the 12 Azarbaijani *mughams* and the Kashmiri *maqām*, have little connection with the several dozen melodic-type *maqāmāt* of the Eastern Mediterranean Turco-Arabic world. The small number of systemic *maqāmāt* in all likelihood represent the spirit of the early classification established by Ṣafī al-dīn which, to a certain extent, also survived in the Persian system (Veksler 272; Karamatov 284; During 313; Jung 316; Powers 319). On the other hand, the conception that predominates the *maqām* treatment in all these traditions refers rather to a small number of standard cycles of separate items; designated by some scholars as 'cyclic genres', the outcome of this treatment is a kind of suite. In this respect, the suite form that coincides with the principles of *maqām* somewhat resembles the Turkish *fasil*, the Iraqi *maqām* or the North African *nūba*; these compound forms will all be discussed in Chapter 10.

Association of modes with ethical and cosmological values

The fervent belief in music's overwhelming power derives from the emergence of ideas associating music with many and varied effects and properties. Ethical and cosmological speculations are linked to the concrete application of modes (both melodic and rhythmic) in diverse circumstances. In the first centuries of Islam, the doctrine of ethos found its highest expression in the writings of al-Kindī and Ikhwān al-Ṣafā (see Chapter 5). Ṣafī al-dīn, whose highly sophisticated system has been discussed above, also referred to the particular expressive properties of modes in the brief Chapter 14 of his *Kitāb al-adwār* entitled 'On the Influence of Modes', where he writes:

> Know thee that each *shadd* of the *shudūd* has a pleasurable effect on the soul, yet this effect varies with respect to the different modes. Some modes inspire force, courage and exaltation; this concerns three modes: *'ushshāq, abūsalīk* and *nawā*, which correspond to the nature of the Turks, the Abyssnians, the Blacks and the mountain-dwellers. Concerning the modes *rast, nawrūz, 'irāq* and *iṣfahān*, they delight the soul with a feeling of subtle pleasure. Concerning the modes *buzūrk, rahāwī, zīrāfkand, zankula* and *ḥusaynī*, their effect stirs a kind of apathetic sadness. Therefore, one should set *shadd* to a poem corresponding to its property. If, for instance, verses describing the state of a happy man were set to the mode *zīrāfkand*, the combination would not be suitable.

Until the nineteenth century almost all available sources dealing with modal theory were concerned with specifying the manifold affiliations of the *maqāmāt* and *awāzāt* to ethical, therapeutical and cosmological values. The detailed lists of correspondences involve categories such as the planets, signs of the zodiac, seasons, day and night, hours, elements, humours, temperaments, virtues, classes of men, colours, odours, raw materials, letters of the alphabet and poetic metres. These multiple correspondences were considered important to the musician, who was expected to select the appropriate mode for each circumstance. They were also useful to the physician, enabling him to administer the treatment suitable for each disease.

Rhythm

Rhythm has always been an essential and predominant component of Near Eastern music. After the advent of Islam, rhythm, called *al-īqā'* (plural *al-īqā'āt*), began to develop its distinctive musical traits, but without severing its previous links with the prosody of Arabic poetry. In this context it is significant that the famous philologist and codifier of the rules of prosody, al-Khalīl (718–791), was also the author of the first theoretical work on rhythm, the *Kitāb al-iqā'* (Book on Rhythm), no longer extant.

Rhythmic modes acquired more definite form under the Umayyads; during their time, six modes were identified as follows: *thaqīl awwal*, *thaqīl thānī*, *khafīf thaqīl*, *hazadj*, *ramal*, and *ramal ṭunbūrī*. Later, with the inception of the scientific approach, rhythm became a principal object of theoretical investigation. Al-Kindī, who defined rhythm as 'art of times relationship' in his *Risāla fī khubr ta'līf al-alḥān* (Treatise Concerning the

Knowledge of Musical Composition), also devoted a special work to it that has since been lost: *Kitāb al-īqā'* (Book on Rhythm). In connection with rhythm, al-Kindī described eight fundamental modes (*uṣūl*): *al-thaqīl al-awwal, al-thaqīl al-thānī, al-mākhūrī, khafīf al-thaqīl, al-ramal, khafīf al-ramal* and *khafīf al-khafīf*. With al-Fārābī the science of rhythm attained its highest analytical level. In addition to its centrality in his *Kitāb al-mūsīqī al-kabīr* (Grand Book on Music), he devoted two important studies to it: *Kitāb al-īqā'āt* (Book on Rhythmical Modes) and *Kitab iḥṣa' al-īqā'āt* (Book on the Enumeration of Rhythmical Modes) – (Neubauer 65; Sawa 143: 35–71). There may also have been a third study, but nothing has remained of it. Famous authors of the following generation such as Ibn Sīnā and Ṣafī al-dīn attributed similar importance to the science of rhythm and followed a similar analytical approach.

In his *Kitāb al-adwār*, Ṣafī al-dīn refers to rhythm as 'a group of beats *naqarāt* (sing. *naqra*) separated from each other by times of determined duration; they are organized into quantatively equal cycles disposed in particular ways'. Generally speaking, rhythm was conceived as the division of a span of time into sections marked off by beats separated from each other by perceptible and measurable durations. To define the time lapse between successive beats and notes, it was necessary to establish a prime time unit from which the different patterns would derive. Theoreticians usually identified this time unit with a light beat in a moderate tempo, of shortest possible – but still perceptible – duration, a duration too short to allow another beat to be placed between it and the one adjacent to it. This prime time, as they called it, was analogous to the Greek *chronos protos*. In attempting to illustrate the stress and duration of separation, theoreticians of the classical period usually borrowed the concepts of prosodic elements and their nomenclature from grammarians and prosodists.

The metrical terms used are *sabab thaqīl,* illustrated by the word *laka*; *sabab khafīf* illustrated by *qad*; *watad* illustrated by *laqad*; and *fāṣila* illustrated by *ghalabat*. These terms correspond respectively to two vocalized or moved consonants (according to the grammatical concept of moved and quiescent consonants); one moved followed by a quiescent; two moved and one quiescent; and three moved followed by a quiescent. When applied to rhythm the theoreticians used the mnemotechnic syllables *ṭana* for the first; *ṭan* for the second; *ṭanan* for the third; and *ṭananan* for the fourth. Therefore, the shortest beat would be ṭa designated by the theorists as 'light'; then comes *ṭan* called 'second light' equalling *ṭana* or two lights in duration; *ṭanan* designated as 'first heavy' and *ṭananan* 'second heavy', corresponding respectively to the duration of three and four light beats. In his systematized prosody al-Khalīl represented the moved or vocalized consonants by a circle (O) and quiescent consonants by a stroke (/). In applying these symbols to represent the metres, some theoreticians changed the stroke to a point (.).

When applied to rhythm, the symbol (O) represents a beat or an attack equivalent to *ṭa*, the point (.) an intervening time unit equivalent in length to the beat. Therefore (O) or *ṭa* would correspond to ♪; *ṭana* to ♪♪; *ṭan* to ♪ 𝄾 or ♩; *ṭanan* ♪♪𝄾 to ♪♩ or *ṭananan* to ♪♪♪𝄾 or ♪♪♩. In prosody the metrical elements are combined into eight basic patterns designated by paradigms derived from the root *f'l*: *fa'ūlun*, *mafā'īlun*, *mustaf'ilun* etc. which correspond respectively to the rhythmic patterns used by the theoreticians: OO.O.; OO.O.O.; O.O.OO. The 16 classical metres were derived from different combinations of the eight basic feet; the theoreticians referred to the same principles in establishing the ideal forms of the fundamental rhythms or rhythmic modes.

On the theoretical level two classes of rhythm were distinguished: conjunctive and disjunctive. They were organized in equal patterns representing recurrent periods or rhythmic cycles parallel to the two-fold division of a poetic verse. In the conjunctive class the sequence of beats is incorporated by equal intervening times; in the disjunctive an additional time is placed between the cycles. Each class is then subdivided differently. The disjunctive forms are generally considered artistically superior, hence preferable.

The commonly used seven rhythmic modes in the classical period were derived from the multiple theoretical patterns; the fundamental modal forms are described in detail and designated by proper names: *al-thaqīl al-awwal*; *al-thaqīl al-thānī*; *khafīf al-thaqīl al-awwal*; *khafīf al-thaqīl al-thānī* or *mākhūrī*; *al-ramal*; *khafīf al-ramal* and *al-hazadj*. To represent the cyclic aspect of the fundamental modal forms, Ṣafī al-dīn, like some other theoreticians, displayed the rhythmic modes in concrete cycles indicating the first beat and the anti-clockwise movement as well as the 'moved' and 'quiescent' beats. Thus, according to him, the cyclic pattern provided on the outer side of the *thaqīl awwal* circle which corresponds to *mafā'ilun*, *fa'ilun*, *mufta'ilun* is: OO. OO. OOO. O. OOO. or *ṭanan ṭanan ṭananan ṭan ṭananan*, representing 16 units altogether. One more interesting example, about which Ṣafī al-dīn writes that 'the Persians called (it) "fundamental rhythm" and "most of their compositions are in this rhythm", is *thaqīl al-ramal*: O . . . O . . . O. O. O. O. O. O. O . . . or *ṭananan ṭananan ṭan ṭan ṭan ṭan ṭan ṭan ṭananan*, equalling 24 units. In addition to the seven classical modes, Ṣafī al-dīn adds the Persian *fākhitī*: O . . . O. O . . . O . . . O. O . . . (20 units), which he maintains '. . . is rarely used in composition'. Interestingly, this mode appears in the writings of subsequent generations of authors.

One should note that, despite their precise definitions, the modal forms provided by the earliest theoreticians only served as basic models subject to variations and embellishments. For example, al-Fārābī described no less than 16 recognized techniques of variation and ornamentation (Sawa 143: 46–53).

Those rhythmic modes later underwent changes in structure, number and name. The first mention of modern rhythmic modes, henceforth called *ḍurūb* (pl. of *ḍarb*), appears in the encyclopedic work *Irshād al-qāṣid* (The Guiding of the Searcher) by Ibn al-Akfānī (d. 1348). In his exposition, he refers to the six ancient Arab modes, adding that the Moderns use four basic modes: *ḍarb al-aṣl*; *ḍarb al-mukhammas*; *ḍarb al-turkī* and *ḍarb al-fākhitī* (the last was mentioned by Ṣafī al-dīn). Subsequently, the famous theorist 'Abdu'l-Qādir ibn Ghaybī (d. 1435), referred exclusively to the ancient modes as described by his celebrated predecessors. Soon after him, the Ottoman author Muḥammad al-Lādhiqī (d. 1495), in his *Risālat al-fatḥiyya fī'l-mūsīqī* (The Epistle of Victory Concerning the Science of Music), paralleled the six modes of the Ancients (which he described in detail) with 18 rhythmic modes of the Moderns (Erlanger 51: IV, 337–350; 485–498). This may indicate that by then the modern modes had gained ground. Some time later we begin to receive concrete descriptions of characteristic patterns of the new modes that are still in practice today, namely the notions of heavy and light accents and timbre designated by *dum*, *tak*, and *taka*. *Dum* (mellow) and *tak* (dry) refer respectively to the beat near the center of the drumhead, and to the strike near or on the rim. The author 'Askar al-Ḥalabī al-Qādirī (the date of his birth and death are uncertain, but we learn of the period in which he lived from the date 1672 on his unique manuscript *Rāḥ al-djām* . . . [Wine of the cap . . .], which may be an autograph) provides examples of 19 rhythmic modes. It is interesting that al-Qādirī refers to the aforementioned Ibn al-Akfānī as an authority representing the new trend in the science of music. Furthermore, the general definition with which the section on rhythm begins is a precise copy of the one offered by Ṣafī al-dīn in his *Kitāb al-adwār*, although his name is not mentioned any place in the treatise. After a general exposition of the ancient prosodic terms *sabab thaqīl*, *sabab khafīf*, *watad*, and *fāṣila*, the author claims that the new terms *dum*, *tak*, and *taka* correspond to them.

According to al-Qādirī, all rhythmic patterns can be described by means of those three elements; indeed he used them in displaying the 19 rhythmic modes known then. Here, for example, is the *ḍarb* called çanbar: *dum tak dum dum tak dum tak taka taka,* which correspond to nine beats. If for the sake of convenience we give the *dum* and *tak* a time value of a quaver with the stem upward and downward respectively, and the *taka* is given two crotchets, we obtain the following scheme:

Çanbar
9/4

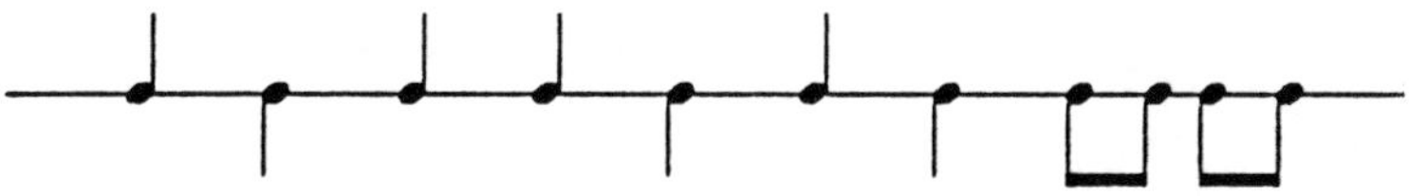

Incidentally, the same mode with the same name and beat scheme occurs in a list of Turkish modes provided by Albert Bobowsky (1610–1675) who assumed the name of ʻAlī Beg or ʻAlī Ukfī, in his collection of Turkish notated songs (Paris, Bibliothéque Nationale, Mss, Turc 292). As a matter of fact, 11 of the *ḍurūb* contained in Ukfī's list have similar names yet only three of them correspond to al-Qādirī's schemes, the others being variations. One more example shows the longest of the *ḍurūb* introduced by al-Qādirī – the *thaqīl*, which corresponds only partially to Ukfī's *thaqīl*: *dum taka dum taka taka dum taka dum tak tak dum dum tak dum tak tak dum taka dum tak dum tak dum dum tak taka taka dum taka dum taka taka dum taka dum tak taka taka*; there are altogether 38 beats.

Thaqil
38/4

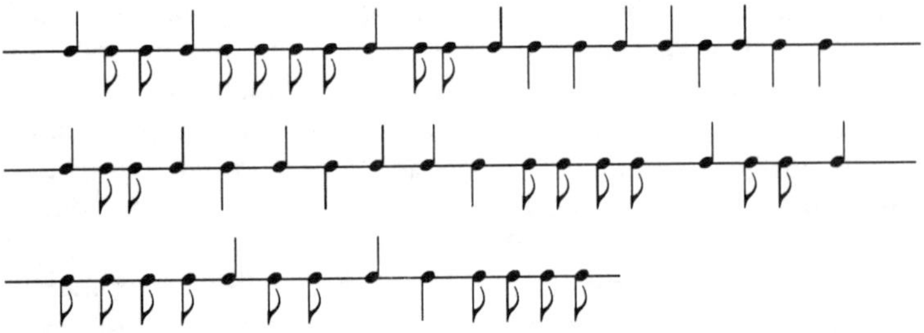

This illustration – which in its basic concept concords with the old method – represents, in the words of C. Sachs, the concept of additive rhythm in contrast to Western divisive rhythm. 'Oriental rhythm', writes Sachs in his book *Rhythm and Tempo*, 'progresses from a note x time units long to another y time units long. The sum of x and y forms the metrical pattern to be repeated. Additive rhythm has of necessity two aspects: metric and accentual. It relies on a clear distinction between the two members of which a pattern consists'. (Sachs 266: 92) A few examples of modern *ḍurūb* follow.

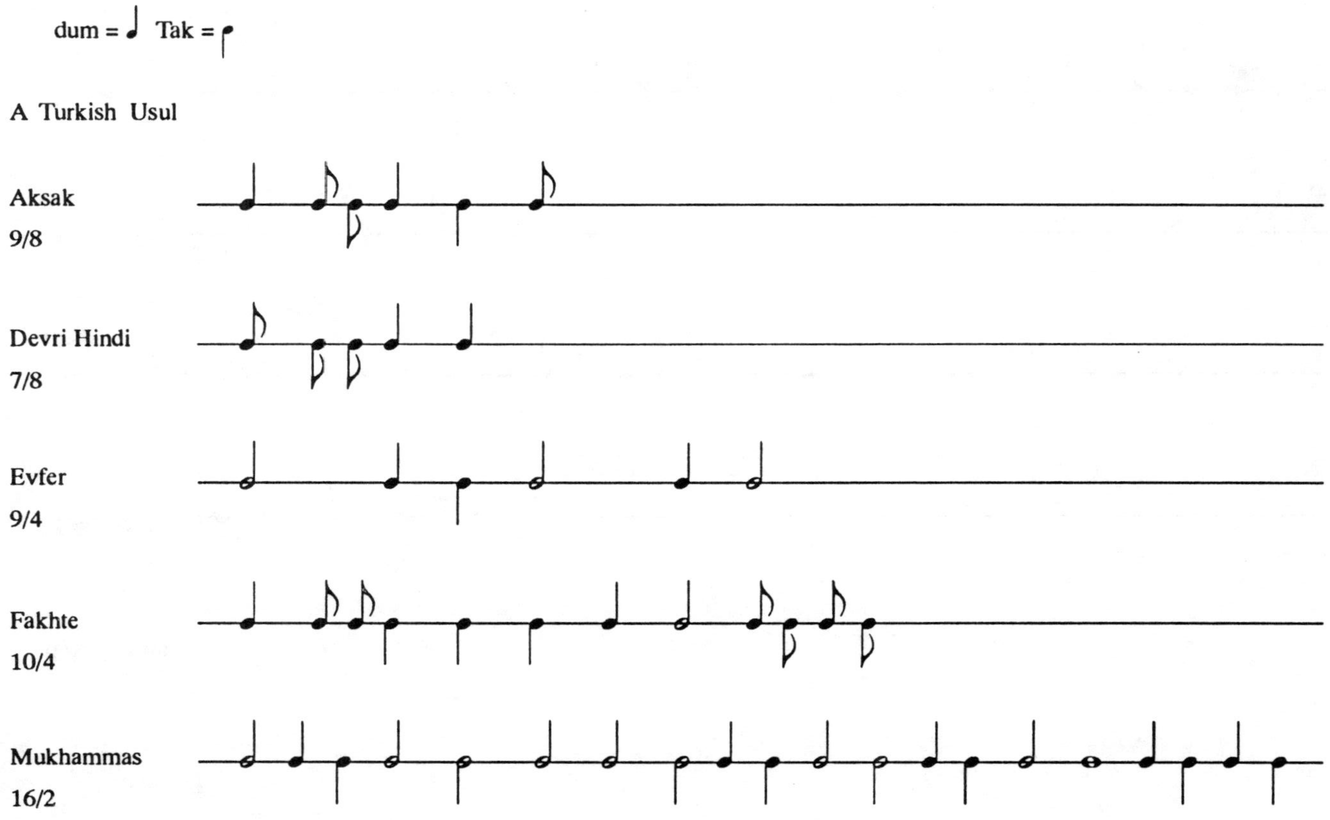
dum =
Tak =
A Turkish Usul
Aksak
9/8
Devri Hindi
7/8
Evfer
9/4
Fakhte
10/4
Mukhammas
16/2

B Arab usul

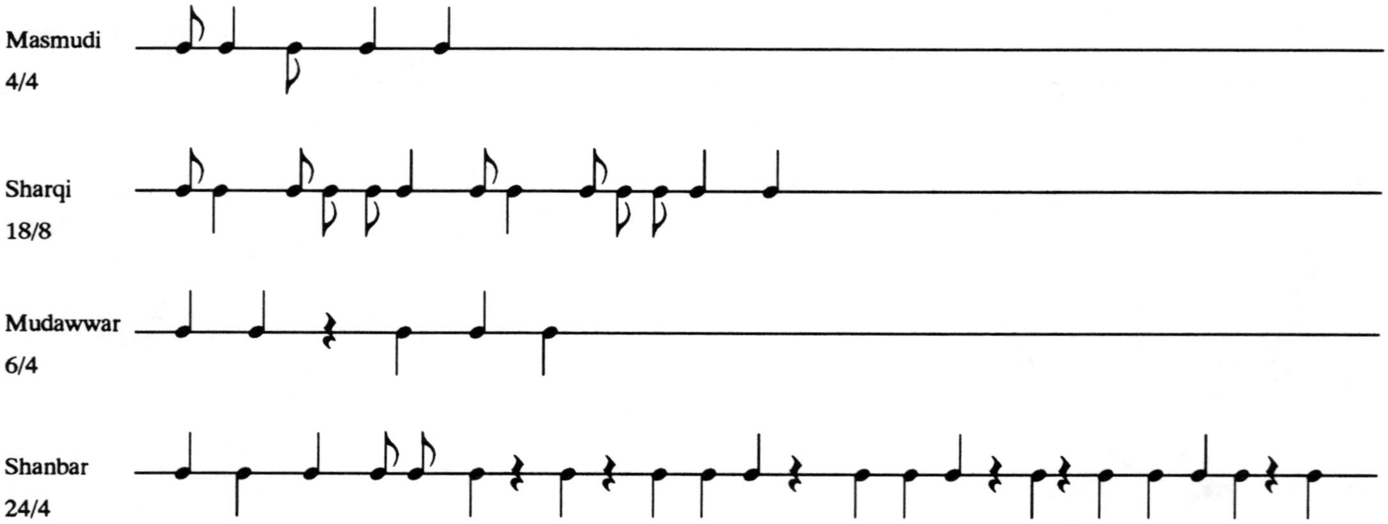

10 Improvised and Compound Compositions

Improvised pieces

Most of the improvised types or styles refer to a scheme or model on the macro level, in which framework the micro details are left to the performer's choice and decision. Thus the performer enjoys a degree of freedom but is nevertheless restrained from permitting his imagination to run rampant; on the whole he continues to rely on culturally conditioned structural notions. However, within the imposed limits, the performer still has a great deal of leeway – especially in the non-metric pieces – for demonstrating his talents and creativeness; he can also convey long-established ideas in his own way and from his own point of view. The Oriental artist has a penchant for the details that constitute a work. Therefore on the micro level, in the course of remoulding the idiomatic vocabulary, the artist allows the model-bound structure, which is usually organized around tonal areas, to emerge empirically in accord with his own personal outlook.

The taqsīm

In the Turco-Arab cultural sphere, *taqsīm* refers to an improvised form for a solo instrument. The term means 'division', probably referring to the high degree of sectionalization that characterizes the form. The improvised material of the *taqsīm* is divided into a chain of sections, the number, shape, and length of which depend largely on the musician's individual abilities, state of mind and, to some extent, the circumstances surrounding the performance. The sections may be delineated by rests or by concluding contours similar to cadences in the sense of typical melodic flow toward the *finalis* with which a musical section ends. The cadences appear several times in the sections of the *taqsīm*.

The sections almost always proceed in an ascending direction: as a rule, they are short at the beginning of the *taqsīm* and increase in length as the piece develops. However, the gradual expansion of range and the temporal extensions, as well as the return to the modal home base, rarely proceed in a straightforward curve from beginning to end. There are indeed several retreats on the way to the *finalis* which create moments of relaxation enabling the performer to regroup forces and permit the tension to grow gradually, several climaxes being produced along the way.

The sections correspond to phases in the development that are centred on a number of focal tones determined in turn by the modal frame of reference. As a rule, there is no thematic development; the melodic elements are essentially the result of stress on central pitches. Thus, the various centres play an important role in the structural design of the *taqsīm*. Central tones can be musically identified in any of the following ways:

1. The tone is heard repeatedly and successively;
2. Its rhythmic value is lengthened;
3. A given tone is used in such a way that it assumes the function of a temporary *finalis*;
4. A centre is created through the use of secondary *maqāmāt* in which the tone is the *finalis* or the first in the tetrachord.

This indicates an important aspect of the *taqsīm* which refers to the possibility that the performer use a given central tone of the basic *maqām* as the point of departure for what we may call a 'modulation' (Marcus 346).

From this it transpires that, on the whole, the development of a *maqām* presumes a shift to one or more secondary *maqāmāt* and a return to the basic *maqām*. The process can be repeated a number of times within the same *taqsīm* on condition that the performer does not remain in any secondary *maqām* too long, thereby obscuring the main *maqām*. There are two schools of thought concerning the modulatory progressions in the *taqsīm*: one sets great store by an artist's ability to properly and frequently move away from the basic *maqām* and then return to it; the other considers it more appropriate for the artist to exhaust the potentiality of the basic *maqām* with almost no deviation.

In conclusion, it should not be assumed that the musician playing a *taqsīm* improvises his material *ex nihilo*; rather, he remakes a cultural tradition which incorporates the cumulative vocabulary of generations of musicians, a tradition that favours recomposition rather than original development – whether compositional or improvisational.

Generally speaking, the rhythmic component can be described as free; the *taqsīm* is not confined to periodic accents (articulation) or to the periodicity of fixed rhythmic formulae, and therefore it may be said to lack meter. However, different levels of rhythmic freedom can be noted in the *taqsīm*, ranging from rhythm that gives the effect of an even pulse to a state wherein the feeling of pulse is totally lacking (Gerson-Kiwi 287; Elsner 288; Spector 289; Olsen 291; Nettl 296; Touma 299 and 333).

The layālī – vocal improvisation

Layālī (pl. of *layla*) is one of the terms designating vocally accompanied improvisation; literally translated the term means 'nights' and is connected with the fact that the singer takes the word as his phonetic base for improvisation. The word is used in invocatory form : *ya leylī* (O my night!) which is occasionally interchanged with *ya 'einī* (O my eye!). This as well as other expressions that serve as meaningless syllables for vocalization, are common in other styles of the region and probably gave birth to the *ay* and *leyli* in certain introductory types of Andalusian *cante hondo*. The treatment of vocalization syllables varies from syllabic (repetition in repeated passages), to melismatic (giving each syllable several notes).

Vocal improvisation is always accompanied by the *'ūd* or some other instrument intended to keep the singer in pitch, to reinforce important tones (especially drones) and to play interludes that enable the singer to rest and marshal his creative imagination, inspiring him to develop his improvisation further. The *layālī*, therefore, interspersed vocal and instrumental parts that evolved according to the principles of the *taqsīm,* which in turn may have adopted vocal material for an instrumental idiom.

The mawwāl

This vocal genre falls between the *layālī* and subsequent metrical rhythmic forms. It is usually improvised on a strophe of varying length which belongs to a genre of folk poem also called *mawwāl.* Such a text may be declaimed in cantillation style or may contain improvised melismatic portions; the overall rhythmic concept, however, is free. This is particularly apparent when one hears the song accompanied by the full ensemble, including percussion, that follows the *mawwāl.* This improvised vocal section is fairly similar in nature to the *bitain* or *muwwāl* of the Moroccan *nūba. Bitain* means two isolated verses that serve as the base for highly melismatic improvised passages which constitute expressive climactic moments in the performance of a *nūba* (see below).

Individual and compound compositions

The muwashshaḥ

The *muwashshaḥ* is a prestigious vocal form based on the classical

Andalusian strophic genre (see Chapter 6), from which its current name *muwashshaḥ andalūsī* is derived. Based on the structure of the classical Andalusian *muwashshaḥ*, the vocal art form practised in some major Near Eastern centres has the following components: a prelude of a line or two called *badaniyya* or *dawr* (Andalusian *madhhab* or *ghuṣn*) with a rhyme scheme:

__________A   __________B   (or x2)

a varying number of two-line strophes with rhymes other than those of the *dawr*, called *khāna* or *silsila* (Andalusian *dawr* or *ṣimt*) with rhyme scheme:

__________c   __________c
__________c   __________c   or
__________c   __________c
__________d   __________d

and a concluding line called *qafla* (Andalusian *qufl*) that has the same rhyme as the prelude but a different text. Then again, instead of the *qafla*, the first line or lines are sometimes repeated.

The musical setting follows the general structure of the poetic text. The first line of the *muwashshaḥ* became a refrain that was repeated after each *khāna* or *silsila*. As regards the strophes, the *silsila* corresponds to the low pitch range of the *maqām* in which the *muwashshaḥ* is sung; the *khāna* corresponds to the high pitch range. The range increases gradually from strophe to strophe and, as it develops, is permitted to shift to a secondary, related *maqāmāt*. The *muwashshaḥ* rests on an isorhythmic texture deriving from one of the established rhythmic modes. The characteristics of these modes are indicated by two types of drums, part of the small instrumental ensemble which also includes the *'ūd* and the *kamandje* (a spike fiddle, eventually a violin). The vocal part is provided by a soloist and one or two male or female choirs singing antiphonally; both soloist and choir frequently add nonsense syllables to the text – a distinguishing characteristic of the *muwashshaḥ*. At given interludes, the instrumentalists play short passages called *lāzima*. The text of the *muwashshaḥ* has no impact on the nature of the music; the latter is rather determined by the nature and possibilities of the *muwashshaḥ's maqām*. Consequently, different texts can be sung to the same music, as one *muwashshaḥ* text can be set to different musical compositions (Faruqi 336).

The *muwashshaḥ*, now in decline, is still considered one of the most important musical genres. In his treatise *Safīnat al-mulk . . .* (The Royal ship . . .), Shihāb al-dīn al-Ḥidjāzī (1795–1857) devotes an extensive section to it, including 350 *muwashshaḥāt* arranged in 30 sections which in turn illustrate 12 *maqāmāt*; the author also gives the rhythmic mode for each composition. In an anthology with musical notations published in 1965 in Beirut, the Lebanese author Salīm al-Ḥilū provides 115 known *muwashshaḥāt* (Ḥilu 328). Finally, mention should be made of the religious *muwashshaḥ* called *tawshīḥ dīnī*. It is usually performed as a solo; the rendition being quite unlike the rendition of an art *muwashshaḥ*.

Compound and cyclic genres

Multisectional forms consisting of several related vocal and instrumental parts are prevalent in the music of Central Asia and the Near East. They are all based on modal unity and conceived as an artistic unit in which musical and prosodic aspects intermingle (Faruqi 343).

The shashmaqom (six *maqāmāt*)

The *shashmaqom* in the traditional art music of the Uzbeks and Tajiks was codified in its present form during the eighteenth century. The six *maqāmāt* according to the standard order are *buzruk*, *rast*, *nava*, *dugah*, *segah* and *iraq*; they all have the same basic internal structure emphasizing the cyclic principle. Each *maqām* consists of two main divisions: one is instrumental and called *mushkilot* (lit. difficulties); the second, considerably larger than the first, is vocal and consists of an extensive set of accompanied songs; it is called *nasr* (Arabic *nathr* meaning lit. prose or scattering). The instrumental section with which each *maqām* begins consists of five parts called *tasnif*, *tarje*, *gardun*, *mukhammas* and *saqil*. With the exception of the *gardun*, all parts of this section have a rondo-like structure consisting of a varying number of *khanas* (episodes) and a recurring phrase *bazgui*. The *gardun* is characterized by a rhythmic formula of irregular and changing metre and contains only *khanas*. The vocal division has a complex internal structure including large subdivisions or groups of *sho'ba* or *shu'ba* (branches), usually between three and four. The first *sho'ba* has a unique configuration containing four extended vocal parts, *sarakhbar*, *talqin*, *nasr*, and *ufar*, the last in dance rhythm. The *sarakhbar* (lit. major information) was referred to as '*maqām*' until the nineteenth century, probably because this part, placed at the beginning of the important vocal section that immediately follows the introductory instrumental section, is said to introduce the essential tonal-melodic characteristics of the cycle as a whole. Its internal subdivisions, which correspond to the stanzas of the poem being sung, depict an asymmetrical arched contour starting with the low register, rising higher and higher until they reach the climax (*auj*) and then again descending to the low register. The gradual extension of the tonal range and the return to the initial pitch level also underline emotional tension and relaxation. This principle reaches its highest expression in the *sarakhbar*, but is also characteristic of other parts of the *maqām*, although to a lesser extent. Lighter compositions called *tarona,* which may be based on folk texts and rhythms, are inserted between the four parts of the first group. The subsequent groups of *sho'ba* invariably have five songs, the fifth being an *ufar*, a finale in dance rhythm (Veksler 272; Jung 316; Matjabukov 317).

The Andalusian nūba

The Andalusian *nūba* has survived in several North African centres; various old Andalusian styles are still extant in Fez, Tlemcen, Algier and Tunis. These *nūba* repertories are called respectively *'āla*, *gharnāṭī*, *ṣan'a*, *ma'lūf*. Some differences notwithstanding, they are very similar in spirit and structure. The individual *nūba* is named after the mode or *ṭab'* (nature or temperament, alluding to its cosmological connotation); for example, *nūba raml-māya*, *nūba dīl*, *sbihān*, *'ushshāq*, *raṣd*, *zīdān*, *ḥsīn,* and so on.

The overall physiognomy of the *nūba* in all centres is more or less alike: it comprises an instrumental prelude or preludes and a series of pre-composed vocal pieces that represent autonomous phases of the *nūba*, each having its own set of poetic texts as well as melodic and rhythmic characteristics. Most of the poems sung in this repertory consist of *muwashshaḥāt* interpreted by a chorus and soloist or soloists. In this fundamentally choral genre the soloist, an octave higher, leads the chorus and instrumentalists and also performs the free-measured pieces that intersperse the various phases. The overall structure and the individual phases as well are governed not only by modal unity but also by rhythmic acceleration that reaches its peak toward the end of the *nūba*. Indeed, the emphasis is on accelerating rhythms rather than on modulation. A number of vocal features distinguish the *nūba*: voice timbres, technical vocabulary, use of nonsense syllables and a wealth of melismatic arabesques.

The Moroccan nūba

The Moroccan *nūba* begins with the *mishālia* or *bughya*, two non-metric semi-improvised instrumental preludes in which the instrumentalists set forth the characteristics of the given mode. It is followed by the *touchia*, a rhythmic piece played by the instrumental ensemble. There are numerous *touchias* in the repertory; about 90 of them are known and serve as preludes to the five parts of the *nūba*. The five parts reflect rhythmic phases: *mayāzīn* (pl. of *mīzān,* lit. metre), followed by *bsīṭ* with the rhythmic pattern 2/4+2/4+2/4 or 6/4; *qā'im wa-nuṣṣ*: 8/4 or 4/4+4/4; *bṭaiḥī*: 3/4+6/8+2/4 or 3/4+3/4+2/4; *quddām*: 3/4 or 6/8; *draj*: 8/4. Each *mīzān* includes a variable number of *ṣan'as* designating songs of the *muwashshaḥ* genre. The term probably implies the art used in the performance of these songs which reached its zenith in the *ṣan'a mashkūla*, that is, ornate artistry, making frequent use of nonsense syllables for embellishment. Each of these phases is conceived as an autonomous unit in which the sequence of songs is arranged in a predetermined order, progressing with occasional lapses from a heavy, slow movement to a light, rapid one; acceleration is greatest in the songs of the *inṣirāf* which are performed in a rapid tempo and conclude with the finale *qufl*. Between the highly regulated *mīzāns*, the skilful soloist called *munshid*, discreetly accompanied by the *'ūd* and the *kamandje*, intones virtuoso vocal improvisations: *bitain* (distich) or *muwwāl,* constituting a highly expressive transition that contrasts with the measured choral songs of the *mīzāns*.

The Algerian nūba

There are two distinctive traditions, one associated with Tlemcen and which has been open to exchanges with those of Oujda, Fez and Tetouan in Morocco; the other is associated with Alger. Proceeding according to the aforementioned principles, the Algerian *nūba* begins with the *dā'ira* – a short, free, rhythmic vocal prelude consisting of vocalised nonsense syllables followed by *mustakhbar al-ṣan'a* (Algiers) or *mishālia* (Tlemcen), a free rhythmic instrumental prelude. It is followed by the *touchia*, a rhythmic piece played by the instrumental ensemble. The five phases of vocal pieces are *mṣaddar*: 4/4; *bṭaiḥī*: 4/4; *draj*: 4/4; *inṣirāf*: 5/8; *khlāṣ:* 6/8.

The Tunisian nūba

This *nūba* begins with an instrumental prelude called *istiftāḥ* (overture) played by the musicians without the support of the percussion, but over a precise rhythm. The *istiftāḥ* provides an exposition of the mode's characteristics. It is followed by a *muṣaddar*, a measured instrumental overture with a 6/4 slow rhythm accelerating to 6/8 and then to 3/8. The *muṣaddar* is conceived in the same style as the *bashraf* of Ottoman origin (see below). It is followed by another short instrumental prelude introducing the *abyāt*, choral songs with instrumental intermezzi: 2/4+4/4. Another set of songs, *bṭaiḥī*: 4/4 is followed by an instrumental *touchia,* an *'ūd* improvisation, some folk songs, and then the *barwal*: 2/4; *dardj*: 6/4 and the *khatm*: 3/8 (Erlanger 51: VI; Rouanet 93: 2845–2866; Chottin 155; Guettat 185: 186–232; Pacholczyk 258).

The nūba or nawba in Eastern traditions

The Eastern *nawba* made its appearance as far back as the Umayyads, but at that time it meant musicians playing or singing in turn (Farmer 95: 153–154; Erlanger 51: IV, 236–239). Only later on does one find the term used to designate the compound form. As such it is mentioned by the fifteenth-century author Mawlāna Fatḥ Allah al-Shirwānī, who refers to it in several different kinds of compositions. Anonymous XIII, in *Fann al-anghām* (The Art of Modes), states that the *nawba* of the masters includes four sections or genres, *qawl*, *ghazal*, *taran*, and *farūdast*, adding that the *ghazal* is always in Persian while the other pieces are in Arabic, and that this *nawba* is a set work composed by known musicians and based on strict rules. Anonymous XXVII, in *Madjmū'a fī 'ilm al-mūsīqī* (A Collection Concerning the Science of Music), provides information on various forms of vocal and instrumental music and enumerates ten *nawbas* named after their accompanying *maqāmāt*. Among other forms mentioned as preceding that of the *nawbāt* are the *silsila*, *khāneh*, *samā'ī*, and *bashraf*; the first two are parts of the *muwashshaḥ*, the others are parts of the *faṣil*, discussed below.

The faṣil

In contrast to the well-conceived and articulated compound form of the Andalusian *nūba*, the Turkish multisectional *faṣil* (lit. section) seems to have grown from the Eastern *nawba*. The *faṣil* was described by D. Cantemir as early as *circa* 1700. At a concert it was customary to perform a fixed sequence of pieces of different genres, allowing a certain amount of freedom to introduce new combinations and compositions in accordance with accepted models. Two restrictions had to be observed – the order of the pieces and modal unity. The *faṣil* begins with one or more *taqsīm* (instrumental improvisation), thereby introducing both performers and listeners to the feeling of the *maqām*; the *taqsīm* is also woven into the middle of the *faṣil*. The following instrumental piece is either a *peshrev* (lit. prelude) or a *sāz semaî*. The *peshrev* is composed of three or four parts called *khāne* (house). Each *khāne* is followed by a refrain called *teslim* – also added after the last *khāne* as a finale. The *peshrev* is a rhythmic composition and allows modulation in the second *khāne*. The *sāz semaî* has a similar form but with an *aksak* rhythm of 10/8 (3+2+2+3). The *sāz semaî* is usually played at the end of the *faṣil*. Between the two imposed instrumental pieces are five song genres: *kar*, *beste*, *agir-semaî*, *şarki*, and *yürük-sema'ī*. There are many pre-composed pieces in one or other genre made to fit the different *maqāmāt*, including the recent light instrumental forms of foreign importations: the Greek *sirto* and the Rumanian Gypsy *longa*. The performer is permitted to either skip or multiply one or more genres in selecting pieces of his choice. The vocal part is rendered by a soloist and chorus, the instrumental part by a small ensemble of musicians.

The waṣla

The Egyptian *waṣla* (lit. link or sequence) is another example of a compound form that flourished in the past but tended to decline after World War I. It was performed by a male vocal soloist *muṭrib* accompanied by a chorus of four or five men, and a *takht*, a small group of instrumentalists who played the *qānūn* (zither), *'ūd* (lute), *nāy* (flute), *riqq* (small frame drum) and *kamandje* (a spike fiddle, which in the late nineteenth century was replaced by the Western violin) (Shawan 408).

The *waṣla* was a sequence of then popular genres combined in an organic unit, although each genre could be used interchangeably in the same *maqām*. To ensure the unity of the *maqām*, all component genres had to begin and end in the *maqām* of the *waṣla*. The sequence of genres opens with a *taqsīm* on the *'ūd*; it is followed by a precomposed metric instrumental introduction, either a *dūlāb* or a *samā'ī*, played by the ensemble. Then there is a *taqsīm* on other instruments followed by a *muwashshaḥ* rendered by the entire chorus. After one or more *taqsīm* the *muṭrib* (vocalist) performs the *layālī* and *mawwāl*, two improvisatory non-metric genres. The *waṣla* ends with the precomposed metric genre *dawr* performed by the entire ensemble. In this final and most crucial phase, the long middle section of the *dawr* allows for considerable flexibility; it presents episodes called *hank* in which the solo singer improvises short passages. Here the coordination and cohesion of the entire ensemble achieves its highest levels (Racy 341).

In a *waṣla* or a *fāṣila* (similar to the Turkish *faṣil*) other vocal and instrumental genres can be represented. One of those is the interesting *taḥmila*, an instrumental genre comprising two parts. The first, light in character, is played in unison by the ensemble at the beginning of the performance and recurs at given moments in the course of the second part. The latter is an improvisation on a theme in which two instrumentalists compete: they demonstrate their skill and virtuosity in creating variations, modulations, transpositions, glissandi and other striking artifices. As the stabilizing and unchanging element, the first part plays a supporting role, so to speak, to the second; hence the name *taḥmila*, which literally means 'to carry a burden'.

Al-maqām al-'irāqī (The Iraqi maqām)

The term *al-maqām al-'irāqī* has unique implications which do not, however, supersede attributes previously ascribed to the *maqām*. It refers to a complex, highly structured genre belonging to types of the compound form, and is usually performed by a specialized group known as *tchalgī Baghdād* (the Baghdad ensemble). The group comprises four instrumentalists who play on the *djawza* (lit. coconut), a spike fiddle with a resonator made of coconut shell covered with sheep skin; the *santūr*, a trapezoidal hammered dulcimer which has twenty-three quadruple metallic courses; the *dunbuk*, a single-skinned drum; and the *daff al-zanjarī*, a tambourine with small cymbals. The central figure is the vocalist known as *qāri' al-maqām (maqām* reader). The term *qāri'* is usually reserved for the *Qūr'ān* reader; hence its use in this context implies the great privilege and respect the genre enjoyed and the seriousness ascribed to its rendition. The *qāri'* was often assisted by a singer of secondary importance, the *pastadjī*, who performed the *pasta* (a light, metric syllabic song) between one *maqām* and the next, while the *qāri'* rested.

As to the general structure, it consists of an instrumental introduction played by the ensemble followed by the first section called the *taḥrīr* (not to be confused with the Persian *taḥrīr*, a type of vocal ornament). In this section, the vocalist introduces the *maqām* by using characteristic syllables and expressions that differ from one *maqām* to another and serve as distinguishing marks; the stock phrases are usually in Arabic, Turkish, Kurmanji (the language spoken by the Kurds) or Persian, and even in Hebrew which indicates active Jewish participation in the performance of this genre. Here, as well as in other parts, the vocalist is expected to demonstrate the rich ornamental devices (glissando, portamento) which are considered an integral part of the performance. The section that develops the low range pitch of the *maqām* includes several vocal sequences, some of which are presented as a kind of dialogue with instrumental responses. This dialogue between the vocalist and the instrumentalists is known as *muḥāsabāt* (sing. *muḥāsaba*). The section of the *taḥrīr* closes with the *taslīm,* a short cadential passage descending to the finalis. The central section that follows is sung on a higher pitch level and usually includes modulation to other related *maqāmāt*; popular folk verses of the *'abūdhīyya* type may be inserted (Wegner 340). The following *miyāna* section evolves in a higher octave, sometimes reaching the double octave; it demands great ability from the vocalist. The performance concludes with the *taslīm*. A *pasta* in the same *maqām* is usually rendered either to end the performance, or as a transition to subsequent *maqām* performances. Finally, it should be noted that the rhythmic component is important for the definition and character of any given *maqām*. The appropriate rhythmic mode may be performed either continuously or in specific portions (Rajab 271; Hassan 262; And 379: 109–110; Tzuge 334).

11 Dance

Art dance

Unlike the science of music which has been treated extensively in numerous studies, art dance has not received much attention either *per se* or in connection with the Great Musical Tradition. From the scattered information we possess, however, it emerges that alongside non-professional dancing, a well-defined form of sophisticated dance did exist. The latter probably referred to the glorious pre-Islamic Iranian dance with its codified rules and aesthetics; the former was probably of a more spontaneous, less formalized character. The paucity of analytical and technical descriptions of art dance in the literature might be due not only to its severe prohibition by the religious fanatics, but also to a basic culture-bound mistrust prevalent in Muslim society, and a deprecatory attitude among intellectuals.

In a brief passage of his major treatise, The Grand Book on Music, al-Fārābī classifies dance with drumming, hand-clapping and mime as inferior to the art of singing and playing melodic instruments, which are higher in the hierarchy. He has nothing more to say about dance. On the other hand, one finds substantial information on art dance in the important historical work *Murūdj al-dhahab wa-ma'ādin al-djawāhir* (Meadows of Gold and Mines of Gems) by the historian and geographer Abū'l-Ḥasan al-Mas'ūdī (d. 956). Al-Mas'ūdī describes a public session at which ibn Khurradādhbih spoke at length on music and its origin in response to a question by the Caliph al-Mu'tamid (870–92). In a session held the next day, the caliph interrogated a dance specialist on the principles of dance. The expert called upon began his reply with a statement on the relation between dance and rhythm, displaying the eight rhythmic modes. Then he described the attributes essential for a proficient dancer, including, among others, a natural inclination, an innate sense of rhythm, appropriate physical properties such as length of neck and hair, flexibility of flanks and fingers, great agility in gyrating the hips and twirling around oneself on the fixed axis of the legs. In this context two dances are mentioned specifically: *al-kurra* (lit. ball) and *al-ibl* (lit. camel).

Al-kurra may correspond to the Persian *kurre,* signifying colt, to be found in Arabic literature in connection with dance under the form of *al-kurrādj* – a saddle-horse or hobby-horse dance. This dance is described by al-Iṣfahānī (d. 950) in his *Kitāb al-aghānī.* It is told there that the Caliph al-Amīn (809–13), who was a man of pleasure, urgently summoned the two famous musicians Muḥammad ibn abī Ṭāhir and prince Ibrāhīm ibn al-Mahdī to his palace. Upon their arrival they found the court brillantly illuminated by hundreds of candles. The monarch was riding on a wooden horse, a *kurrādj,* dancing to the loud accompaniment of a band of reed-pipes (*surnāyāt*) and drums (*ṭubūl*) as well as many singing-girls. The capricious caliph, indifferent to the two singers' fatigue, ordered them to sing throughout the night along with the instrumentalists. The *kurrādj* is also described as a favourite dance among the Andalusians by the famous historian ibn Khaldūn who wrote: 'The *kurrādj* is a wooden figure resembling a saddled horse and is attached to robes such as women wear. (The dancers) thus look as if they have mounted horses. They attack and withdraw and compete in skill (with weapons)' (Rosenthal 63: II, 404–405). It may be inferred from this camouflaged horse dance that *al-ibl* might have been a camouflaged camel dance (Shiloah 356).

It should nevertheless be noted that there was a dance called *al-kurra* meaning 'ball'. We have noted in Chapter 5 an interesting example of this as danced by an automaton, described and illustrated in the *Kitāb fī ma'rifat al-ḥiyal al-handasiyya* (Book of Knowledge of Ingenious Mechanical Devices) by the twelfth-century Iraqi author, al-Djazarī. The device merits a full description in the present context: three musicians, slave-girls, are shown on a balcony, one holding an oboe-like instrument (*mizmār*) to her lips, another holding a lute (*'ūd*) and the third with a frame drum (*daff*) slung around her neck; on a platform above their balcony a dancer holding batons in both hands balances himself on a ball. He dances to the harmonious sounds and rhythms played by the slave-girls. He twirls a half-circle to his left and a quarter-circle to his right, moving his head and waving the batons while keeping his feet – sometimes only one foot – on the ball (Shiloah 76: 96–98).

The belly dance

As viewed by a westerner, belly dancing certainly seems to be the best known and most characteristic of all Near Eastern dances, the vehicle most typical of female dancers. At its best it can symbolize pleasant reveries and a kind of 'paradise lost'; at its worst, it is an exhibit of highly suggestive sexuality akin to prostitution. What in fact is this dance? Is it an art dance, folk dance or burlesque? Has it a unique defined form of its own, or is it a combination of patterns and expressive forms representing different dance genres? Is it exclusively female, or can it also be danced by men? Descriptions recorded by European eyewitnesses at various times and places may afford us an insight into the different aspects and characteristics of belly dancing.

In the 1530s, Guillaume Postel, a French scientific attaché at the embassy in Constantinople, described a band of female minstrels who sang and played on a harp, a tambourine and pieces of hard wood. 'Then', he writes:

> to vary the material, the eldest and most beautiful girl gets up to dance in their fashion; removing her scarf and gold cap, she puts on a turban –which is the headdress of a man – and does a mime, so strongly mimicking the gestures of love that describing it to men who do not see it would excite more desire than pleasure. First, she undulates sinuously, presenting herself for appraisal to the penetrating glances of the principal personages in the party, and pretending to offer herself; waving a pretty kerchief she seems to wind a string to the one she has aroused, only to stop short – until Mercy tempers these ends. . . . (Postel 142)

The gliding, twisting movements of the dancer's body and the use of the kerchief as a basic accessory appear in a more detailed description in the travel record of an Italian Jew, Samuel Romanelli, who visited Morocco in 1787. Romanelli referred to a dancing girl in the framework of a Jewish wedding in an urban milieu –Tangier. The character of the dancing he described, with his appended value judgement, has much in common with the usual perception of belly dancing. He wrote thus:

> . . . And a dancing girl, her head tilted sideways, holds an edge of a kerchief in each hand, one high above her head, the other pointing below her waist to her stomach, and then slowly, suggestively, she reverses the position of her arms. I thought she was mad, but they told me that was how they dance in their city. This was accompanied by young girls beating quietly on goblet drums . . . the drumming was entirely random, conforming to no known rules of composition. How could anyone present at this performance refrain from laughing? (Schirmann 358: 29)

The erotic aspect was stressed by the famous orientalist E. W. Lane in his book *The Manners and Customs of Modern Egyptians*. He devoted a whole chapter entitled 'Public Dancers' to the special class of dancing girls known as *ghāziyeh* or *ghawāzī*. On festive occasions these girls would perform in public on the streets of Cairo, in houses, and in the harem. In addition to the sound made by the rapid percussion of tiny brass cymbals, two of which are attached to the thumb and middle finger of each of the dancer's hands, the musical accompaniment was provided by musicians who played on a spike fiddle (*rabāb*), a tambourine (*ṭār*) or a goblet drum (*drabukka*). 'Their dancing,' Lane wrote, 'has little of elegance; its chief peculiarity is a very rapid vibrating motion of the hips, from side to side.' He admits, however, that by 'more animated looks' and 'by increased energy in every motion, they exhibit a spectacle' that women and men delight in witnessing. But in some cases, he adds, their performances were lascivious, eliciting the disapproval of persons from the higher classes and among the more religious (Lane 420: 384–388). Indeed, in the year 1834, soon after he had written that description, public female dancing was prohibited by the ruler of Egypt, Muḥammad ʻAlī. As a result of that prohibition, the number of male dancers increased and they were even more audacious than the girls.

As to the possible origin of belly dancing, while Lane perceived similarities between it and the pharaonic dances depicted in tomb-paintings (Lane 420: 387), other observers have suggested links with late Etruscan prototypes in Italy, or even with ancient Near Eastern ritual (Berger 352: 8).

The belly dance of today is much the same as it was in past centuries; it continues to entertain in show business, fancy cabarets, night clubs and cinema houses, although to a lesser extent, due to changes in social context brought about by the impact of modernization and the growing importance of mass communications media. It has also begun to throw off its doubtful reputation and to shore up its status as an artistic dance by stressing the aesthetic foundations that were lost sight of, due to the emphasis on sexual excitation and vulgarity.

A genuine belly dance is based on expressive movement of the body, arms, hands, head and eyes, rather than the legs as is the case with many dances of other cultures. Thus its salient characteristic is not locomotion but intensive development of, and improvisation on, a form within a narrow compass. The set sequence of movements that compose the dance should therefore be executed with supple grace; the dancer must exercise full control of abdominal muscles as well as of torso and arm muscles. The dancer's keen rhythmic feeling comes to the fore mainly as she claps out rhythmic patterns with the brass cymbals. Some of the complex twisting, undulating movements are made only by the belly, others are made by rolling the hips while simultaneously thrusting the belly in the opposite direction; still other patterns include arching backward until the dancer's head touches the floor, or performing circular undulations reminiscent of a serpent's slithering glide.

In a comprehensive article called 'The Arab Danse du Ventre', Morroe Berger has likened this dance to Arab art as a whole:

> The effect of the dance is somewhat like that of Arab art in general. That is, it depends upon form, the arrangement of parts within a compressed area, as in a mosaic. It is an art of abandon, but has a large measure of restraint and control. (Berger 352: 23)

This comment corresponds to a basic concept in the composition of music that was referred to in Chapter 5, pp. 61–63.

Dance among the mystics

Islam's attitude toward dancing is fully explicated in the polemical literature about the sacred dance of the mystic orders. Secular dance as practised in the rulers' courts or the homes of the aristocracy is ignored in this literature, its illegitimacy apparently taken for granted. Folk dance, if mentioned, is usually tolerated both because of its function in enhancing festive occasions in the life of the individual and community, and because of the general belief that the concept dance, like music, should be applied to forms associated with diversion and relaxation.

In the rich literature about the sacred dance of the mystics, we find that dancing, as stated above, is usually associated with singing, hand-clapping and the playing of instruments, a composite known as *samāʿ*.

The mystics' ecstatic dance is said to demonstrate their infinite love for God; it serves as a means to attain sublime heights. In this context reference is often made to King David who sought divine inspiration through dance. Ecstatic dance helps those who have reached advanced gnosticism to come nearer to God. But the practice by a novice, who has not yet been saved from the clutch of his carnal soul, is considered dangerous. Eventually, when the mystic reaches perfection, he ceases to need all these things; he realizes mystical union through concentration and meditation (Molé 211; Rouget 222: 405–410).

Nevertheless, certain old masters of mysticism expressed dissatisfaction with dance and physical excitation as methods of reaching an ecstatic trance because so often the trance was simulated artificially. Indeed, some extravagant practices roused strong opposition among the mystic authorities; their ire was directed especially against the deceitful, exhibitionist dervishes who would dance in the market-place, undress in public, sit on hot coals, swallow glass, engage in acts of self-mutilation and, in general, misuse the ceremony of *samāʿ*.

Naturally the most violent attacks against the dancing of the Ṣūfīs came from canonists and theologists who considered any form of dancing a vice or worse. They saw it as temptation by the devil, a heretical and polytheistic act; the Ṣūfīs' dance would turn Muslims away from God's word, being similar in nature to the atheism expressed in the dancing around the Golden Calf.

Beyond all legalistic and theological considerations, one finds references to what appear to have been conventional standards of good behaviour. Indeed, it was not fitting for a thoughtful, ponderous man to behave in a frivolous manner, clapping hands like a woman or prancing like an animal.

In its simplest form, dancing that came to be an attendant element of the *samāʿ* was nothing more than physical movements performed collectively by initiates all standing in the same line or circle. Shoulder to shoulder, occasionally clapping hands and obsessively repeating fixed phrases, the devotees would sway to and fro in place, raising and lowering themselves, nodding energetically. They sway ever more vigorously, breathing deeply to the modulating voice of the precentor and occasionally to the beating of a drummer or cymbalist.

The most spectacular and sophisticated dance is that of the Mevlewis, named after *Mawlāna* (our master) Djalāl al-dīn al-Rūmī (d. 1273), the greatest Persian-language mystic poet. Under his teaching and influence, 'Music and dance,' in the words of the great expert Fritz Meier, 'intermingled to create so indivisible a unity that the dances were performed as rituals in praise of God and as stimulants to an exalting experience of inner harmony' (Meier 205: 122). In the works of al-Rūmī and other writers the symbolic meaning of music and dance is emphasized by such utterances as: The sounds of music awaken spirits deep in the slumber of ignorance and make them stand up and dance like the dead who will rise at the resurrection to the sound of the trumpet. Human spirits whose origin is the world above recall their homeland when they hear music; they shake off their bodily cage and manifest their emotion by dancing. Dance helps man to free his foot rooted in the terrestrial mud and transports him upward to the summit of the world.

All details of their ceremony, called *mukabele*, are highly formalized. An ensemble of well-trained singers and instrumentalists, sitting apart according to rank, perform the different parts of the ceremony, in which dancing is most important. The *semazen* (dancers) stand on a huge octagonal platform near the sheikh, they and their leader – the *semazen bashi* – wearing white gowns symbolizing a shroud, black mantles and peaked caps symbolizing the tomb. After a ritual prayer, the singing of the *na't sherif* (praise to the prophet) and a flute improvisation, the dancers walk around the platform three times in stylized fashion to the sound of a prelude. Then they throw off the black mantle, the leader asks the sheikh for permission to begin and one after another they kiss the sheikh's hand and begin to dance. Each dancer spreads out his arms, his right palm facing up and his left down, his head inclined to the right. The right is said to receive divine emanation and the left to transmit it to lower spheres. In this posture each dancer starts whirling, his white dress floating around him to form a revolving discus. Each whirling slowly around his own axis, the dancers complete a full circle; in the centre an aged dancer usually whirls in place. The ceremony includes three or four dancing phases separated by musical interludes and characterized by different rhythm and tempi (Ritter 201; Molé 211: 229–251). (See music example 10 on page 230.)

This refined and highly spiritual dance stands in sharp contrast to the frenetic trance entered into by certain popular societies in the framework of the Ṣufī practice of invocation – the *dhikr* – which in this case usually includes extreme manifestations of ecstatic dancing and other extravagant behaviour. This type of ecstatic ritual presents us with the magical version of the roots of music and dance, as related to another important aspect found in the practices of some confraternities – the ritual of healing and exorcism (Rouget 22: 374–382; 422–428). In the performance of such rituals, ecstatic dancing is always emphasized and stimulated by corresponding rousing music played on appropriate instruments. Among the latter the various kinds of drums predominate, providing an essential accompaniment that leads to ecstasy by means of an obsessive, exciting beat. Among the best illustrations of this kind of ritual are those found in North Africa – more specifically, in Morocco (Meier 205: 126–127).

'Isāwa or 'Isāwiyya

The *'Isāwiyya*, one of the most popular religious confraternities, is named after its founder Sīdī (saint) Aḥmed ben 'Īsa who died in Meknes (Morocco) in 1523. This very pious man was an accomplished mystic and adhered to the basic classical orthodox Ṣūfī methods of attaining spiritual perfection. During his lifetime he enjoyed great popularity, was said to possess remarkable powers of healing and to have obtained for his followers the boon of immunity from scorpion and snake poisoning as well as from the dangerous prick of cactus thorns. The growing number of his disciples spread word of the confraternity and led to the establishment, during the lifetime of Sīdī 'Īsa, of several *zāwiyas* (sanctuaries) outside of Meknes, fanning out to Algeria, Tunisia, Lybia, Syria, Cairo and Mecca.

The session at which the invocations and dancing take place is called *ḥaḍra* which corresponds to the ecstatic dancing known as *taḥayyur* (ravishment). After a rhythmic intoning of litanies comes the first phase of the *ḥaḍra* – the *rabbānī*, or slow section. The dancers stand in line holding hands, raise and lower their chests, perform bending and upright movements, toss their heads energetically from side to side and stamp the ground first with one foot and then the other. The musicians accompanying the dances play on four *bendirs* (frame drums) and the (oboe-like) *ghayta*; forming a semi-circle, they refrain from entering an ecstatic state, gradually preparing the transition to the second phase. After this transitional dance during which some disciples may quit the group in quest of individual ecstasy, the ceremony reaches its climax with the *mudjarrad* (denuding) – the rapid section – during which the dancers remove the *djallāba*, form a circle around the *muqaddam* (the leader) and manifest extreme excitement. When performed by couples or groups the dances may assume interesting forms, although they often end in displays of *fakirism* wherein the disciples pick up burning coals in their bare hands and place them between their lips, swallow fragments of broken bottles, or strike themselves with swords. These characteristics of ecstatic dancing as well as what they call *firsa* – bloody feasts – can be best observed at the time of the *mawlid*, the anniversary of the prophet, when the *'Isāwiyya* of all lands congregate at the tomb of their patron saint (Dermingham 203).

Do disciples of the confraternity who reside in different lands all observe the same extravagant *ḥaḍra* practices at their respective *zāwiyas*? Fortunately, we possess a detailed colourful eyewitness report on an *'Isāwiyya ḥaḍra* celebrated in Cairo in the first half of the nineteenth century by disciples who were almost all Maghrebans. Its author is the famous British orientalist, E. W. Lane, who spent most of the years between 1825 and 1849 in Egypt, and reported on the *'Isāwiyya ḥaḍra* he attended. The way he describes what he witnessed for an hour or so reflects the overwhelming effect produced on him by the wildly extravagant behaviour of the disciples performing the ecstatic dance. A few excerpts from that report are very much in place here.

In his lengthy description Lane tells of a group of 20 dervishes sitting on the floor; while they beat different types of drums, six other dervishes commenced a strange kind of dance.

> There was no regularity in their dancing; but each seemed to be performing the antics of a madman; now moving his body up and down; the next moment turning around, then gesticulating strangely with his arms; next the dancer jumps and sometimes screams. In short, if a stranger observing them were not told that they were performing a religious exercise, supposedly the involuntary effect of enthusiastic excitement, he would certainly think that these dancing *derweeshes* were merely striving to excel one another in playing the buffoon.

Among those dancing dervishes were two principal performers who gradually became wild and extravagant, seizing pieces of live charcoal which they put in their mouths, deliberately chewing and swallowing the live coals 'without evincing the slightest symptom of pain'. The younger of them

> displayed a remarkably fine and vigorous form . . . after having danced not much longer than the former, his actions became so violent that one of his brethren held him: but he released himself from his grasp, and, rushing towards the chafing-dish, took out one of the largest live coals and put it into his mouth. He kept his mouth wide open for about two minutes, during which period, each time he inhaled, the large coal appeared to be of almost white heat; and when he exhaled, numerous sparks were blown out of his mouth. . . .'

After having described another party of the same sect performing near the centre of the great portico, Lane concluded:

> After I had witnessed these extraordinary performances for about an hour, both parties of derweeshes stopped to rest; and as there was nothing more to see worthy of notice, I then left the mosque. (Lane 420: 466–468)

This eyewitness report restricted to the ritual performed at the Cairo *Zāwiya* does not of course refer to other elements of the magic-religious complex that apply to other activities of the *'Isāwiyya* confraternity. Of those, the practices of healing, of conjury and exorcism, as well as the mimicking of animals, should be mentioned.

Animal dances

It is notable that among the most striking dances of the confraternity are those in which a certain number of disciples impersonate animals whose behaviour they mimic very realistically. One impersonating a camel, for instance, should carry enormous burdens, devour cactuses without showing signs of pain; the impersonator of a jackal or panther consumes raw meat; dancers who mimic wild boars and dogs confront each other in ferocious fights; in the dance of lions and lionesses, the latter are represented by women who squat while the men execute acrobatic figures. These and other animal dances may have derived from ancient Saharan rituals. In his book *The History of Dance,* Curt Sachs expresses the opinion that dances imitating animals have been part of human life since the dawn of mankind. Among the roles Sachs assigned to these dances, the closest to the *'Isāwa* might be 'the attempt to control or dominate the power or magical virtues that characterised the animals being imitated' (Sachs 355: 79–85).

Healing rituals

The magical-religious healing practices are usually performed by the *'Isāwiyya* at special therapeutic *ḥaḍra* held in the houses of patients in need of a cure for some mysterious disease or psychological disturbance, or, as commonly believed, seeking release from an evil spirit that has possessed them. The healing process depends very much on the use of exciting music and frenzied, ecstatic dancing by both healers and patient. Unable to resist the obsessive rhythm and powerful effect of the sonorous music, the patient becomes agitated, stands up and makes frenetic gestures, dancing himself into a trance. He finally reaches a state of exhaustion which supposedly indicates his release from the spirit that has possessed him.

The *'Isāwiyya* healing ritual is closely related to the *ḥaḍra Gnāwī* called *derdeba*, or its Tunisian equivalent *stambalī*; fairly frequently the *'Isāwa* and *Gnāwa* collaborate in performing therapeutic *ḥaḍras*.

The *Gnāwa* in Morocco, or the Sudanis – as they are known in Algeria and Tunisia – are black Muslim descendants of slaves who may have been brought to North Africa from the coast of Guinea. However that may be, they seem to have maintained a cultural affinity with West Africa and they can be found in most Maghreban towns. On the occasion of pilgrimages (*mousem*) their brotherhood, dedicated to the patron Saint Sidi Bilal, celebrates Ṣūfī-affiliated rituals in *zāwiyas* at its own special sanctified locales and tombs. Their healing ritual, like that of the *'Isāwiyya*, is held in the dwellings of patients suffering from mysterious illnesses. It comprises three phases: a procession through the town to the patient's house; the *kuyu* and *ouled bambara* which include entertaining dances that end close to midnight; and, finally, conjuring the haunting spirit to leave the body of the patient – this final stage marked by ecstatic dancing. In performing the *kuyu*, each dancer winds a pair of iron clappers or castanets (*karākeb*) around his palms and beats them together. To this metallic beat the dancers display their choreographic skills in a sequence of acrobatic figures performed with impressive rapidity. Couples dance face to face, becoming mutually provocative as they whirl around, bending and stretching their legs horizontally, stamping in a variety of positions, thus creating different rhythmic nuances. Because the rhythmic metallic sound of the *karākeb* predominates, the corresponding spectacular dances in the Algerian maraboutic feasts of the *Gnāwa* are called *karākabus*. The songs *ouled bambara* belonging to the same phase, often tell stories of black ancestors; they are accompanied by the *gunbrī*, a long-necked three-stringed lute. A little before midnight the lute is purified with incense before the last phase, when it is used with the *ganga* (side drum) to accompany the ecstatic dance of exorcism.

It should be noted in this context that both ancient sources and recent accounts have extolled the talent for rhythm and dance displayed by the blacks. In his book *Risāla fi shirā' al-raqīq wa-taqlīb al-'abīd* (Tract on How to Buy Slaves and How to Detect Body Defects), Ibn Buṭlān, a Christian physician (d. 1068), praised the blacks' inherent sense of rhythm in the following colourful manner: 'If a black were to fall from the sky to the earth he would fall in rhythm'. In his monumental history book The *Muqaddima*, the eminent historian Ibn Khaldūn (d. 1406) referred to the aptitude and fondness of the blacks for rhythm and dance, in his discussion of racial differences and the influence of climate on human character (Rosenthal 63: I, 174–175). In recording their impressions, many European travellers to the Maghreb particularly noted the dancing of blacks. Describing the Moroccan instruments then in vogue, the Jewish traveller Samuel Romanelli mentioned the *karākeb* as being typical of the blacks 'who dance as spryly as new-born colts' (Shirmann 358: 55-56). The Frenchman J. J. Tharand, in his book *Rabat ou les heures marocaines*, vividly described a black ritual dance on the occasion of their pilgrimage to the tomb of their patron saint. He wrote:

> A seated Negro, impressive in his barbaric dignity, a string of shells around his neck, holds a guitar [probably a *gunbrī*] in his hands. Around him other negro musicians shook cymbals [*karākeb*] . . .This metallic orchestra created a fierce uproar in a rapid monotone . . . under the effect of its hallucinating rhythm the silent crowd was deeply moved . . . one man stands up, then another . . . by now there are ten of them dancing in front of the musicians, jumping from one leg to

the other, and stamping their heels so violently that one feels the ground trembling underfoot. (Tharand 151: 29–32)

The Ḥamādisha

In connection with the therapeutic *ḥaḍra*, the *Ḥamādisha* should be mentioned. This is a Moroccan society more aptly described as a community of exorcists on the fringe of both Islam and Ṣūfīsm. Its name derives from the founder Sīdī 'Alī ben Ḥamdūsh (fl. seventeenth century) whose tomb is found in the mountains of Zerhoun, near Meknes. Their ritual *ḥaḍra*, which resembles the Egyptian *zār* or Tunisian *būrī*, has two parts: hot and cold. The 'hot' is collective in character, loud and fast, the dancers holding hands in a line. They sharply swing chest and head back and forth as they spring up and down with agility, vigorously stamping their feet. The 'cold' is quieter and is danced individually. The *ḥaḍra* is designed to whip performers and patient into a trance meant to mollify the spirits that have possessed the patient. The melodies played by the oboe-like *ghayta* usually allude to those particular spirits. The participants line up opposite the musicians, forming an outer boundary ringing the dance area. In the centre of this ring formed by most of the dancers, some of the women and the patient perform a wilder dance until they fall into a convulsive state as each dancer hears his special spirit. Acts of self-mutilation are performed in the course of this individual dance (Crapanzano 391).

This and the other therapeutic dancing we have mentioned has much in common with the *zār,* whose frenzied movements are designed to contact the invading spirits and drive out those that are evil. The *zār* practised in Egypt and Sudan is part of a ceremonial ritual intended to exorcise evil spirits and mysterious diseases. Specialized ensembles of singers, dancers and instrumentalists, particularly players on the *simsimiyya* (a lyre), fulfil an important role in this ceremony that may be based on an Ethiopian model (Shiloah 375). Indeed, the word *zār* is Amharic – the language spoken in Ethiopia – and designates a demon or other spirit that can possess a person. However, the Ethiopian *zār* cult functions as a form of group therapy, since no patient is ever discharged as cured; consequently, he will be enrolled in the *zār* society of fellow-sufferers for the rest of his life. This is reflected in the social hierarchy that prevails in the organization. Interestingly, the *zār* spirits themselves are divided according to basic human categories of age, sex, social class, education, religion and ethnicity.

The foregoing examples all display certain similar musical procedures in the healing rituals: the use of exciting music which stimulates spontaneous locomotion in the patient; the predominancy of a rhythmic component as an essential agent of the stimulation sought; the escalating release and arousal attained by drumming, clapping, stamping and beating of body idiophones; the obsessive rhythmic excitation affecting the body and its movements, gradually intensifying until the participants enter the ecstatic trance without which the healing process is impossible. At the climax of the trance the evil spirit that caused the malady is exorcised.

In an attempt to clarify in modern therapeutic terms these universal phenomena testifying to the influence of music and dance on body and mind, H. Sekeles writes:

> The sound of ecstatic drumming and the movement reacting to it leads to auditory driving as well as to auditory and visual imagery, particularly in stress conditions. It is easier to transmit increased energy to the brain by accelerated drumming at high amplitude and low frequencies than, for example, by the sound of a flute or a violin. The effectiveness of the drumming is enhanced by a multiplicity of rhythms, especially at moments of multi-sensory stimulation.
>
> The ecstatic healing ritual allows the participants to release sexual energy and aggression. It can be compared to the pubertal phase where the subliminal mechanism is most effective for mental hygiene. Catharsis and sublimation in the ecstatic healing ritual are attained through sound stimulation and vigorous locomotion. The group plays an all-important role in supporting the individual and his bizarre behaviour during the ritual.
>
> Processes of guided imagery help the patient to withdraw temporarily from reality and commune with his inner experiences; often he undergoes a kind of 'rebirth'. (Sekeles 419: Introduction)

Folk dance

Folk dances reflect the great variety of ethnic groups and sub-groups that dwell in the region; they encompass nomads, semi-nomads, peasants and city-dwellers, most of whom speak different languages and dialects. Due to the multiple functions fulfilled by folk dances performed on special occasions in the life of individuals and communities, and their role in enhancing festive social gatherings, the number and types of dances representing ethnic and regional styles is enormous; experts enumerate close to a thousand in Anatolia alone (And 351). There are collective and communal group dances in which all members of the community participate, as well as solos performed by skilled amateurs, semi-professional and professional male or female dancers. The group dances may have simpler or more complex forms and patterns; some of them are danced only by women, some only by men, while others are danced by both sexes together. Throughout the region circle, line and frontal dances are the oldest and most common forms. Most dancing takes place outdoors, in the course of festive events, social gatherings or pilgrimages to holy shrines.

Communal and Group Dances

The communal dances are more participatory activities than performances.

Their social character is expressed by the dancers' close contact: arms are linked tightly in different holds, sometimes hands are placed on the adjacent dancer's shoulders or hips. This aspect of closeness may be what is implied by the term *destbend*, meaning hand in hand, that designates certain *chori* dances in Khorasan, or the Turkish dance *baru-haru* which means in choir (in unison). In the simplest form of open-circle, line and frontal dances the main activity is in the legs, the trunk is treated as a single unit and there is limited play of the body in space.

Open-circle dances

These dances are characterized by mass participation. Short, repetitive and relatively simple step patterns characterize the Iranian *rostai* or *tavaifi*; ten to twenty young men, hand in hand, form an open-circle, the lead dancer rhythmically waving one or two scarfs. From time to time, without stopping, the dancers toss a coin to the musicians who accompanying them.

In Turkey there is a large category of rounds and communal dances called *halay*, *bar* and *horon*. The *halay* is danced by men only, their rhythm contrasting with the vehement accompaniment performed, as in many other dances of the region, by the oboe-like *zurna* and the double-headed drum, the *davul*; the leader of the dance usually signals to the instrumentalists when it is time to change the rhythm. The *horon* is a vigorous dance from the east coast of the Black Sea. It calls for the male dancers to shake all their members, to squat and rise abruptly. The Palestinian male dance *far'awiyya* is a simple rural dance form which starts as an exhortatory song. The participants stand in a long line clapping hands and singing short responses; then, very slowly, they start moving to the right in a simple pattern until they form a full circle.

Frontal and line dances

The frontal dances include examples such as the Turkish category of *karşilama* in which two lines facing each other execute certain forms and patterns; the dance form is usually reflected in the responsorial singing. The spoon dances – *kaşik oyunu* and *çifte telli* – also belong to this category: either the dancers themselves or musicians accompany the dancing by striking a pair of wooden spoons against each other. In Yemen and possibly in the entire Arabian peninsula, the frontal dance *radīḥ* is antiphonal – choreographically as well as musically. In the Bedouin *daḥḥiya*, the dancers form a row facing the poet-singer. The latter sings improvised stanzas and the group sings responses and claps while moving alternately backward and forward; there is no other accompaniment. When the dance reaches its climax an unmarried woman clad entirely in black appears. Brandishing a sword or stick, she takes up a position opposite the row of men, moving in long strides and leaps. The dancers alternately move toward her and away, driven back by the sword. This mimetic part of the dance is closely associated on the one hand with amorous play and war dances, and on the other, with frontal dances.

Sword dances

Martial sword dances are still extant throughout the region. Known as *djengi*, forms of battle dances have survived in the mountainous parts of Iran. In the *chappi* dance, men form a tight circle holding each other by their belts; they move around stamping in cadence and raising one foot, the toe pointing up. The leader conducts the dance while singing and waving a scarf; he dances independently of the others. More typical is the individual sword dance in which one dancer – occasionally two – simulates combat. The most famous battle dance is the *zeybek* that became almost a national dance in Turkey. Its characteristic pattern consists of sharply rapping the knee against the ground while dancing. Another interesting characteristic of this dance is its asymmetric rhythm.

In Yemen this type of dance embodies a more sophisticated choreography. In the tribal dance *bara‘*, a term meaning literally to excel, the dance represents a sequence of three or four parts. A group of dancers, whose number may reach 50 or more, form an open circle and while brandishing daggers (*djanbiyya*) in a manner suggesting combat, they perform a series of highly stylized movements with their legs, arms, and heads; these movements are expected to accord perfectly with those of the leader. As the dance becomes progressively more complex, the poorer dancers drop out of the circle while the better ones, usually those who are older and more experienced, proceed to execute rapid, intricate figures. The climax is reached with only two or three outstanding performers left to bring the dance to its dazzling end. This dance has several variations and is usually accompanied by two special drummers, one on the *marfa‘*, the other on the *ṭāsa*; the former beats out the basic pulse while the latter embroiders subtle patterns (Lambert 418: 297–300).

Such communal dances can be organized in a sequence of dances like the Yemenite *mizmār* (a double clarinet) suite, which is vocal–instrumental in urban centres and purely instrumental in rural areas. The suite played by the *mizmār*, *ṭabl* (drum) and *ṣaḥn* (a copper plate), comprises three major rhythms that develop in a progressive crescendo: the *manta*, an asymmetric rhythm of seven beats similar to the *ṣan‘āni da‘sa*; the *shaniya*, a 4/4 rhythm in moderate tempo; and a similar rhythm in a rapid tempo. The passage from one phase to the next is usually indicated by conventional musical transitions uttered by the players or the singers (Lambert 418: 297–300).

A sequence of dances characterizes other traditions, such as the Kurdish and North African Berber group dances. In these cases either the dances follow one another without a break, the transition being indicated by the instrumentalist or dance leader, or they are separated by a very short pause.

Mixed male and female dances

The mixed dances typical of certain groups and regions can be open-circle, line or frontal. Women participate in the Turkish open-circle bar dance; mixed groups are also quite common in Kurdistani dances. Many of the powerful, vigorous open-circle and line dances are performed by mixed groups, with participants linked closely together. The steps include bounces and leaps, accompanied by energetic rhythmic swinging of the arms. The two rows of the Iranian-Kurdish *chori* represent the two sexes. Slowly swinging their arms, the groups move toward and away from each other. The women cross over to exchange places with the group of men. This is a signal for the men to stop dancing and start singing and clapping hands, while the women continue to dance.

Women are frequently included among the large numbers who participate in the *aḥidou* and *aḥwāsh* dances performed by the Berbers of the high, anti- and middle Atlas (Morocco). A sequence of dances linked to each other and progressing from slow to more rapid movement, the *aḥidou* and *aḥwāsh* are frequently performed by mixed groups either in two lines, one of women and the other of men, or in a circle with men and women alternating. These dances, often nocturnal, go on for many hours; they usually start with a solo vocal improvisation followed by the first phase of the group dance characterized by the dancers' relative immobility. Standing shoulder to shoulder or holding hands and bending backward and forward, the performers move in a line while singing antiphonally and clapping hands, sometimes forming a circle; they are accompanied by an ensemble of frame drums (*bendīr*) that emphasizes the slow patterns. The *bendīr* players hold the drum horizontally and beat the skin stretched underneath with an upward movement. In neighbouring Algeria, the Ouled Nail tribe perpetuates an interesting couple dance called *saadaoui*. The two dancers perform basically the same patterns, moving to the sounds of the (oboe-like) *ghayta* and the *bendīr* (frame-drum), without jumping or gliding (Chottin 423).

At Tindouf (an oasis in the Algerian Sahara) a ritual dance is performed in front of men by young girls who have reached puberty. The girls dance in couples facing each other, their arms engaging in a kind of dialogue. Another interesting dance young unmarried girls perform in front of young men is the Lybian and south Tunisian 'hair' dance, called *nakh*. Kneeling, their hair loose, the girls sway, moving the head and upper torso in time to the accompanying music. Thus their hair is flung forward and back. At the same time a group of young men moves toward them and away to the rhythm of the music. It is interesting to note that in a similar dance executed in south Yemen the women attach tiny jingles to their braids so that when they toss their heads, they produce soft metallic sounds.

Individual dancing

Among nomadic and rural societies it is not uncommon to find individual dancing. The entertaining Yemenite *luʿba* (lit. play, game) danced by both men and women, but separately, belongs in this category. This intricate, highly refined dance that enhances family celebrations and social gatherings, calls for skilful, agile dancers with extraordinary bodily control. It is performed by two dancers facing one another; in a kind of mirror-play they are expected to imitate each other's subtle movements – this involves highly skilled acrobatic performances. To endow their dancing with a sense of serious respectability, they exert strict control over their facial expressions (Lambert 418: 345–350).

The Kurdistani *diwānki* dance, a form of evening entertainment, essentially consists of people sitting in a circle telling stories and singing. Dancing inside the circle (*diwān*) is performed by one, two or three soloists, while those seated around clap their hands. The dance is improvised, each dancer modifying the patterns to suit his own personal style. When there are two dancers, one dances in front of the other holding a sword or kerchief.

A fascinating individual dance for women is the Moroccan *guedra* (lit. pot); actually, the name designates the drum that accompanies the dance – it has a ceramic pot-like base over which a camel skin is stretched. The dance is practised in the region of Goulimine situated in the vast reaches of the Moroccan south. Surrounded by a circle of singing, clapping men and women, a kneeling woman begins to move the upper part of her body. Her arms outstretched, she sways alternately from left to right, performing subtle hand motions that set off a delicate play of fingers; the movements of her upper torso are in syncopation with the percussive rhythm, her head swinging back and forth. The rhythm is gradually intensified and the dancer's movements become increasingly rapid and frenzied, until she reaches a state of exhaustion.

Individual dancing is fairly typical of folk dances in urban and semi-urban centres. The dancers usually treat the torso as two separate units, the hips gyrating or shaking; the more skilful and acrobatic performances are closely related to the belly dancing described above. In addition to acrobatic, comic and erotic dances, considered an inferior genre, in Iran one finds more dignified individual dances such as the *bezlei* or pantomime dance. In gestures and dance patterns the performer depicts the life and deeds of the hero whom the accompanying song extols; using symbolic gestures, the dancer also simulates abstract emotions.

In Morocco professional itinerant musician-dancers travel as troupes throughout the country. They often perform at Marrakesh where, clad in white robes, they dance, sing and play on the *gunbrī* (lute) and a single-stringed, skin-bellied fiddle.

12 Folk Musical Traditions

This chapter primarily refers to those forms of music-making that address broad segments of the population inhabiting the vast area we have been discussing. In the main, therefore, we are excluding the more eclectic, sophisticated traditions of 'art music', as well as certain forms of religious practice and dance already treated in previous chapters.

Someone attempting to acquire an overview of the folk traditions practised in these lands, stretching from Central Asia in the east to North Africa in the west, finds himself confronted with a bewildering multiplicity of musical idioms and poetic-musical genres. These in turn reflect a wide range of human responses to varying ecological conditions, and enormous ethnic, linguistic, religious, and economic diversity. Indeed, this intricate mosaic involves peoples belonging to many different ethnic groups and sub-groups who adhere to diverse denominations and sects, ranging from Muslim, *Sunnī*, *Shī'ī* and Druze to important religious minorities that include Armenian and Assyrian Christians, Jews, Zoroastrians, Bahā'is and Gypsies. They speak and sing in numerous languages, idioms and dialects and live in conditions ranging from desolate arid zones to flourishing urban centres. Repertories practised by amateurs and professional or semi-professional specialists, whose activities extend from cities to villages to nomad encampments, have developed countless forms and genres with texts that span a wide gamut of tongues, from colloquial vernaculars to elegant classical forms. As a result of a long process of interaction among peoples who have shared languages such as Arabic, Turkish, Iranian, Kurdish, Berber, individual repertories manifest an overall kinship expressed in linguistic and musical affinities that cut across political boundaries. Today, therefore, hardly any country has a homogenous folklore. The effect of interaction between certain high folk musical genres and neighbouring urban art-music must also be taken into consideration.

In view of the vast arena indicated above, it is clearly impossible for this survey to attempt a full exposition of the almost endless store of folk musical traditions involved. At best, only salient common traits and distinctive particularities can be singled out. The great importance of poetry and a predominantly vocal conception of music, closely associated with the memorizing and declaiming of texts that is characteristic of both nomadic and sedentary people of all social levels, should nevertheless be stressed; in large measure this also pertains to dance genres that are usually accompanied by singing and clapping (see Chapter 11). The poetry referred to here is less a form of literary expression than an accompaniment to ceremonial and other events; *de facto*, however, it is based on consistent forms and methods of composition. Many, many forms and genres of folk poetry are sung; in both quantity and fecundity, folk songs surpass classical songs. This prolific richness finds expression in the plethora of categories and terminology applied by the folk themselves. The types of music-making include several forms of religious recitation and singing, work songs, narrative, didactic and lyric songs, songs and dances that provide entertainment at weddings and other musical gatherings.

In songs and dances of a communal nature, responsorial forms are frequently used, which indicates the importance attributed to audience participation. Social and group folk songs usually comprise the oldest category and throughout the region they are characterized by relative simplicity and absence of embellishment, in contrast to later melismatic and variegated treatment. Also, a general distinction is often drawn between long, serious, heavy genres and lighter, more diverting ones.

Work songs

Among the collective functional songs are work songs that originated in an agricultural and rural life. Songs of cattleherders and shepherds are characteristic of the *Kazakhs* and *Kirgiz*. Songs mark the ploughing, reaping, threshing and grinding of grain; among the predominantly agricultural peoples of Tajikistan, Uzbekistan and Turkey, those songs are sometimes antiphonal. The Yemenite *mahdjal* is primarily a harvest song but it also relates to other collective work such as that of masons; it consists of improvised verses sung by a soloist to which the group repeats an identical refrain after each verse. The musical rhythm, corresponding to the rhythm of the work, has a stimulating effect. The Yemenite women's work song *ḥādī* is linked to stripping off the Sorgho foliage; it is a melismatic song performed by a soloist and group (Lambert 418: 74–80). A remarkable work song is the *ifdjerī* of the pearl-fishers along the coast of the Persian Gulf, namely in Bahrain, Kuwait and Qatar. The *ifdjerī* include songs to accompany particular tasks aboard ship; one of them, the *khrāb*, sung as the anchor is weighed, is of particular musical interest because the crew sings the chorus in preternaturally deep voices, akin to Tibetan Lamaist chanting. The soloist sings on a high pitch while the crew intones a background chant two octaves lower. According to H. Touma, 'an *ifdjerī* song consists of a series of sections . . . each section is characterised by the rhythmic structure which accompanies the vocal part, and is named accordingly . . . only percussion instruments are used: double-skin drums (*ṭabl* and *mirwas*), frame-drum (*ṭār*), little metal cymbals (*ṭūs*) and water-jars (*ghalah*)' (Touma 451). This ensemble, and the clapping that accompanies it, performs highly sophisticated rhythmic patterns.

The performers

In the realm of performing practice, the folk poet-musician specialist has a uniquely important position: both narrator and spokesman, he articulates the moods and aspirations of his fellow men. Without in any way minimizing the role of non-specialists in cultivating specific song genres, it is arguable that the transmission and constant revitalization of all repertories depend largely on the presence and activities of gifted bards found in tribal encampments, villages and towns from Central Asia to North Africa. Whether itinerant or permanently settled inhabitants, in verse and music they interpret the memorable events, customs and manners of their surroundings, enhancing joyous or sorrowful public and private occasions. Among them are professionals, semi-professionals or specialists in one genre or another; they either provide their own poems or paraphrase and present traditional heroic and didactic narratives as well as other song forms. Such a bard is endowed with an exceptionally fine memory, has a good – or at least pleasant – voice, a measure of poetic, dramatic talent, and when singing epic and lyric songs he usually accompanies himself on a fiddle, lute or drum.

The bards are known by appellations that usually allude to the type of activity or particular genre in which they distinguish themselves. The terms *maddāḥ* or *meddāḥ* (panegyrist), the *naqqāl* and the Yemenite *nashshād* (singer of *nashīd*) and the like, designate professional performers of religious poetic genres such as the *qaṣīdas*, *nashīds*, and *tasābīḥ*, as well as a wide range of doctrinal verses. The term *shā'ir* (poet) or *sāz ṣairler* – as he is known in Turkish-speaking areas – meaning poet-musician, who accompanies himself on the long-necked lute *sāz*, obviously refers to the poetic talent of the performer. It also, however, indicates the predominance of the text over the musical component, as does the term *qawwāl* or *gawwāl* (one who says, for example poetizer), or the Kurdish *beytbig* (singer of verses) and *ḥaddāy* (singer of *ḥidā'* – a folk poetic genre).

Narrative and didactic songs

The itinerant poet-musician *'āshik* (lover), a name that came into being in the sixteenth century, probably under the influence of Ṣūfīsm, is a bard found in the northern highlands of Iran, Anatolia, Afghanistan and Azarbayjan. After having spent a number of years with teachers, whom he serves with utmost respect, he begins to perform in urban coffee houses and private homes. His repertory encompasses short lyric poems with amorous, moral, patriotic or religious content; it also includes long narratives (*hikaye*) in which spoken prose alternates with sung verse. He accompanies his songs on the *sāz* and may be joined by other men playing the *daff* (drum) and/or *balaban* (double-reed pipes). The *'āshiq,* who receives cash from his patrons and listeners, is expected to conduct long sessions: an epic may sometimes last longer than ten consecutive sessions. He must also be capable of adapting and improvising his texts to suit his audience (Blum 173; Reinhard 445).

Other professional and semi-professional performers such as the Balushi *dom* and *lori*, the Kurdish *beytbidj* and the Khorasani *bakhshi* play a prominent role in the transmission of narrative songs celebrating the origins and heroic deeds of an outstanding hero or tribe. In Kurdestan the context of epic song is mixed rural and urban, rather than 'tribal'. The Kurdish bard exercised his art in the home of the upper classes, in urban tea houses, and in villages. Both 'heroic' and 'romantic' narratives included in his repertory serve a didactic purpose. The Iranian *qesse-khwan* and the Turkish *hikayeler* (story-teller) recount realistic stories in verse or prose, often singing and using extensive vocal mimicry. It should be noted in this respect that the story-teller's art in Turkey and Iran has important affinities with the dramatic forms known as *pahlavan-kachal* (Iranian marionette theatre), *orta oyunu* (Turkish folk theatre), which include instrumental pieces, and the Turkish *karagöz* (shadow plays), which contain interpolated songs (Menzel 425; Ritter 349; And 357). In Egypt and elsewhere one finds a singer of narratives known as *abū zaydīyyah* (specialist in relating the story of the life and adventures of Abū Zayd al-Hilālī). This romance about the famous Arab hero is usually performed in the evenings during Ramadan.

Most of the above designations refer to poetic forms and indicate the poetic talent of the performer. 'Creativeness', however, often implies skill in adapting or rearranging existing material from the traditional store of poetic and musical motifs and formulae. This in no way detracts from the performer's interrelated talents as poet, composer, singer, instrumentalist, improviser and sometimes actor.

Lyric song

Whereas narratives and didactic songs fall largely within the orbit of professional and semi-professional specialists, the intimate, individual singing of non-professionals – men and women in all walks of life – is characterized by several types of 'lyric' songs. The caravan song *hujaynī* or *djammālī* belongs to the oldest strata of the Bedouin repertory and corresponds to the pre-Islamic *ḥudā'*. This simple caravan and camel song which we have discussed in another context in Chapter 1, with its narrative, nostalgic melody, is said to help break the infinite desert silence and encourage the lonely traveller and his mount. Among the forms sung by non-professionals individually or for small groups of friends are love songs. Lovers are addressed in the second person in the form of a monologue or dialogue, or there may be an actual dialogue between a man and woman as in the Moroccan *'rūbī*. The Yemenite *ḥomaynī* is both lyric and elegiac; it exalts genteel love, juxtaposing platonic themes with sensual features. Privately sung love songs belong to the realm of women.

Female musicians

The phenomenon of women singing for other women on various occasions was undoubtedly a way of circumventing restrictions engendered by religious and social bias that limited their public musical activities. Women's performances encouraged the emergence and crystallization of songs in which the women could express their world of experiences and the female values they upheld. The songs of women, like those of the men, reflect themes of everyday life, including public and political events, individual personal experiences and various communal happenings. Among the latter, wedding ceremonies are the most important. Many of the wedding songs indicate an attempt to offer the frightened girl, who in traditional societies marries very young, a measure of psychological preparation and assistance at this crucial turning-point in her life. During the relatively long period prior to the drastic change, a variety of rituals and, above all, songs help to fortify the girl's spirit. There are many types of songs for weddings and other occasions, some of which have specific relevance and some generalized content; they include lyric, humorous and dance songs.

The songs are sung in public on occasions of a folk nature and at semi-private gatherings of women, by either a group or one individual with a good voice. There are also professional performances by female musicians who are specialists in specific genres; particularly notable is the performance of funeral laments and dirges which are considered the province of women who excel as keeners. The Hebrew scriptural text of the Mishna contains a statement setting forth the bond between marriage and death: 'The pipe is for the bride and death'. Interestingly, a suggestion of this bond symbolizing the continuance of a person's existence may be found in the affinity between the *Kirghiz kiz uzatuu* (a bridal lament) and the *koshok* (funeral lament) which is similar to it. Professional performances are given by one or two specialists – the main singer and her 'assistant'. They usually accompany themselves on the region's most characteristically feminine instrument, the frame drum: *doira*, *ṭār*, *bendīr* or *daff*. In the Persian Gulf, larger all-female ensembles are known as *'adīd*. While singing at weddings and other family celebrations, they beat out complex rhythms on *ṭārs* (frame drums). Another larger group is the Baghdadian *daqqāqāt* (drummers), which at one time was a Jewish ensemble comprising four to five women beating various drums (frame drum, kettle drum and a two-headed drum). The leader of such a little band was noted for her fine voice and, being a talented performer, she was the soloist. While singing she accompanied herself on small kettle drums. Besides the drum, which in biblical times already appears as a feminine instrument, in Central Asia and Afghanistan the Jew's or jaw's harp is widely considered an instrument for women and children. In Central Asia, Turkey, Kurdistan, among the Berbers in North Africa and elsewhere, songs and dances are performed by alternating groups of women and men. A few such instances are described in Chapter 11.

An important aspect still awaiting thorough and systematic investigation is the extent to which, from the musical standpoint, women's songs differ from those of men. In this respect Bartok's view of the unique and archaic nature of women's music should be noted, as it may well apply to the singing of women in the Arabic and Islamic culture. The great composer, who studied the folk songs of Hungary, Romania, Turkey and Biskra in Algeria, was of the opinion that they preserved an ancient strata of song because in traditional societies the women who sing are bound to the home: their opportunities for contact with the external world are far fewer than those of the men (Bartok 448: 18).

Strophic forms

In all folk traditions text and music are inseparably linked; the texts are of many types, differing from one another in prosodic form, mode of performance, and social or musical function. Strophic forms, particularly quatrains with or without refrains, are usually predominant; the number of syllables per line varies, as does the rhyme scheme. The quatrain – known in different places under different names: *murabba'*, *rubā'ī*, *muthamman* (double quatrain), *mubayyat*, *dubeiti*, *charbeiti*, *'rūbī* or *'rūbī zā'id* (augmented) – may be a simple communal song with a limited number of melody types or an ornamented lyrical solo song; the rhyme scheme may be simple, such as AAAB, or ABAB, or AABA, AABB, or may comprise a variety of more complex forms. Certain specific types of quatrain are used by both men and women, alone or alternately, in 'dialogue', 'disputation' and 'competition' songs known as *ḥiwār*, *mu'ārada* (Near East), *'rūbī* (North Africa), *mani* (Turkey) and *aitis* (Central Asia) (Emsheimer 163). In this largely improvisational genre, which also includes certain Turkish and Kurdish dance-songs, two soloists – men or women, sometimes a man and a woman as in the Moroccan *'rūbī* – professional and semi-professional poet-musicians compete, exchanging improvised verses bound by strict rhythmic and melodic conventions. In the folk poetry of Tajiks, Iranians, Turks, and other peoples, the 'dialogue' is sometimes performed by a single person; certain romances are sung by only one singer who represents the two lovers executing an exchange of quatrains.

Strophic types can include a varied number of lines in a stanza, accommodating a varying number of syllables. Compared with the Tunisian *'rūbī*, the Moroccan *'rūbī* is more flexible, sometimes having six to seven lines per stanza, similar to the Baghdadi *mawwāl* which has a rhyme scheme of AAABBBA. The Egyptian *mawwāl* has only five lines, while the Moroccan ranges between three and six. Other than textual structure and prosody, the small poetic forms are characterized primarily by the recurrence of certain vowels and consonants, repetition of part or all of a line, interpolation of meaningless syllables, vocatives and expletives, as well as the refrain. The meaningless syllables can be added at the beginning, middle, or end of a line. In some cases, vocables such as the Turkish '*hey*' and '*aman*', the Arabic '*of*', or the Kurdish '*le lei*' or '*lolo*' are used to extend the melodic line; in other cases, as in some Kurdish songs, the extra vocables may be of longer duration than the text proper. In Hadramaut (Yemen) there is a category of songs called *dana dana*; a refrain of meaningless vocables: *dana dana ya dani/ ya dani dana dana* is sung by the audience after each of the soloist's improvised stanzas (Sergeant 427).

Non-strophic forms

Non-strophic forms comprise simple exhortatory or exclamatory single-line or independent-line songs that accompany marches, processions, political manifestations and other special genres such as the Yemenite work songs *mahdjal* and *ḥādī*, or the *tanṣura*, *hanhunnāt* and *zaghārīd* sung by women on joyful occasions. They consist of improvised verses which start with the interjection *ayha* or *iyha* on a high pitch, followed by verses sung in a fast parlando style, interrupted by the traditional *yuyu* (ululation or shrill trills). This category includes more developed genres such as the *qaṣida* or *nashīd* that reflect the highly regarded classical poetic form, as well as some narrative and epic songs that are popular throughout the area and among all classes of people. They are performed by special bards in nomad encampments, villages, market-places and urban coffee or tea houses; the performers often accompany themselves on either fiddle or lute (Hoerburger 428; Alexandru 433; Chadwik 435; Blum 442).

In their narratives and epics they celebrate heroic deeds, past events that often carry current political overtones, customs and moral values of their respective groups.

Relation of text to melody

For the folk-singer, text and melody form an integral unit, a cohesion implying that in most cases they are conceived simultaneously by the same performer. Nevertheless, there is a category of skilful musicians who perform verses composed by others. Length of line is often determined by melodic or rhythmic texture; in some instances the text may determine the nature of the melody and rhythm. As a rule, in the different traditions one finds intentional differentiation between cruder, simpler, syllabic songs of narrow range, and those that are melismatic and of a more complex texture. The former are usually communal, performed at social and group functions; the latter are soloistic, lyrical, and to a large extent fulfil individual and psychological functions. This category includes songs in which the melodic component seems to prevail (Blum 446). When discussing Maghreban folk music, J. Rouanet claims that vocalizing is the passion of the Maghreban singer and that his pronounced taste for ornamentation leads him to pay little attention to the union of poetry and music; he favours melody at the expense of words. But, he adds, this tendency is restricted to urban folksingers and does not apply to rural or Berber singing (Rouanet 93: 2902–2906). K. Reinhard stresses the important place occupied in Turkish folk music by the class of *uzun hava* ('long melodies') which supersedes the class of *kirik hava* ('broken melodies') including syllabic and dance songs. The 'long melodies' are rhythmically free, ornamented, and stress the importance of the melody. Reinhard views the *uzun hava* as a synthesis of 'Central Asian' and 'Near Eastern' practices (Reinhard 171: 210–212).

Instrumental music and musical instruments

Most instrumental music is closely linked to singing and dancing. However, some forms of independent folk instrumental music can be found, mainly in Turkey, Iran and Central Asia. The players, incidentally, are usually professionals who are remunerated for their services. An instrumental ensemble in

Iran, for instance, might be composed of *ṭār* (a long-necked fretted lute with five or six strings tuned in pairs, its double belly covered with two sheepskin membranes), *kemenche* (a long-necked spike fiddle with three or four strings) or violin, and *zarb* (goblet-shaped drum). Another combination might include *sorna* (double-reed pipes), *qushma* (double-clarinet) and *kemenche*. The Egyptian instrumental ensemble *ṭabl baladī* comprises three shawms (two large and one small), a pair of kettledrums and the cylindrical drum *ṭabl baladī*, which gives the ensemble its name.

String instruments include a variety of long-necked lutes. In Iran, Turkey and Central Asia, where they are often used to accompany singing, one finds the *dambura* or *setār* that generally has three strings and a pear-shaped belly; two forms of *dūtār* with two strings; and, in particular, the half-pear-shaped *sāz* (lit. instrument) that has many sizes and a varied number of strings; the smallest, *cura,* is portable and used by itinerant musicians. A plucked lute called *genibrī* or *gunbrī* with a rectangular, skin-covered body and round neck is common in the Maghreb. The spike fiddle exists in many different forms; it is known as *rabāb* in the Near East and North Africa, *amzad* in Mauritania, *kemenche* and *kopuz* in Iran and Turkey and *geishek* or *sarinda* in Baluchestan; the latter is a short-necked fiddle with from one to three bowed strings and several resonating drone strings. The fiddle is usually played by singer-poets to accompany performances of narrative and epic songs. A five-stringed lyre known as *simsimiyya* or *ṭambura* is found around the Red Sea and the Persian gulf area. According to K. Reinhard, Turkish peoples started using string instruments fairly early (Reinhard 171: 125). The aerophones or wind instruments constitute a rich class that includes double-reed pipes with tubes of conical and cylindrical shape; they are known as *sorna* or *zurna, balaban, ghayta* and *zukra.* The common combination of this oboe-like instrument and *dohol, dawul* or *ṭabl* (a barrel drum with two membranes) provides music for dancing, processions, weddings and other outdoor festive gatherings; in some places it also announces the beginning of the Ramadan fast. Simple and double clarinets are known as *duzele* or *zimare, zummāra, qushma, çifte, arghūl, mudjwiz, maqrūna* and *'affāta.* There is a variety of flutes named *nei* or *nāy, kaval, qaṣṣāba, shabbāba* and *duduk*; as a rule the flute is deemed the appropriate instrument for shepherds and lovers, yet it often accompanies dances and the singing of quatrains. A bagpipe with a double chanter known as *nei-arbūn, zummāra bi-soan,* and *djirba* can still be found in scattered places, as can long trumpets such as the *nafīr* and *karna.*

The membranophones or drums are by far the most varied in type and function. They include a variety of frame drums, plain or with metal discs, metal rings, or snares, such as the *daff, bendīr, daira* or *doira*; barrel drum such as the *ṭabl, mirwās, dohol* or *dawul*; kettledrums *naqqārāt*, and goblet drums *darbukka* and *zarb.*

The most common idiophones are struck against one another to accompany dancing. They include the *zeng* or *ṣunūdj* and *ṭūs* (small copper or bronze cymbals), the *chahar pare* (four pieces of bone, two held in each hand) which are attached to the thumb and middle finger, one or two pairs of spoons and the iron clappers or castanets *karākeb* used by the *Gnāwa* in North Africa. *Ṣaḥn* is a copper plate on which female and male singers beat the rhythm with a ring. Jingles (*khalkhal*) may be attached to the feet or arms; in South Yemen as we mentioned in Chapter 11 the women attach tiny jingles to their braids so that as they toss their heads, they produce soft metallic sounds. In the Persian Gulf the dancer sews the *mangūr* (goats' hooves) to a kind of short skirt covering his hips and they strike each other as the performer sways.

The great variety of instruments referred to above only partially reflects the bewildering multiplicity of musical idioms, poetic-musical genres, performing practices and ethnic diversity we have attempted to portray in this final chapter. These traditions, which existed well before the advent of Islam, also included the musical heritage that evolved in the Arabian Peninsula; it is with them that we embarked on our story. Following the Muslim armies' conquests the folk traditions pursued an independent existence in the overwhelming shadow of the Great Musical Tradition and its offshoots, in some cases interacting with it or absorbing its influence, and in other cases evading it and more or less devotedly elaborating the tradition's original traits. However, while art music has been extensively described and its theory discussed in a multitude of scientific and literary writings, this type of literature has almost entirely ignored folk musical traditions.

Viewed against their historical background these more or less old musical strata can supplement and enrich the more general information treated in the earlier chapters of this work.

Thematic bibliography (references)

Abbreviations

AcM	Acta Musicologica
JAMS	Journal of the American Musicological Society
JbfMVV	Jahrbuch für Musikalische Volks- und Völkerkunde
JIFMC	Journal of the International Folk Music Council
JRAS	Journal of the Royal Asiatic Society
REI	Revue des Etudes Islamiques
SIMg	Sammelbände der Internationale Musikgesellschaft
TGUOS	Transactions of the Glasgow University Oriental Society
YIFMC	Yearbook of the International Folk Music Council
YFTM	Yearbook for Traditional Music
ZfMw	Zeitschrift für Musikwissenschaft

I. Bibliographical works

(see also 76)

1. Waterman, R. A., W. Lichtenwanger, V. H. Hermann, 'Bibliography of Asiatic Musics', *Notes*, V, 1947–8, 21, 178, 354, 549; VI, 1948–9, 122, 281, 419, 570; VII, 1949–50, 84, 265, 415, 613; VIII, 1950–51, 100, 322.
2. Saygun, A., 'Ethnomusicologie turque', *AcM*, 32, 1960, 67–68.
3. Farmer, H. G., *The Sources of Arabian Music*, Leiden: Brill, 1965.
4. Arseven, V., *Bibliography of Books and Essays on Turkish Folk Music*, Istanbul, 1969 (in Turkish).
5. Laade, W., *Gegenwartsfragen der Musik in Afrika und Asien: Eine Grundlagende Bibliographie*, Heidelberg, 1971.
6. Reinhard, K., 'Grundlagen u. Ergebnisse der Erforschung türkischer Musik', *AcM*, 44, 1972, 266–280.

7. Massoudieh, M. T., 'Die Musikforschung in Iran', *AcM*, XXXVIII, 1976, 12; 52, 1980, 79–83.
8. Hassan, Sh. Q., *Maṣādir al-mūsīqā al-'irāqiyyah, 1900–1978*, Baghdad, 1981.
9. Hassan, Sh. Q., 'Die Entwicklung und Gegenwärtige Stand der Musikforschung im Iraq', *AcM*, 54, 1982, 148–162.
10. Krüger-Wust, W. J., *Arabische Musik in Europäischen Sprachen: Eine Bibliographie*, Wiesbaden, 1983.
11. Poché, Ch., *Music of the Arab World: A Research Guide*, to be published.

II. Lexicographical works

12. Kāẓim, A., *Al-isṭilāḥāt al-mūsīqiyyah*, Baghdad, 1964.
13. Faruqi, L. Ibsen, *An Annotated Glossary of Arabic Musical Terms*, Westport, 1981.

III. General works on Muslim history, literature, religion and civilization

14. Nasir-i-Khusraw, *Sefer Nameh* (Relation de voyage), Paris: Eernest Leroux, 1881.
15. Nicholson, R. A., *Studies in Islamic Mysticism*, Cambridge, 1923.
16. Brockelmann, K., *Geschichte der Arabischen Literatur*, Leiden: Brill, 1943, 5v.
17. Rosenthal, F., *The Technique of Scholarship*, Rome, 1947 (Analecta Orientalia, 24).
18. Villard, Ugo Monneret de, *La Pittura musulmane al soffito della Cappela Palatina in Palermo*, Rome, 1950.
19. Grunebaum, G. E. von, 'The Problem: Unity or Variety' in Grunebaum, G. E. von (ed.), *Unity and Variety in Muslim Civilization*, Chicago: Chicago University Press, 1955.
20. Bartold, V. V., *Four Studies on the History of Central Asia*, trans. from Russian by V. and T. Minorsky, Leiden: Brill, 1956.
21. Grunebaum, G. E. von, 'The Problem of Cultural Influence', *Charisteria Orientalia*, Prague, 1956, 86–99.
22. Trimingham, J. S., *Islam in West Africa*, Oxford, 1959.
23. *Études d'orientalisme dédiées à la memoire de Lévi-Provençal*, Paris, 1962, 2 tomes.
24. Gibb, H. A. R., 'The Social Signification of the *Shu'ūbiyya*', *Studies on the Civilization of Islam*, Boston, 1962, 62–73.
25. Goldziher, I., *Muslim Studies*, vol. I. London, 1967, 137–163.
26. Rosenthal, F., *The History of Muslim Historiography*, Leiden, 1968.
27. Lewis, B., *Islam in History: Ideas, Men and Events in the Middle East*, London: Alcove Press, 1973.

28. Pellat, Ch. 'Jewelers with Words', in *The World of Islam* (see 31), 141–60.
29. Sabra, A. I. 'The Scientific Enterprise', in *The World of Islam* (see 31), 181–200.
30. Mottahedeh, R. P., 'The *Shu'ūbiyya* Controversy and the Social History of Early Islamic Iran', *International Journal of Middle East Studies*, 7, 1976, 161–182.
31. *The World of Islam: Faith, People, Culture*, ed. by Bernard Lewis, London: Thames and Hudson, 1976. First paperback edition, 1992.
32. *The Cambridge History of Arabic Literature, vol. 1: Arabic Literature to the End of the Umayyad Period*, ed. by A. F. L. Beeston, T. M. Johnston, R. B. Serjeant and G. R. Smith, Cambridge University Press, 1983.
33. Granit, D., 'The Music Paintings of the Capella Palatina in Palermo', *Imago Musicae*, 2, 1985, 9–49.
34. Levzion, N., 'Islam in Sub-Saharan Africa', in Eliade, M. (ed.), *Encyclopedia of Religion*, New York: Macmillan, 1987.
35. *The Cambridge History of Arabic Literature, vol. 2: 'Abbāsid Belles Lettres*, ed. by Julia Ashtiani, T. M. Johnstone, J. D. Latham, R. B. Serjeant and G. Rex Smith, Cambridge University Press, 1991.

IV. Writings

(see also 54, 366, 367)

36. Kosegarten, J. G. L., *Alii Ispahanensis liber cantilenarum magnus Arabice editus adjectaque translatione ad notationibus que illustratus*, Greifswald, 1840.
37. Smith, E., 'A Treatise on Arab Music. Being a tr. of Mikhā'īl Mashāqa, *al-Risāla al-Shihābiyya fī'l ṣinā'ah al-mūsīqiyya*', *Journal of the American Oriental Society*, 1, 3, 1847, 171–217.
38. Carra de Vaux, B., 'Le traité des rapports musicaux ou l'épître à Sharaf Ed-Din, par Safi Ed-Din. . .', *Journal Asiatique*, 8, 18, 1891, 279–355.
39. Macdonald, D. B., 'Emotional Religion in Islam as Affected by Music and Singing. Being a Translation of a Book of the *Iḥyā' 'ulūm al-dīn* of al-Ghazzālī, with Analysis, Annotation and Appendices', *JRAS*, 1901, 195–252 and 705–748; 1902, 1–28.
40. Yafil, N. E. (ed.), *al-Ḥā'ik, Majmū' al-aghānī*, Alger, 1904.
41. Hujwīrī, 'Alī ibn, 'Osman, al-, *The Kashf al-Maḥjūb, the Oldest Treatise on Ṣufīsm by al-Hujwīrī*, trans. by R. A. Nicholson, Gibb Memorial Series n. 17, London, 1911, reprinted 1970.
42. Farmer, H. G., *Al-Fārābī's Arabic-Latin Writings on Music*, Glasgow, 1934 (London, 1965).

43. Farmer, H. G., 'Greek Theorists of Music in Arabic Translation', *Isis*, 1929–30, 325–33.
44. Ḥefni, M. A. al-, *Ibn Sīnā's Musiklehre*, Berlin, 1930.
45. Farmer, H. G., *The Organ of the Ancients: From Eastern Sources*, London, 1931.
46. Lachmann, R., M. al-Ḥefni (eds and trans.), *Ja'ḳūb ibn Isḥāq al-Kindī, Risāla fī khubr ta'līf al-alḥān*, Leipzig, 1931.
47. Farmer, H. G., *An Old Moorish Tutor: Being four Arabic Texts from Unique Manuscripts. . .*, Glasgow, 1933.
48. Farmer, H. G., *Turkish Instruments of Music in the Seventeenth Century, as Described in the 'Siyahat Nama of Ewliya Chelebi*, Glasgow, 1937.
49. Robson, J. (ed. and trans.), 'The Kitāb al-malāhī of Abū Ṭālib al-Mufaḍḍal ibn Salāma . . .', *JRAS*, 1938, 231–49. Appeared as a separatum under a new title: *Ancient Arabian Musical Instruments. . .*, Glasgow, 1938.
50. Robson, J. (ed. and trans.), *Tracts on Listening to Music: Being Dhamm al-Malāhī by ibn abī'l Dunyā and Bawāriq al-ilmā 'by Majd al-dīn al-Ṭūsī al-Ghazzālī*, London, 1938.
51. Erlanger, R. de, *La Musique Arabe*, Paris, 1930–59, 6 vols. Vol. I: *Al-Fārābī, Kitāb al-mūsīqī al-kabīr*, livres I-II, 1930; vol. II: *Al-Fārābī, Kitāb al-mūsīqī*. livre III, and *Ibn Sīnā. Kitāb al-shifā'*, 1935; vol. III: *Ṣafī ad-dīn, al-Risāla al-sharafiyya* and *Kitāb al-adwār*, 1938; vol. IV: *Traité anonyme dédié au sultan Osmanli Muḥammad II (XV. s.)* and, *al-Lādhiqī, Traité al-fatḥiyya(XVI s.)*; vol. V: *Essai de codification des règles usuelles de la musique moderne, échelle générale des sons, système modal; vol. VI: Essai de codification . . . le système rythmique. Les diverses formes de composition artistique moderne.*
52. Robson, J., 'A Maghribi Ms. on Listening to Music', *Islamic Culture*, 26, 1, 1952, 113–31.
53. Farmer, H. G., 'The Song Captions in the *Kitāb al-Aghānī*', *TGUOS*, 15, 1953/54, 1–10.
54. Farmer, H. G., *The Science of Music in Mafātīḥ al-'ulūm*, London: Hinrichsen, 1959.
55. Hefni, M. al- (ed.), *al-Muslim al-Mawṣilī, al-Durr al-naqī*, Baghdad, 1964.
56. Yūsuf, Z. (ed.), *Risālat Naṣr al-dīn al-Ṭūsī fī 'ilm al-mūsīqī*, Cairo, 1964.
57. Yūsuf, Z., *Mu'allafāt al-Kindī al-mūsīqiyyah*, Baghdad, 1965.
58. Cowl, C. (trans.), 'The *Risāla fī khubr ta'līf al-alḥān* of al-Kindī', *Consort*, 3, 1966, 129–166.
59. Muṭlaq, A. H. (ed.), al-Ṣafadī, Ṣalāḥ al-dīn, *Tawshi' al-tawshīḥ*, Beirut, 1966.

60. Shiloah, A., (trans.), 'Epître sur la musique des Frères sincères', *Revue des études islamiques*, 1965, 125–162; 1966, 125–168.
61. Wright, O., 'Ibn al-Munajjim and the Early Arabian Modes', *The Galpin Society Journal*, 1966, 26–48.
62. Ghaṭṭās, 'Abd al-Malik Khashaba (ed.), *Kitāb al-mūsīqī al-kabīr of al-Fārābī*, Cairo, 1967.
63. Rosenthal, F., (trans.), *The Muqaddimah of ibn Khaldūn: An Introduction to History*, (3 vols), Princeton, 1967.
64. 'Uthmān, M. A. (ed.), of *al-Fārābī*, *Iḥṣā' al-'ulūm*, 3rd printing, Cairo, 1968.
65. Neubauer, E., (trans.), 'Übersetzung des *Kitāb al-Īqā'āt* von Abu Naṣr *al-Fārābī*', *Oriens*, 21–22, 1968–1969, 196–232.
66. Shawqi, Y., *Risālat al-Kindī fī khubr ṣinā'at al-ta'līf*, Cairo, 1969.
67. Shiloah, A., 'Problème musical de Thābit b. Qurra', *Orbis Musicae*, 1, Tel-Aviv, 1971, 303–315.
68. Shiloah, A., (trans. and comm.), *La perfection des connaissances musicales by al-Ḥasan al-kātib*, Paris: Geuthner, 1972.
69. Shiloah, A., 'Ibn Hindū le médecin et la musique', *Israel Oriental Studies*, 2, 1972, 447–462.
70. Avenary, H. (ed.), 'The Hebrew Version of Abū l-Ṣalt's Treatise on Music', *Yuval*, 3, 1974, 7–82.
71. Shiloah, A., 'Traité sur le 'ūd d'Abū Yūsuf al-Kindī', *Israel Oriental Studies*, 4, 1974, 179–205.
72. Ghaṭṭās, A. M. Khashaba (ed.), *al-Kātib: Kamāl adab al-ghinā'*, Cairo, 1975.
73. Shawqī, Y., *Risālat ibn al-Munajjim fī'l mūsīqā wa-kashf rumūz kitāb al-aghānī*, Cairo, 1976.
74. 'Abd al-Qādir ibn Ghaybī: *Maqāṣid al-alḥān*, T. Binish, ed., Teheran, 1977.
75. Shiloah, A. (trans. and comm.), *The Ikhwān al-ṣafā's Epistle on Music*, Tel-Aviv U., 1978.
76. Shiloah, A., *The Theory of Music in Arabic Writings (ca 900 to ca 1900)*, Series B of the RISM, München, 1979.
77. Neubauer, E., 'Der Essai sur la musique oriental von Charles Fonton' (Text-teil), *Zeitschrift für Geschichte der Arabisch-Islamischen Wissenschaften*, 2, 1985, 277–324.
78. Neubauer, E., 'Der Essai sur la musique von Charles Fonton (Einleitung und Indices)', *Zeitschrift für Geschichte der Arabisch-Islamischen Wissenschaften*, 3, 1986, 335–76.
79. 'Abd al-Qādir ibn Ghaybī, *Jāmi' al-alḥan*, T. Binish, ed., Teheran, 1987.
80. Behar, C., *18. Yüzilda Türk Müziği: Charles Fonton*, Istanbul, 1987.
81. Liu, B. and J. T. Monroe, *Ten Hispano-Arabic Songs in Modern Oral*

Tradition: Music and Poetry, Berkeley–Los Angeles–Oxford, 1989 (University of California Publications in Modern Philology 125).

82. Shiloah, A., *The Dimension of Music in Islamic and Jewish Culture*, Aldershot: Variorum, 1993 (Collected Studies Series CS393).

V. Historical – General studies

(see also 152, 165, 167, 170, 171, 175, 177, 185, 191, 199a, 233–235, 324a, 354–357, 378, 409, 414)

83. Rousseau, J. J., 'musique', in *Dictionnaire de la musique*, Paris, 1768, 314 and planche N.
84. Laborde, J. B. de, *Essai sur la musique ancienne et moderne*, Paris, 1780.
85. Villoteau, G. D. *De l'état actuel de l'art musical en Egypte*, (vol. xiv of *Description de l'Egypte*, 2nd edn) Paris, 1826.
86. Kiesewetter, R. G., *Die Musik der Araber*, Wiesbaden, 1968 (first publ. 1842).
87. Christianowitsch, A., *Esquisse historique de la musique arabe aux temps anciens, avec dessins d'instruments et 40 melodies notées et harmonisées*, Köln, 1863.
88. Caussin de Perceval, A. P., 'Notices anecdotiques sur les principaux musiciens arabes des trois premiers siècles de l'islamisme', *Journal Asiatique*, 7 ser., 2, 1873, 397–592.
89. *Revue et Gazette musicale de Paris*. VIe année, no. 23, Juin 1889, p. 188.
90. Khulaʿī, M. K. al-, *Kitāb al-mūsīqā al-sharqī*, Cairo, 1904.
91. Collangettes, M., 'Etude sur la musique arabe', *Journal Asiatique*, 2 ser., 4, 1904 (Nov–Dec), 365–422; 10 ser., 7, 1906 (Jul-Aug), 149–190.
92. Mitjana, R., 'L'orientalisme musical et la musique arabe', *Le Monde Oriental*, 1, 1906, 121–184.
93. Rouanet, J., 'La musique arabe' and 'La musique arabe dans le Maghrib', *Encyclopédie de la musique et dictionnaire du conservatoire*, Paris, 1922, vol. I, V, 2676–2812; 2813–2944.
94. Ribera y Tarrago, J., 'La ensñanza entre los Musulmanes Españoles – la musica', *Dissertaciones y Opusculos*, Madrid, 1928, 1, 298–302.
95. Farmer, H. G., *A History of Arabian Music to the XIIIth Century*, London, 1929 (reprinted 1967).
96. Lachmann, R., *Musik des Orients*, Breslau, 1929.
97. *Receuil des Travaux du Congrès de Musique Arabe*, Le Caire, 1934.
98. Ḥefni, M. A. al-, *al-Mūsīqā al-naẓariyya*, Cairo, 1946, first publ. 1937.
99. Sachs, C., *The Rise of Music in the Ancient World: East and West*, New York: Norton, 1943.

100. Farmer, H. G., *The Minstrels of the Arabian Nights: A Study of Music and Musicians in the Arabic Alf Laila and Laila*, Bearsden, 1945.
101. Barkechli, M., *L'art Sassanide base de la musique arabe*, Teheran, 1947.
102. Allawerdi, M., *Falsafat al-mūsīqā al-sharqiyya fī asrār al-fann al-'arabī* (*The Philosophy of Oriental Music*), Damas, 1948.
103. 'Azzāwī, 'A., *al-mūsīqā, al-'irāqīyyah fī 'ahd al-mughul wa'l turkumān*, Baghdad, 1951.
104. Avenary, H., 'Abū'l-Ṣalt's Treatise on Music', *Musica Disciplina*, VI, 1952, 27–32.
105. Larrea-Palacin, A., *La musica Hispano-arabe en Marruecos*, Madrid, 1956.
106. Farmer, H. G., 'Al-Kindī on the Ethos of Rhythm, Color and Perfume', *TGUOS*, 16, 1957, 29–38.
107. Farmer, H. G., 'The Music of Islam', in *The New Oxford History of Music*, London, 1957, vol. I, 421–64.
108. Hickmann, E., *al-Fārābī*s Musiklehre, Hamburg, 1960 (Diss.).
109. 'Amrūshī, F., al-jawārī al-mughanniyāt, Cairo, 1961.
110. Shiloah, A., *Caractéristiques de l'art vocal arabe au Moyen Age*, Tel-Aviv, 1963.
111. Taymour, A., *al-Mūsīqā wa'l-ghinā' 'ind al-'arab*, Cairo, 1963.
112. 'Alwatshī, 'A., *Rā'id al-mūsīqā al-'arabiyyah*, Baghdad, 1964.
113. Wardī, H. al-, *al-Ghinā' al-'irāqī*, Baghdad, 1964.
114. Neubauer, E., *Musiker am Hof der frühen 'Abbāsiden*, Diss. Frankfurt am Main: Goethe-Universität, 1965.
115. Farmer, H.G., *Musikgeschichte in Bildern*, Bd. III, Leiferung 2: Islam, Leipzig, 1966.
116. Rajab, H.M. al-, *Ḥall rumūz kitāb al-aghānī li'l muṣṭalaḥāt al-mūsīqiyyah al-'arabiyya*, Baghdad, 1967.
117. 'Allāf, 'A. al-, *Qiyān Baghdād fī'l 'aṣr al-'abbāsī wa'l 'usmānī al-akhīr*, Baghdad, 1969.
118. Hickmann, H., 'Die Musik des arabisch-islamischen Bereichs', in *Orientalische Musik*, ed. by H. Hickmann, W. Stauder, Leiden and Cologne, 1970, 1–134.
119. Alvarez, A.B., *Handbook of Arabic Music*, Beirut, 1971.
120. Jargy, S., *La musique arabe*, Paris, 1971.
121. Günther, R. (ed.), *Musikkulturen Asiens, Afrikas und Ozeaniens im 19 Jh*, Augsenburg, 1973 (Studien zur Musikgeschichte des 19 Jh. 31).
122. Harrison, F., *Time Place and Music: An Anthology of Ethnomusicological Observation c. 1550 to c. 1800*, Amsterdam: Fritz Knuf, 1973.

123. Anati, Emanuel, *Rock-Art in Central Arabia*, Louvain: Institut Orientaliste, Université Catholique, 1974 (Corpus of the Rock Engravings, 4).
124. Bencheikh, J. E., 'Les musiciens et la poésie: les écoles d'Isḥāq al-Mawṣilī et d'Ibrāhīm ibn al-Mahdī', *Arabica*, 22, 1975, 114–52.
125. Stigelbauer, M., *Die Sängerinnen am Abbasidenhof um die Zeit des Kalifen al-Mutawakkil nach dem K. al-Aghānī*, Wien, 1975.
126. Randel, D. M., 'Al-Fārābī and the Role of Arabic Music Theory in the Latin Middle Ages', *JAMS*, 24, 2, 1976, 173–188.
127. Salvador-Daniel, F., *The Music and Musical Instruments of the Arab*, ed. by H. G. Farmer, Portland, Maine, 1976 (first publ. 1915).
128. Shiloah, A., 'Dimension of Sound – Islamic Music', in *The World of Islam* (see 31), 161–180.
129. Touma, H. H., *La musique arabe*, Paris, 1977.
130. Shiloah, A., 'The Status of Art Music in the Near East', *Asian Music*, 12, 1, 1979, 40–55.
131. Wright, O., 'Music', in Schacht, J., Bosworth, C. E. (eds), *The Legacy of Islam*, second edn, Oxford, 1979, 489–505.
132. Collaer, P. and J. Elsner, *Musikgeschichte in Bildern, Bd. 1, Musikethnologie Lieferung 8 – Nordafrika*, Leipzig, 1983.
133. Racy, J. A., 'Music in 19th Century Egypt: An Historical Sketch', *Selected Reports in Ethnomusicology*, 4, 1983, 157–80.
134. Wright, O., 'Music and Verse', in *The Cambridge History*, (see 32), 433–459.
135. Haas, M., 'Arabische und Lateinische Musiklehre – ein Vergleich von Strukturen', in Zimmermann, A. (ed.), *Miscellanea Mediaevalia Bd. 17 Orientalische Kultur und Europäisches Mittelalter*, Berlin, 1985, 358–75.
136. Bardakçi, M., *Maragali Abdülkadir*, Istanbul, 1986.
137. Bohlman, Ph., 'R. G. Kiesewetter's Die Musik der Araber', *Asian Music*, 17, 1, 1986, 164–196.
138. Shiloah, A. and A. Berthier, 'A propos d'un petit livre arabe sur la musique', *Revue de Musicologie*, 71, 1–2, 1986, 164–177.
139. Oesch, H., M. Haas and H. P. Haller, *Aussereuropäische Musik*, II, Laaber-Verlag, 1987.
139a. Wright, O. 'Aspects of Historical Change in the Turkish Classical Repertoire; *Musica Asiatica*, 5, Cambridge University Press, 1988, 1–108.
140. Belon, P. 'L'observations de plusieurs singularités…', an excerpt cited in *Turkish Music Quarterly*, 2, 2–3, 1989, 11–12.
141. Menavino, G. E. 'I Costumi, e la vita dei Turchi', an excerpt cited in *Turkish Music Quarterly*, 2, 2–3, 1989, 7.
142. Postel, G. 'De la République des Turcs', an excerpt cited in *Turkish Music Quarterly*, 2, 2–3, 1989, 6.

143. Sawa, D.G., *Music Performance Practice in the Early 'Abbāsid Era 132–320 AH/ 750–932 AD*, Toronto: Pontifical Institute of Medieval Studies, 1989.
144. Touma, H. H., *Die Musik der Araber*, Wilhemshaven: Florian Noetzel Heinrichsen, 1989.
145. de la Valle, Pietro, 'Viaggi', an excerpt cited in *Turkish Music Quarterly*, 2, 4, 1989, 11.
146. Blount, Henry, *A General Account of the Turkish Empire*, an excerpt cited in *Turkish Music Quarterly* 3, 2–3, 1990, 14.
147. Shiloah, A., 'Techniques of Scholarship in Medieval Arabic Treatises', in Barbera, A. (ed.), *Music Theory and its Sources – Antiquity and the Middle Ages*, South Bend: U. of Notre Dame, Indiana, 1990, 85–99.
148. Racy, A. J., 'Historical Worldviews of Early Ethnomusicologists: An East–West Encounter in Cairo, 1932', in Blum, S. Ph. V. Bohlman, Neuman D. M. (eds), *Ethnomusicology and Modern Music History*, Chicago: University of Illinois Press, 1991, 68–91.
149. Shiloah, A., 'Musical Modes and the Medical Dimension: the Arabic Sources (c. 900–c. 1600)', in Kessler, J. (ed.), *Metaphor – A Musical Dimension*, Sydney: Currency Press, 1991, 147–159.
149a. Behar, C., *Zaman, Mekân, Müzik: Klasik Türk Musikisinde Eğitim (Meşk), Icra ve Akatarim*, Istanbul, 1993.

VI. Regional studies

(see also Country Index on pages 189 to 190)

150. Hornbostel, E. M. von, 'Phonographierte tunesische Melodien', *SIMG*, 8, 1906–7, 1–63.
151. Tharand, J. J., *Rabat ou les heures marocaines*, Paris, 1921.
152. Yekta, R., 'La musique Turque', in Lavignac, A. (ed.), *Encyclopédie de la musique et dictionnaire du conservatoire*, Paris, 1922, I, V, 2845–3064.
153. Kösemilhalzade, M. R., *Anadoli Türkuleri ve Musiki Istikbalimiz*, Istanbul, 1927.
154. Belyayev, V., and V. Uspensky, *Türkemnskaya Muzika*, Moscow, 1928.
155. Chottin, A., *Corpus de musique marocaine*, Paris, 1931.
156. Belyayev, V., *Muzikalnie instrumenti Uzbekistana*, Moscow, 1933.
157. Ezgi, S., *Nazari ve Ameli Türk Musikisi*, Istanbul, 1933–53.
158. Vaziri, N., *Musiqi-ye Nazari*, Tehran, 1934.
159. Chottin, A., *Tableau de la musique marocaine*, Paris, 1939.
160. Borrel, E., 'Les poètes Kizil Bach et leur musique', *REI*, 15, 1947, 157–190.

161. Sergeant, R.B., *South Arabian Poetry and Prose of Hadramaut*, London, 1951.
162. Khaleqi, R., *Sargozasht-e musiqi-ye Iran*, Teheran, 1954–55.
163. Emsheimer, E., 'Singing Contests in Central Asia', *JIFMC*, 8, 1956, 26–29.
164. Reinhard, K., 'Tanzlieder der Turkmenen in der Südtürkei', *Kongressbericht der Gesellschaft für Musikforschung Hamburg 1956*, Kassel, 1957.
165. Chottin, A., 'Nordafrikanische Musik', *MGG*, 9, 1961, col. 1558–1569.
166. Karelova, I. N. (ed.), *Voprosy muzykal'noi kul'tury uzbekistana*, Tashkent, 1961.
167. Reinhard, K., *Türkische Musik*, Berlin, 1962.
168. Caron, N. and D. Safvate, *Iran: Les traditions musicales*, Paris, 1966.
169. Reinhard, K., 'Musik am Schwarzen Meer', *JbfMVV*, 2, 1966, 9–58.
170. Popesco-Judet, E., 'Dimitrie Cantemir et la musique turque', *Studia et Acta Orientalia*, 7, 1968, 199–213.

170a. Alexandru, T. 'Dimitrie Cantemir si musica Orientalia' (see 379a), 233–251.

171. Reinhard, K. and U., *Turquie*, Paris, 1969.
172. Massoudieh, Moh. T., 'Die *Mathnawi*-Melodie in der Persischen Kunst-Musik', *Orbis Musicae*, 1, 1971, 57–67.
173. Blum, S., 'The Concept of the *'asheq* in Northern Khorasan', *Asian Music,* 1972, 4, 1, 34–42.
174. Barkechli, M., 'Musique de zour-khaneh et ses rythmes caractéristiques', *JIFMC*, 13, 1973, p. 73.
175. Farhat, H., *The Traditional Music of Iran*, Teheran, 1973.
176. Guignard, M., *Musique, honneur et plaisir au Sahara: étude psychologique et musicologique de la société Maure*, Paris, 1973.
177. Zonis, E., *Classical Persian Music: An Introduction*, Cambridge, Mass.: Harvard University Press, 1973.
178. Khaleqi, R., *Sargozasht-e Musiqi-e Iran*, 2 vol, Teheran, 1954, 1974.
179. Belyayev, V., *Ocherki po istorii muziki narodov SSSR* [Essays on the Musical History of the Peoples of the USSR], Moscow, 1962–63; Eng. trans. 1975.
180. Kuckerz, J. and M. T. Massoudieh, *Musik in Busehr, Sud-Iran*, Linz, 1975.
181. Slobin, M., *Music in the Culture of Afghanistan*, Tucson, 1976.
182. Slobin, M., *Music of Central Asia and of the Volga-Uralic Peoples*, Bloomington: Indiana University, 1977.
183. Schuyler, Ph., 'Moroccan Andalusian Music', *World of Music,* 1, 1978, 33–44.

184. Racy, A. J., 'Music of Tunisia: A Contemporary Perspective', *Arabesque* 1, 1979, 18–24.
185. Guettat, M., *La musique classique du Maghrib*, Paris: Sindbad, 1980.
186. Lortat-Jacob, B., *Musique et fêtes au haut Atlas*, Paris, 1980.
187. Baily, J., 'A System of Modes Used in the Urban Music of Afghanistan', *Ethnomusicology*, 25, 1, 1981, 1–40.
188. Cherki, S., *Musique marocaine. Moroccan Music,* in English and French, Sale, 1981.
189. Caton, M., *The Classical Tasnif: A Genre of Persian Vocal Music,* Los Angeles: University of California, 1983.
190. Zokhrabov, R., *Azerbaidzhanskie tesnify*, Moscow, 1983.
191. During, J., *La musique Iranienne: tradition et evolution*, Paris, 1984.
192. Schuyler, Ph., 'The Rwais and the Zāwia Professional Musicians and the Rural Religious Elite in Southwestern Morocco', *Asian Music*, 17, 1, 1985, 114–131.
193. Qureshi-Burckhardt, R., *Ṣūfī Music of India and Pakistan: Sound, Context and Meaning in Qawwālī*, New York, 1986.
194. Behar, C., *Klasik Türk Musikisi Üzerine Denemeler*, Istanbul, 1987.
195. Petrovic, A., 'Paradoxes of Muslim Music in Bosnia and Herzegovina', *Asian Music*, 20, 1, 1988, 128–147.
196. Zeranska-Kominek, S. 'The Turkmen Bakhshy: Shaman and/or Artist', in *VII European Seminar in Ethnomusicology, Pre-publication of the Conference Papers*, Berlin: International Institute for Comparative Music, 1990, 497–508.
197. Feldman, W. 'Cultural Authority and Authenticity in the Turkish Repertoire', *Asian Music*, 22, 1, 1990/91, 73–112.
198. Zeranska-Kominek, S., 'The Classification of Repertoire in Turkmen Traditional Music', *Asian Music*, 21, 2, 1990, 90–109.
199. During, J., Z. Mirabdolbajhi and D. Safvat, *The Art of Persian Music*, Washington DC: Mage Publishers, 1991.
199a. Bardakçi, M. *Fener Beyleri'ne Türk, Şarkilari*, Istanbul, 1993.

VII. Religious music (attitude, cantillation and Ṣūfī music)

(see also 39, 41, 51, 53, 76, 192, 193, 332, 409, 410)

200. Friedlander, G. (trans. and ed.), *Pirque de-Rabbi Eli'ezer*, London, 1916.
201. Ritter, H., 'Der Reigen der Tanzenden Derwische', *Zeitschrift für Vergleichende Musikwissenschaft*, 1, 1933, 28–40.
202. Borrel, E., *Sur la musique secrète des tribus turques, Alevi*, Paris, 1936.

203. Dermengham, E. and L. Barbes, 'Essai sur la hadhra des Aissoua d'Algérie', *Revue Africaine*, 95, 1951, 289–314.
204. Farmer, H. G., 'The Religious Music of Islam', *JRAS*, 1952, 60–65.
205. Meier, F., 'Der Derwischtanz', *Asiatische Studien*, 8, 1954, 107–136.
206. Schneider, M., 'Le verset 94 de la sourate VI du Coran étudié en une version populaire et en trois *maqāmāt* de tradition Hispano-Musulman', *Anuario Musical*, 9, 1954, 80–96.
207. Ritter, H., *Das Meer der Seele*, Leiden, 1955.
208. Roychoudhury, M. L., 'Music in Islam', *Journal of the Asiatic Society of Bengal*, 23, 2, 1957, 43–102.
209. Talbi, M., 'La qirā'ah bi'l alḥān', *Arabica*, 5, 1958, 183–190.
210. Rossi, E. and A. Bombaci, *Elenco di drammi religiosi persiani*, Vatican, 1961.
211. Molé, M., 'La danse extatique en Islam', *Les danses sacrées*, Paris, 1963, 147–280.
212. Parson, T., summary to Weber's theory in the introduction to Max Weber's *The Sociology of Religion*, trans. by Ephraim Fischoff, Boston: Beacon Press, 1964.
213. Meier, F. 'The Mystic Path', in *The World of Islam* (see 31), 117–140.
214. Boubakeur, S. H., 'Psalmodie coranique', in Porte, J. (ed.), *Encyclopédie des musiques sacrées*, Paris, 1968, I, 414–21.
215. Mokri, M., 'La musique sacrée des Kurdes fidèles de verité en Iran', Porte, J. (ed.), *Encyclopédie des Musiques Sacrées*, Paris, 1968, I, 441–452.
216. Nasr, S.H., 'The Influence of Ṣūfism on Traditional Persian Music', *Studies of Comparative Religion*, 6, 4, 1972, 225–234.
217. Pacholczyk, J., 'Vibrato as a Function of Modal Practice in the Qur'an Chant of Shaik 'Abdū-l-Basīṭ 'abdū-s-samād', *Selected Reports of Ethnomusicology*, 2, 1, 1974, 33–41.
218. Nasr, S.H., 'Islam and Music', *Studies in Comparative Religion*, 10, 1976, 37–45.
219. Faruqi, L., 'Accentuation in Qur'ānic Chant, A Study in Musical *Tawāzun*', *YIFMC*, 10, 1978, 53–68.
220. Poché, Ch., 'Zikr and Musicology', *World of Music*, 20, 1, 1978, 59–73.
221. Random, M., *Mawlāna Djalāl al-dīn al-Rūmī, le soufisme et la danse*, Tunis, Sud-Editions, 1980.
222. Rouget, G., *La musique et la transe*, Paris: Gallimard, 1980.
223. Qureshi-Burckhardt, R., 'Islamic Music in an Indian Environment: the Shī'a Majlis', *Ethnomusicology*, 25, 1, 1981, 41–72.
224. During, J., 'Revelation and Spiritual Audition in Islam', *World of Music*, 3, 1982, 68–84.
225. Nelson, K., 'Reciter and Listener: Some Factors Shaping the

Mujawwad Style of Qur'ānic Reciting', *Ethnomusicology*, 25, 1, 1982, 41–48.
226. Poché, Ch., 'David and the Ambiguity of the Mizmār according to Arab Sources', *World of Music*, 2, 1983, 58–73.
227. Qureshi-Burckhardt, R., *Ṣūfī Music of India and Pakistan. Sound, Context and Meaning in Qawwālī*, New York, 1986.
228. Faruqi, L.I., 'The Cantillation of the Qur'ān', *Asian Music*, 19, 1, 1987, 2–25.
229. During, J., *Musique et Mystique dans les traditions de l'Iran*, Paris-Teheran, 1989.
230. Qureshi-Burckhardt, T., 'Ṣūfī Music and the Historicity of Oral Tradition', in Blum, S., Ph. V. Bohlman, D. M. Neuman, (eds), *Ethnomusicology and Modern Music History*, Urbana & Chicago: University Press, 1991, 103–120.
231. Gribetz, A., 'The *Samā'* Controversy: Ṣūfī vs. Legalist', *Studia Islamica*, 74, 1991, 43–62.

VIII. Influences

(see also 81)

232. Ribera y Tarrago, J., *Discursos leidos ante la Real Academia Español*, Madrid, 1912.
233. Farmer, H.G., 'Clues for the Arabian Influence on European Musical Theory', *JRAS*, 1925, 61–88.
234. Schlesinger, K., *Is European Musical Theory Indebted to the Arabs?*, London, 1925.
235. Farmer, H. G., *Historical Facts for the Arabian Musical Influence*, London, 1930 (Hildesheim, 1970).
236. Ursprung, O., 'Um die Frage nach dem Arabischen bzw. maurischen Einfluss auf die abendländische Musik des Mittelalters', *ZfMw*, 16, 1934, 129–41; Nachtrag, 355–57.
237. Farmer, H.G., 'Oriental Influences on Occidental Military Music', *Islamic Culture*, 15, 1941, 235–42.
238. Ribẹra y Tarrago, J., *La musica Arabe y su influencia en la Española*, Madrid, 1942.
239. Angles, H., *La musica de las Cantigas de Santa Maria del Rey Alfonso el Sabio. Facsimil, transcripcion y estudio critico*, 3 vols., Barcelona, 1943–1964.
240. Schneider, M., 'A proposito del influjo arabe: ensayo de etnografia musical de la España Medieval', *Anuario Musical*, 1, 1946, 31–141.
241. Stern, S. M. 'Les vers finaux en español dans les *muwashshaḥs* hispano-hébraiques', *Al-Andalus*, 13, 1948, 299–343.
242. Denoumy, A.J., *Concerning the Accessibility of Arabian Influence in the Earliest Provençal Troubadours*, Toronto, 1953.

243. García-Gómez, E. 'La poésie hispano-arabe et l'apparition de lyrique romane', *Arabica*, 5, 1958, 113–130.
244. García-Gómez, E., 'Una extraordinaria pagina de Tīfāshī y una hipotesis sobre el inventor del zejel', in *Études d'orientalisme dediées ā la mémoire de Levi-Provençal*, Paris, 1962, vol. II, 517–529.
245. Rihthman, C., 'Orientalische Elemente in der Traditionellen Musik Bosniens und der Herzegovina', *Grazer und Münchener Balkananalogische Studien*, 2, 1967, 97–105.
246. Anderson, L. A., 'The Interrelation of African and Arab Musics', *Essays on Music and History in Africa*, ed. K.P. Wachsmann, Evanston, 1971, 143–179.
247. Bowles, E. A., 'Eastern Influences on the Use of Trumpets and Drums in the Middle Ages', *Anuario Musical*, 26, 1971, 1–28.
248. Signell, K., 'Mozart and the Mehter', *The Consort*, 26, 1972, 310–22.
249. Perkuhn, E. V., 'Die arabische Theorie und die Ursprungsfrage der Troubadourskunst', *Studia Musicologica*, 15, 1973, 129–39.
250. Kwabena Nketia, J. H., *The Music of Africa*, New York: Norton, 1974.
251. Stern, S. M., *Hispano-Arabic Strophic Poetry*, Oxford, 1974.
252. Reinhard, K., 'Über die Beziechungen zwischen byzantinischer und türkischer Musik', *Musica Antiqua Europeae Orientalis*, 4, Bydgoszcz, 1975, 623.
253. Simon, A., 'Islamische und Afrikanische Elemente in der Musik des Nordsudan am Beispiel des Dikr', *Hamburger Jahrbuch zur Musikwissenschaft*, 1975, 249–78.
254. Perkuhn, E. R., *Die Theorien zum arabischen Einfluss auf die europäischen Musik des Mittelalters*, Walldorf-Hessen: Verlag für Orientkunde, Bd. 26 of Beiträge zur Sprach- und Kulturgeschichte des Orients, 1976.
255. Simon, A., 'Islamic influences', in *International Music Society Report of the 12th Congress, Berkeley 1977*, Kassel; Basle; London: Bärenreiter, 1981.
256. McGee, T.J., 'Eastern Influence in European Dance', in Falck, R. and Rice, T., (eds), *Cross Cultural Perspectives on Music, in Honor of M. Kolinski*, Toronto, 1982.
257. Wulstan, D., 'The Muwashshaḥ and Zadjal Revisited', *Journal of the American Oriental Society*, 102, 2, 1982, 247–264.
258. Pacholczyk, J., 'The Relationship Between the Nawba of Morocco and the Music of the Troubadours and Trouvères', *World of Music*, 25, 2, 1983, 5–16.
259. Katz, I., 'Higinio Angles and the Melodic Origins of the "Cantigas de Santa Maria": A Critical View', *Alfonso X of Castile the Learned*

King (International Symposium Harvard University, 17 November 1948). Harvard, 1985, 46–75.

260. Manzano, F. R., *De las melodias del reino Nazari de Granada a las estructural musicales Cristianas*, Granada, 1985.
261. Alvarez, R., 'Los instrumentos musicales en los codices Alfonsinos: su tipologia, su uso y su origen. Algunos problemas iconograficos', *Revista de Musicologia*, 10, 1, 1987, 1–38.
262. Hassan, Sh. Q., 'Some Islamic non-Arabic Elements of Influence on the Repertory of *al-maqām al-ʿirāqī*', in *Maqām-Raga-Zeilenmelodik*, (see 314), 148–155.
263. Burnett, Ch., 'Teoria e Pratica musicale arabe in Sicilia e nell'Italia meridionale in età normanna e sveva', *Nuove effemeridi*, 11, 3, 1990, 79–89.
264. Simon, A. 'Musical Traditions, Islam and Cultural Identity in Sudan', in Bender, W. (ed.), *Perspectives on African Music*, Bayreuth: Breitinger, 1989.
265. Shiloah, A., 'The meeting of Christian, Jewish and Muslim musical cultures on the Iberian Peninsula (before 1492)', *AcM*, 64, 1, 1991, 14–20.
266. Shiloah, A., 'Development of Jewish Liturgical Singing in Spain', in Beinart, H. (ed.), *The Sephardi Legacy*, vol. II, Jerusalem: Magnes Press, 1992, 423–437.

IX. Scales and modes

(see also 51, 93, 102, 155, 157–159, 162, 167, 175, 177, 185, 187, 191, 322, 380a, 387a)

267. Idelsohn, A. Z., 'Die Maqamen der arabischen Musik', *SIMG*, 15 Jg. H. 1, 1913, 1–63.
268. Farmer, H. G., 'The Old Persian Musical Modes', *JRAS*, 1926, 495–99.
269. Sachs, C., *Rhythm and Tempo*, New York: Norton, 1952.
270. Oransay, G., 'Das Tonsystem der Türkischen Musik', *Die Musikforschung*, X, 1957, 250–64.
271. Rajab, H. M. al-, *al-Maqām al-ʿirāqī*, Baghdad, 1961.
272. Veksler, S., 'Uzbeskie makomy', in Karelova, I.N. (ed.), *Voprozy muzykal'noi kul'tury uzbekistana*, 1961, 72–99.
273. Khatshi, K., *Der Dastgah: Studien zur Neuen Persischen Musik*, Regensburg, 1962.
274. Land, J. P. N., 'Recherches sur l'histoire de la gamme arabe', *Actes du VI congrès international des Orientalistes. . .*, Leiden, 1883 II, 35–138.

275. Ma'rufi, M., *Les systèmes de la musique traditionnelle de l'Iran (Radif)*, Teheran, 1962.
276. Barkechli, M., *Les systèmes de la musique traditionnelle de l'Iran avec transcription en notation musicale par M. Ma'roufi*, Teheran, 1963.
277. Gerson-Kiwi, E., *The Persian Doctrine of Dastghah Composition*, Tel-Aviv, 1963.
278. Cohen-Carmi, D., 'An Investigation into the Tonal Structure of the *maqāmāt*', *JIFMC*, 16, 1964, 102–106.
279. Farmer, H. G., 'The Old Arabian Melodic Modes', *JRAS*, 1965, 99–102.
280. Szabol'si, Bente, *A History of Melody*, London, 1965, 205–215.
281. Kaufmann, W., *Musical Notations of the Orient*, Bloomington, Indiana, 1967.
282. Massoudieh, M.T., *Awaz-e-sur: Zur Melodiebildung in der Persischen Kunstmusik*, Regensburg, 1968.
283. Cohen, D., 'Patterns and Frameworks of Intonation', *Journal of Music Theory*, 13, 1, 1969, 66–92.
284. Karomatov, F. R., 'Schashmaqom', *Beiträge Musikwissenschaft*, 11, 2, 1969, 91–99.
285. Manik, L., *Das Arabische Tonsystem im Mittelalter*, Leiden, 1969.
286. Shawqī, Y., *Qiyās sullam al-mūsīqā al-'arabī*, Cairo, 1969.
287. Gerson-Kiwi, E., 'On the Technique of Arab *Taqsim* Composition', Feschrift Walter Graf, Wiener, 1970, 66–73 (Wiener Musikwissenschaftliche Beiträge 9).
288. Elsner, J., *Der Begriff des Maqam in Aegypten in Neueren Zeit, HabSchr. Musicology*, Berlin, 1970.
289. Spector, J., 'Classical '*Ūd* Music in Egypt with Special Reference to *Maqāmāt*', *Ethnomusicology*, 14, 1970, 243–57.
290. Cohen, D., 'The Meaning of the Modal Framework in the Singing of Religious Hymns by Christian Arabs in Israel', *Yuval*, 2, 1971, 23–57.
291. Olsen, R.P., 'Six versions de *taqsīm* en *maqām rast*', *Studia Instrumentorum Musicae Popularis* 2, 1974, 197–202.
292. Neubauer, E., 'Drei Makamen des Ashiq Divani', *Orbis Musicae*, 1, 1971, 39–56.
293. Nettl, B. and B. Foltin, *Daramad of Chahargah, A Study in the Performance Practice of Persian Music*, Detroit, 1972.
294. Nettl, B. 'Thoughts on Improvisation: A Comparative Approach', *Musical Quarterly*, 60, 1974, 1–19.
295. Seidel, H.P., 'Die Notenschrift des Hamparsun Limonciyan', *Mitteilungen der Deutschen Gesellschaft für Musik des Orients*, 12, 1973–74, 72–119.

296. Nettl, B. and R. Riddle, '*Taqsīm Nahawand*, A Study of Sixteen Performances by Jihad Racy', *YIFMC*, 5, 1974, 11–50.
297. Elsner, J., 'Zum Problem des Maqām', *AcM*, 47, 1975, 208.
298. Massoudieh, M.T., *Radif vocale de la musique traditionnelle de l'Iran par Mahmud Karimi. Transcription et analyse*, Teheran, 1976.
299. Touma, H.H., *Der Maqām Bayātī im Arabischen Taqsim*, Hamburg: Verlag der Musikalienhandlung Karl Dieter Wagner, 1976 (Beiträge zur Ethnomusikologie, Band III).
300. Signell, K., *Maqām-Modal Practice in Turkish Art Music*, Seattle: Asian Music Publications, 1977.
301. Wright, O., *The Modal System of Arab and Persian Music AD 1250–1300*, London, 1978.
302. Pacholczyk, J. '*Sufyana Kalam*, the Traditional Music of Kashmir', *Asian Music*, 10, 1, 1978, 1–16.
303. Shiloah, A., 'Arabic Modal Concept', *JAMS*, 34, 1, 1981, 19–42.
304. Sha'ūbī, I Kh. al-, *Dalīl al-anghām li-ṭullāb al-maqām*, Baghdad, 1982.
305. Nettl, B. and D. Shenassa, 'Toward Comparative Study of Persian Radifs: Focus on Dastgah-e Mahur', *Orbis Musicae*, 8, 1982–83, 29–43.
306. Karomatov, F. and J. Elsen, 'Maqām i makom', *Muzyka Narodov Azii i Afrikii*, 4, 1984, 88–135.
307. During, J., 'Acoustics Systems and Metaphysical Systems in Oriental Traditions', *World of Music*, 1987, 2, 1, 19–31.
308. Nettl, B., 'The Radif of Persian Music', in *Studies of Structure and Cultural Context*, Champaign: Elephant and Cat, 1987.
309. Ogger, T., *Maqām Segah/Sīkah: Vergleich der Kunstmusik des Iraq und des Iran anhand eines Maqam-Modells*, Hamburg, 1987 (Beiträge zur Ethnomusikologie, 15).
310. During, J., *La musique traditionnelle de l'Azerbayjan et la science des muqams*, Baden-Baden, 1988.
311. Brandl, R. M., 'Konstantinopolitanische Makamen des 19. Jh. in Neumen: Die Musik der Fanarioten', in *Maqām-Raga-Zeilen-melodik*, (see 314), 156–169.
312. Dshani-Zade, T., 'Prinzipy Konstruirovanija Azerbajdshanskogo mugama (Bauprinzipien des Azerbaidshanischen mugam)', in *Maqām-Raga-Zeilenmelodik*, (see 314), 86–132.
313. During, J., 'The Modal System of Azerbayjani Art Music', in *Maqām-Raga-Zeilenmelodik*, (see 314), 133–147.
314. Elsner, J. (ed.), *Maqām-Raga-Zeilenmelodik*, Materialen der 1. Arbeitstagung der Study Group 'maqam' beim International Council for Traditional Music, vom 28. Juni bis 2. Juli 1988 in Berlin, 1989.

315. Elsner, J., 'The Maqām Principle, Melodies of Tone Groups as Base and Building Stone for Musical Production' in *Maqām-Raga-Zeilenmelodik*, (see 314), 26–39.
316. Jung, A., 'The Maqām Principle and the Cyclic Principle in the Uzbek-Tajik Shashmaqam', in *Maqām-Raga-Zeilenmelodik*, (see 314), 200–215.
317. Matjabukov, O., ' Shashmaqam v XX veke (Der Shashmaqam im 20. Jh.)', in *Maqām-Raga-Zeilenmelodik*, (see 314), 181–199.
318. Muchambetova, A., 'Zapadnokazachstanskij Tokpe-Kjuj i maqam (Der westkasachische Tokpe-Kjuj und der maqam)', in *Maqām-Raga-Zeilenmelodik*, (see 314), 216–247.
319. Powers, H., 'International *segah* and its Nominal Equivalents in Central Asia and Kashmir', in *Maqām-Raga-Zeilenmelodik*, (see 314), 40–85.
320. Sakata, H. L. 'Afghan Regional Melody Types and the Notion of Modes', in *Maqām-Raga-Zeilenmelodik*, (see 314), 170–180.
321. Pacholczyk, J. 'Musical determinants of *maqām* in *Sufyana kalām* of Kashmir', in *Maqām-Raga-Zeilenmelodik*, (see 314), 248–258.
322. Behar, C., *Ali Ukfî ve Mezmurlar*, Pan Yayincilik: 11, Istanbul, 1990.
323. Matyakubov, O., '19th Century Khorezmian Tanbur Notation', *YfTM*, 22, 1990, 29–35.
324. Farhat, H., *The Dastgah Concept in Persian Music*, Cambridge: Cambridge University Press, 1991.
324a. Behar, C. 'La notation écrite dans la musique turque classique', *Etudes Turques et Ottomans*, 2, Institut d'études turques, Paris 1993, 15–31.

X. Forms and genres

(see also 189, 190, 241, 243, 251, 262, 287, 291, 294)

325. Reinhard, K., 'Zur Variantenbildung im türkischen Volkslied', in *Festschrift H. Besseler*, Leipzig, 1961, 131–69.
326. Christensen, D., 'Tanzlieder der Hakkari-Kurden. Eine Material Kritische Studie', *JbfMVV*, 1, 1963, 11–47.
327. Ḥanafī, G. al-, *al-Mughannūn al-baghdādīyyun wa'l maqām al-'irāqī*, Baghdad, 1964.
328. Ḥilou, S. al-, *al-Muwashshaḥāt al-andalusīyya*, Beirut, 1965.
329. Christensen, D., 'Zur Mehrstimmigkeit in Kurdischen Wechselgesangen', *Festschrift W. Wiora*, 1967, 571–77.
330. Reiche, J. P., 'Stilelemente Südtürkischen, Davul-Zurna Stücke', *JbfMVV*, 5, 1970, 9–54.
331. Tahar, M., *Recherches sur le rythme, les mètres et les formes du melhun algerien*, Paris, 1971.

332. Seidel, H. P., 'Studien zum Usul 'Devri Kabir' in den Peşrev der Mevlevi', *Mitteilungen der Deutschen Gesellschaft für Musik des Orients*, 11, 1972–3, 7–70.
333. Touma, H.H., 'The Maqām Phenomenon: An Improvisation Technique in the Music of the Middle East', *Ethnomusicology*, 15, 1, 1971, 38–48.
334. Tsuge, G., 'A Note on the Iraqi Maqām', *Asian Music*, 4, 1, 1972, 59–66.
335. Schuyler, Ph., *Al-Milḥūn: the Fusion of Folk and Art Traditions in a Moroccan Song Poem*, Washington, 1974.
336. Faruqi-Ibsen, L., 'Muwshashaḥ: A Vocal Form in Islamic Culture', *Ethnomusicology*, 19, 1, 1975, 1–29.
337. Okyay, E., *Melodische Gestaltelemente in den Türkischen Kirik Hava*, Ankara, 1976.
338. Faruqi, L. Ibsen., 'Ornamentation in Arabian Improvisational Music: A Study of Interrelatedness in the Arts', *World of Music*, 20, 1, 1978, 17–32.
339. Kholy, S. A. al-, *The Tradition of Improvisation in Arab Music*, Cairo, 1978.
340. Wegner, U., *Abūdiya und Mawwāl*, 12, Hamburg, 1982 (Beiträge zur Ethnomusicologie).
341. Racy, A. J., 'The Waṣlah: A Compound-Form Principle in Egyptian Music', *Arab Studies Quarterly*, 5, 1983, 396–403.
342. Elsner, J., 'Zum Problem von Komposition und Improvisation', *Beiträge zur Musikwissenschaft*, H. 3/4, Berlin, 1984, 174–184.
343. Faruqi, L., 'The Suite in Islamic History and Culture', *World of Music*, 17, 3, 1985, 46–64.
344. Braune, G., *Die Qaṣīda im Gesang von Umm Kulthūm: die Arabische Poesie im Repertoire der grossten Aegyptischen Sängerin unserer Zeit*, Hamburg, 1987 (Beiträge zur Ethnomusicologie, 16).
345. Shiloah, A., 'La voix et les techniques vocales chez les Arabes', *Cahiers de musiques traditionnelles*, 4, 1991, 85–101.
346. Marcus, S. L., 'Modulation in Arab Music: Documenting Oral Concepts, Performance Rules and Strategies', *Ethnomusicology*, 36, 2, 1992, 171–195.
346a. Suliteanu, G. '*Gir, Beyt, Meyt* in the Musical Folklore of the Dobroudja Tatars', *Milletlerarsi Türk Halk Kültüru Kongresi Bildireleri*, III, Ankara, 1992, 257–281.

XI. Dance

(see also, 161, 164, 201, 205, 211, 215, 221, 256, 391, 418, 420, 423, 427)

347. Buonaventura, W., *Belly Dancing – the Serpent and the Sphinx*. London, 1938.

348. Abdullah, A., 'Dancing East of Suez', *Dancing Times*, new ser., n. 333, 1938, 274.
349. Ritter, H., *Karagöz: Türkische Schattenspiele*, Bd. I, Hannover, 1924; Bd. II, Istanbul, 1941; Bd. III, Wiesbaden, 1953.
350. Murray. M. A., 'Ancient and Modern Ritual Dances in the Near East', *Folklore*, 66, 1955, 401–409.
351. And, M., 'Dances of Anatolian Turkey', *Dance Perspectives*, 3, 1959.
352. Berger, M., 'The Arab Danse du Ventre'. *Dance Perspectives*, 10, 1961, 2–41. 335.
353. La Meri, 'Learning the Danse du ventre', *Dance Perspectives*, 10, 1961, 43–47.
354. Rezvani, M., *Le théâtre et la danse en Iran*, Paris, 1962.
355. Sachs, C., *World History of the Dance*, New York: Norton, 1963.
356. Shiloah, A., 'Réflexions sur la danse artistique musulmane', *Cahiers de civilisation mediévale*, 4, 1962, 463–474.
357. And, M., *A History of Theatre and Popular Entertainment*, Ankara, 1963–64.
358. Schirmann, H. (ed.), *Romanelli's Selected Writings,* Jerusalem: Mosad Bialik, 1969 (Hebrew).
359. Kendal, N., 'Kurdish Music and Dance', *World of Music,* 1979, 1, 19–29.
360. Lievre, V., *Danses du Maghreb d'une rive à l'autre*, Paris, 1984.
361. Racy, J.A., 'Music and Dance in Lebanese Folk Proverbs', *Asian Music*, 17, 1, 1985, 83–97.
362. 'Abd al-Ḥalīm, Soye, S., H. Zaya, *Danse Orientale*, Paris, 1987.

XII. Instruments

(see also 45, 48, 71, 127, 156, 261, 397, 430, 449, 455)

363. Villoteau, G. A., *Des instruments de musique des Orientaux,* Paris, 1823; 1826 (Description de l'Egypte, 2nd ed, vol. XIII-XIV).
364. Wiedemann, E., 'Über Musikautomaten bei der Arabern', *Centenario Amari*, 2, 1910, 164–85.
365. Carra de Vaux, B., 'Notes d'histoire des sciences I: Muristos, inventeur des orgues', *Journal Asiatique*, XI série, X, 1917, 449–51.
366. Farmer, H. G., 'A Maghribi Work on Musical Instruments', *JRAS*, 1935, 339–53.
367. Farmer, H. G., *Ancient Arabian Musical Instruments as Described by al-Mufaḍḍal ibn Salāmah*, Glasgow, 1938.
368. Hickmann, H., *Terminologie arabe des instruments de musique*, Cairo, 1947.
369. Hickmann, H., 'La daraboukkah', *Bulletin de l'Institut d'Egypte*, 33, 1952, 229–245.

370. Hickmann, H., 'Aegyptische Volkinstrumente', *Musica*, 8, Kassel, 1954, 49–52; 97–100.
371. Golos, G., 'Kirghiz Instruments and Instrumental Music', *Ethnomusicology*, 5, 1, 1960, 42–48.
372. Alexandru, T., 'Les instruments musicaux du folklore Egyptien et ceux des pays des Balkans', *Kongress saveza Udruzenya Folklorista Yugoslavie*, Jayce, 1968, 327.
373. Elsner, J., 'Remarks on the Big Arghul', *YIFMC*, 1, 1969, 234–239.
374. Kuckerz, J., 'Origin and Development of the Rabāb', *Sangeet Nalak*, 15, 1970, 16.
375. Shiloah, A., 'The Simsimiyya – A Stringed Instrument of the Red Sea Area', *Asian Music*, 4, 1, 1972, 15–26.
376. Picken, L., *Folk Musical Instruments of Turkey*, London, 1975.
377. Jenkins, J. and P. Olsen, *Music and Musical Instruments in the World of Islam*, London, 1976.
378. Shiloah, A., 'The *'ūd* and the Origin of Music', in *Studia Orientalia, Memorae D.H. Baneth*, Jerusalem, 1979, 395–407.
379. Hassan, Sh. Q., *Les instruments de musique en Iraq et leur rôle dans la société traditionnelle,* Paris, 1980.
379a. Alexandru, T. *Folkloristica Organologie Muzicologie Studie*, Bucarest, 1980: 'Privire asupre instrumentalor muzicale populare din Egipt', 202–218; 'De la *kissar* la *semsemiya*, 219–232.
380. Wegner, U., 'Afrikanische Musikinstrumente im Südirak' *Baessler-Archiv*, 55/N.F. 30, 1982, 394–442.
380a. Rashīd, S.A., *al-ālāt al-mūsīqiyya al-muṣāḥiba li'l l-maqām al-'irāqī*, Baghdad, 1989.

XIII. Social dimensions

(see also 71, 78, 379)

381. Archer, W. K. (ed.), *The Preservation of Traditional Form of the Learned and Popular Music of the Orient and the Occident*, Urbana, 1964.
382. Merriam, A., *The Anthropology of Music*, Northwestern University Press, 1964.
383. Gerson-Kiwi, E., 'The Oriental Musician', *World of Music*, 10, 4, 1968, 8–18.
384. Laade, W., *Die Situation von Musikleben und Musikforschung in der Ländern Afrikas und Asiens und die neuen Aufgaben der Musikethnologie,* Tutzing, 1969.
385. Mirimonde, A. P. de, 'La musique orientale dans les oeuvres de l'Ècole française du XVIII siècle', *Revue du Louvre*, 19, 1969, 231–246.

386. Redfield, R. and M. Singer, 'The Cultural Role of Cities', in Sennett, R. (ed.), *Classical Essays in the Culture of Cities*, New York: Appleton-Century-Crofts, 1969, 206–33.
387. Nettl, B., 'Attitudes toward Persian Music in Tehran 1969', *Music Quarterly*, 56, 1970, 183–97.
387a. Spector, J., 'Musical Tradition and Innovation' in *Central Asia: A Century of Russian Rule*, ed. by E. Allworth. Columbia University Press: New York, 1967, 434–84.
388. Slobin, M., 'A Muslim Shaman of Afghan Turkestan', *Ethnology*, 10, 2, April 1971, 160–73.
389. Nettl, B., 'Persian Popular Music in 1969', *Ethnomusicology,* 16, 2, 1972, 218–239.
390. Cachia, P., 'A 19th Century Arab's Observations on European Music', *Ethnomusicology,* 17, 1973, 41–51.
391. Crapanzano, V., *The Hamadsha – A Study in Moroccan Psychiatry*, Berkeley, 1973.
392. Christensen, D., 'Musical Style and Social Context in Kurdish Songs', *Asian Music,* 6, 1975, 1–6.
393. Nettl, B., 'The Role of Music in Culture: Iran, A Recently Developed Nation', in Hamm, Ch., B. Nettl, R. Byrnside. (eds), *Contemporary Music and Music Cultures*, Prentice-Hall, 1975, 71–100.
394. Racy, A. J., 'Record Industry and Egyptian Traditional Music, 1904–1932', *Ethnomusicology*, 20, 1976, 23–48.
395. Racy, A. J., 'Musical Aesthetics in Present-Day Cairo', *Ethnomusicology*, 26, 3, 1982, 391–406.
396. Blum, S., 'Changing Roles of Performers in Meshhed and Bojurn', in Nettl, B. (ed.), *Eight Urban Musical Cultures*, Urbana, 1978, 19–95.
397. Chabrier, J-C., 'New Developments in Arabian Instrumental Music', *World of Music*, 20, 1, 1978, 94–109.
398. Nettl, B., 'Persian Classical Music in Tehran: the Process of Change', in Nettl, B. (ed.), *Eight Urban Musical Cultures*, Urbana, 1978, 146–185.
399. Racy, A.J., 'Arabian Music and the Effects of Commercial Recording', *World of Music*, 20, 1, 1978, 47–58.
400. Levin, Th. C., 'Music in Modern Uzbekistan: The Convergence of Marxist Aesthetics and Central Asian Tradition', *Asian Music*, 12, 1, 1979, 149–158.
401. Nettl, B., 'Musical Values and Social Values, Symbols in Iran', *Asian Music*, 12, 1, 1979, 129–148.
402. Powers, H. (ed.), 'Symposium on Art Musics in Muslim Nations', *Asian Music*, 12, 1, 1979, 5–39.
403. Shawan, S., 'The Socio-Political Context of *al-Mūsīqā al-'arabiyya* in Egypt: Policies, Patronage, Institutions, and Musical Change', *Asian Music*, 12, 1, 1979, 86–128.

404. Shawan, S., *al-Mūsīqā al-'arabiyya – A Category of Urban Music in Cairo–Egypt, 1927–77*, Diss., Columbia University, 1980.
405. Shawan, S., 'The Role of Mediators in the Transmission of *al-Mūsīqā al-'arabiyya* in Twentieth Century Cairo', *YFTM*, 14, 1982, 55–74.
406. Sakata, H. L., *Music in the Mind: The Concepts of Music and Musician in Afghanistan*, Kent, Ohio, 1983.
407. Shiloah, A. and E. Cohen, 'The Dynamics of Change in Jewish Oriental Ethnic Music in Israel', *Ethnomusicology*, 27, 2, 1983, 227–252.
408. Shawan, S., 'Traditional Arab Music Ensembles in Egypt since 1967', *Ethnomusicology*, 28, 1984, 271–288.
409. Shiloah, A., 'Transformation et phenomènes d'influence dans les musiques du Proche et Moyen Orient, hier et aujourd'hui', *Douze cas d'interaction culturelle*, Paris: UNESCO, Conseil International de Philosophie et Sciences Humaines, 1924, 259–278.
410. Faruqi, L., 'Music, Musicians and Muslim Law', *Asian Music*, 17, 1, 1985, 59–82.
411. Engel, H., *Die Stellung des Musikers im arabisch-islamischen Raum*, Bonn, 1987.
412. Jones, L. J., 'A Sociohistorical Perspective on Tunisian Women as Professional Musicians', in Koskoff, E. (ed.), *Women and Music in Cross-Cultural Perspective*, New York, 1987, 69–84.
413. Sakata, H. L., 'Hazara Women in Afghanistan: Innovators and Preservers of a Musical Tradition', in Koskoff, E. (ed.), *Women and Music in Cross-Cultural Perspective*, New York, 1987, 85–95.
414. Shiloah, A., 'An Eighteenth-Century Critic of Taste and Good Taste', in Blum, S., Bohlman, Ph., Neuman, D. (eds.), *Ethnomusicology and Modern Music History*, Urbana & Chicago: University of Illinois Press, 1991, 181–189.
415. Feldman, W. 'Cultural Authority and Authenticity in the Turkish Repertoire', *Asian Music*, 22, 1, 1990/91, 73–112.
416. Merkhoff, J. 'The Ideology of Musical Practice and the Professional Turkish Folk Musician: Tempering the Creative Impulse', *Asian Music*, 22, 1, 1990/91, 113–128.
417. Schuyler, Ph. D. 'Music and Tradition in Yemen', *Asian Music*, 22, 1, 1990/91, 51–72.
418. Lambert, J., *La Médecine de l'âme: musique et musiciens dans la société citadine de Ṣan'a* (Yemen), PhD Diss., University of Paris, 1990.
419. Sekeles, H., *Music as a Therapeutic Agent*, PhD Diss., The Hebrew University, 1992.

XIV. Folk music

(see also 159, 161, 163, 164, 169, 173, 176, 177, 180, 181, 182, 184, 186, 196, 329, 330, 335, 359, 361, 369–376, 380, 391, 396, 417, 418)

420. Lane, E. W., *An Account of the Manners and Customs of the Modern Egyptians*, 5th edn, London, 1860; reprinted 1963.
421. Idelsohn, A. Z., *Hebräisch Orientalischer Melodienschatz*, Leipzig–Berlin–Jerusalem, 1914–1932.
422. Bartok, B., 'Die Volkmusik der Araber von Biskra', *ZfMw*, 2, 1, 1919–20, 489–522.
423. Chottin, A., 'Chants et danses berbères', *Revue de Musicologie*, 7, 15, 1934, 65–78.
424. Toschi, P., 'Musica popolare tripolina', *Lares*, 8, 1937, 136.
425. Menzel, T., *Meddah, Schattentheater und Orta Ojunu*, Prague, 1941.
426. Hickmann, H., 'Commentaire sur la musique militaire Egyptienne à l'époque du Khedive Ismail', *Cahiers d'Histoire Egyptienne*, 1, 1948, 230–33.
427. Serjeant, R. B., *The Ḥadrami Song: Prose and Poetry from Ḥadramaut*, London, 1951.
428. Hoerburger, F. 'Correspondence between Eastern and Western Folk Epics', *JIFMC*, 4, 1952, 23–26.
429. Rasheed, B.S., *Egyptian Folk Songs*, New York and Cairo, 1958.
430. Snoussi, M., 'Folklore Tunisien, musique de plein air: l'orchestre de ṭabbāl et zokkar', *REI*, 1, 1961, 148–157.
431. Krader, L., *Peoples of Central Asia*, Bloomington, Indiana, 1963.
432. Alexandru, T., *La musique populaire d'Egypte*, Cairo, 1967.
433. Alexandru, T., 'Les chansons épiques d'Egypte', *XV Kongress saveza Udruzenya Folklorista Yugoslavie, Jayce*, 1968, 243.
434. Caron, N., Pourtorab, M., 'Expressions musicales de la vie quotidienne en Iran', in *La musique dans la vie*, vol. II, Paris, 1969, 43–69.
435. Chadwick, N. and V. Zhirmunsky, *Oral Epics of Central Asia*, Cambridge, 1969.
436. Havas, M. A., *The Contemporary Arab Folk Song*, Moscow, 1970.
437. Reiche, J. P., 'Stilelemente Südtürkischen, Davul-Zurna Stücke', *JbfMVV*, 5, 1970, 9–54.
438. Chiavzzi, G., 'Alcune cantilene relative a ceremonie e ricorenze libiche', *Studi Magrebini* 4, 1971, 77–111.
439. Simon, A., 'Feld Forschungen in Aegypten und dem Sudan, 1972–74', *Mitteilungen der Deutschen Gesellschaft für Music des Orients*, 13, 1971.
440. Simon, A., *Studien zur Aegyptischen Volkmusik*, Hamburg, 1972, 2 Bd.

441. Massoudieh, Moh. T., 'Hochzeitlieder aus Balucestan', *JbfMVV*, 7, 1973, 59–69.
442. Blum, S., 'Persian Folksong in Meshhed', *YIFMC*, VI, 1974, 86–114.
443. Shiloah, A., 'A Group of Arabic Wedding Songs from the Village of Deir al-Asad', *Studies of the Folklore Research Center*, 4, Jerusalem, 1974, 267–296.
444. Kuckerz, J. and M. T. Massoudieh, 'Volkgesänge aus Iran', *Beiträge zur Musik des Vorderen Orients und seinen Einflussbereichen, K. Reinhard zum 60 Geburstag*, Berlin, 1975, 217.
445. Reinhard, K., 'Bemerkung zu den Asik, den Volkssängern der Türkie', *Asian Music*, 4, 1975, 189–206.
446. Slobin, M., 'Buz-Baz: a Musical Marionette of North Afghanistan', *Asian Music*, 4, 1975, 217–224.
447. Bartok, B., *Turkish Folk Music from Asia Minor*, ed. by B. Suchoff, Princeton, 1976.
448. Bartok, B., 'Why and How we Collect Folk Music', in *Essays Selected*, ed. by B. Suchoff, London, 1976.
449. Simon, A., 'Zur Oboen-Trommel Musik in Aegypten', *Festschrift Felix Hoerberger*, Laaber, 1977, 153–66.
450. Jargy, S., 'The Folk Music of Syria and Lebanon', *World of Music*, 1978, 1, 79–92.
451. Touma, H. H., 'Music of the Gulf: The Song of the Pearl-Fishers', *The Unesco Courier*, October 1979, 28–31.
452. Shiloah, A. 'Arab Folk Music', in *New Groves Dictionary of Music*, ed. S. Sadie, I, 1980, 528–39.
453. Naji, M. M., *al-Ghinā' al-yamanī al-qadīm wa-mashāhiruhu*, 1983.
454. Fāri', Tāha, *Lamaḥāt fī ta'rīkh al-ugniya al-Yamanīya al-mu'āṣira*, Aden: Dār al-Mahdānī, 1985.
455. Elsner, J., 'Trommeln u. Trommelnensembles im Jemen', in Michel, A. and Elsner, J. (ed.), *Beitr. zur Traditionellen Musik*, Berlin, 1990, 18–37.
456. Danielson, V., '*Min al- Mashāyikh*: A View of Egyptian Musical Tradition', *Asian Music*, 22, 1, 1990/91, 113–128.
457. Grimaud, Y., *Chants de verité*, Fribourg /Pro Musica, 1993, 'Musique vocale berbère de Kabylie', 51–100.

Country index

(List of regional studies references included in the thematic bibliography)

170, 171, 178a, 194, 197, 199a, 201, 202, 252, 270, 295, 311, 322, 324a, 325, 330, 332, 337, 345, 351, 357, 376, 414–416, 437, 445, 457.
Yemen 161, 417, 418, 427, 453–455.

List of sources

The following are fully described in Shiloah, *Theory of Music in Arabic Writings* (RISM) (see 76 in bibliography). The numbers appearing in square brackets refer to the numbering in the above mentioned book.

Appolonius of Perga (262 bc–190 ce). *Ṣan'at al-zāmir* (On the Construction of the Wind Instrument Automaton) [002]

al-Adfuwī (1286–1347). *al-Imtā' bi-aḥkām al-samā'* (The Benefit of the Laws of Listening to Music) [003]

al-Anṭākī, Dā'ūd (–1599). *Tadhkirat 'ulī'l-albāb wa'l-djāmi' li'l-'adjāb al-'udjdjāb* (Memorial for Wise Men and Gatherer of Wonderful Things) [013]

al-'Aṭṭār, Muḥammad b. Ḥusayn 'Aṭṭārzāde (1764–1828). *Rannat al-awtār fī djadāwil al-afkār fī fann al-mūsīqār* (The Sounds of Strings [arranged] in Rubrics to Bring to Mind what Concerns the Musician's Art) [016]

Ayrun (Heron of Alexandria) (fl. 62). *Madjmū 'ālāt wa ḥiyal* (Collection of Apparatuses and Machines) [017]

Banū Mūsa b. Shākir (10th c.). *al-'Āla allatī tuzammir bi nafsiha* (The instrument which Plays by Itself) [022]

Būlos. *'Unṣur al-mūsīkī wa ma iftarakat 'alayh al-falāsifa min tarkībih wa māhiyatih* (The Principle of Music and the Disagreement of the Philosophers about its Elements and Essence) [028]

al-Dhahabī, Shams al-dīn al-Ṣaydāwī (14th c.). *Kitāb al-an'ām bi ma'rifat al-anghām* (Book of Attentive Consideration of the Science of Melodies) [035]

al-Djāḥiẓ (776–898/9). *Kitāb al-ḥayawān* (Book of Animals) [040]

al-Djāḥiẓ. *Risālat al-ḳiyān* (Treatise on the Singing Girls) [045]

al-Djāḥiẓ. *Ṭabaḳāt al-mughannīn* (Book of the Classes of Singers) [046]

al-Djazarī, Badi 'al-zamān (12th-13th c.). *Kitāb fī ma'rifat al-ḥiyal al-handasiyya* (The book of knowledge of ingenious mechanical devices) [050]

al-Fārābī (–950). *Iḥṣā' al-'ulūm* (Classification of the Sciences) [055]

al-Fārābī. *Kitāb fi'l-īqā'at* (Book on Rhythms) [056]

al-Fārābī. *Kitāb al mūsīqī al-kabīr* (The Grand Book on Music) [057]
al-Fāsī, 'Abd al-Raḥmān (1631–1685). *al-Djumū' fī 'ilm al-mūsīqī wa'l-ṭubū'* (The Gatherings in the Theory of Music and the Musical Modes) [059]
al-Ghazālī, abū Ḥāmid (1058–1111). *Iḥyā' 'ulūm al-dīn* (The Revival of Religious Sciences) [061]
al-Ghazālī, Madjd al-dīn (–1121). *Bawāriḳ al-ilmā fī'l radd 'ala mann yuḥarrim al-samā'* (The Lightening Flashes Concerning the Refutation of those who Declare Listening to Music is Forbidden) [063]
Ḥadjdjī Khalīfa (–1657). *Kashf al-ẓunūn 'an asāmī al-kutub wa'l funūn* (Clarification of Conjectures about the Names of Books and Sciences) [065]
al-Ḥā'ik (18th c.). [*Madjmu'at nawbāt*] ([A Collection of Nawbat-I]) [066]
al-Ḥasan al-Kātib (11th c.). *Kitāb kamāl adab al-ghinā'* (The Book of Perfection of Musical Knowledge) [070]
Ḥunayn ibn Isḥāḳ (808–873). *Kitāb ādāb al-falāsifa* (Book of the Aphorisms of the Philosophers) [078]
ibn 'abd Rabbih (860–940). *al-'Iqd al-farīd* (The Unique Necklace) [082]
ibn Abī'l-Dunyā (823–894). *Dhamm al-mālahī* (The Book of the Censure of Instruments of Diversion) [083]
ibn al-Akfānī (–1348). *Irshād al-qāṣid ilā asnā'l-maqāṣid* (The Guiding of the Searcher to the Most Sublime Purposes) [087]
ibn al-'Arabī (1165–1240). *al-Futuḥāt al-makiyya* (Meccan Revelations) [091]
ibn Bisṭām, Muḥammad (–1685). [*Risāla fī'l-fiqh*] (Tract on Jurisprudence) [098]
ibn Buṭlān, abū'l-Ḥasan (–1066 or 1068). *Risāla fī shirā' al-raqīq wa taqlīb al-'abīd* (On How to Buy Slaves and How to Detect Bodily Defects) [099]
ibn Djamā'a, Burhān al-dīn (1325–1388). *Djawāb su'āl sa'alahu shakhs min al-fuqarā' fī'l-samā'* (Response to a Fakīr Concerning the Samā') [100]
ibn al-Djawzī, 'Abd al-Raḥmān (1126–1200). *Kitāb rawḍat al-madjālis . . .* (Book of the Garden of Companies . . .) [102]
ibn Ghaybī, 'Abd al-ḳādir (mid 14th c.–1435). *Dhikr al-anghām wa uṣūliha* (Enumeration of the Modes and their Roots) [107]
ibn Ghaybī, 'Abd al-ḳādir. *Djāmi al-alḥān* (Compiler of Melodies) [108]
ibn Ghaybī, 'Abd al-ḳādir. *Maḳāṣid al-alḥān* (Purports of Melodies) [109]
ibn al-Ḥādjdj (–1336). *Madkhal al-shar' al-sharīf* (Introduction to the Venerable Law) [113]
ibn Hindū, abū'l-Faradj (–1019). *Kitāb miftāḥ al-ṭibb* (The Key of Medicine) [116]
ibn Khaldūn (1332–1406). *al-Muqaddima* (The Prolegomena) [122]
ibn Khurradādhbih (820–911). *Kitāb al-lahw wa'l-mālahī* (Book of Diversion and Musical Instruments) [125]

ibn al-Munadjdjim, Abū Aḥmad b. 'Alī (–912). *Risāla fī'l-mūsīqī* (Treatise on Music) [131]
ibn al-Nadīm (–995 or 998). *Kitāb al-fihrist* (Book of the Index to Arabic Books) [132]
ibn Radjab, Zayn al-dīn (1335–1392). *Nuzhat al-asmā' fī mas'alat al-samā'* (Pleasure of the Ears Concerning the Practice of Listening to music) [134]
ibn Sīnā (Avicenna) (980–1037). *al-Qānūn fī'l-ṭibb* (The Canon on Medicine) [138]
ibn Sīnā (Avicenna). *Kitāb al-nadjāt* (Book of the Delivery) [139]
ibn Sīnā (Avicenna). *Kitāb al-shifā'* (Book of Healing [of the Soul]) [142]
ibn Taghrī Birdī (1409/10–1470). *al-Nudjūm al-ẓāhira* (The Resplendent Stars) [143]
ibn Taymiyya (1263–1328). *Risāla fī'l-samā' wa'l-raqṣ wa'l-ṣarākh* (Tract on Listening to Music, Dance and Screaming) [147]
ibn Zayla (–1048). *Kitāb al-kāfī fī'l-al-mūsīqī* (Book of Sufficiency in Music) [152]
Ikhwān al-Ṣafā (10th c). *Risāla fī'l-mūsīqī* (Tract on Music) [154]
al-Iṣfahānī, abū'l-Faradj (897–967). *Kitāb al-aghānī* (Book of Songs) [156]
al-Qādirī, 'Askar al-Ḥalabī (17th century). *Rāḥ al-djām fī shadjarat al-anghām* (Wine of the Cup Regarding the Tree of Melodies) [160]
al-Khawārizmi abū 'Abdallah (–997). *Mafātīḥ al'ulūm* (The Keys of Sciences) [170]
al-Kindī (–870). *Kitāb al-muṣawwitāt al-Watariyya min dhāt al-Watar al-Wāḥid ilā dhāt al-'asharat al-awtār* (Book of Sounding Stringed Instruments of One to Ten Strings) [173]
al-Kindī. *Risāla fī adjzā' khabariyya fī'l-mūsīḳī* (Treatise Concerning Concise Information on Music) [174]
al-Kindī. *Risāla fī khubr ta'līf al-alḥān* (Treatise Concerning the Knowledge on the Composition of Melodies) [175]
al-Kindī. *Risāla fī'l-luḥūn wa'l-nagham* (Treatise on the Melodies and the Notes) [176]
Kushādjim, abū'l-Fatḥ (–961 or 971). *Kitāb adab al-nadīm* (Book on the Conduct of the Boon Companion) [180]
al-Lādhiqī (–1495). *Risālat al-fatḥiyya fī'l-al-mūsīqī* (The Epistle of Victory Concerning the Science of Music) [182]
al-Maqqarī(1591–1632). *Nafḥ al-ṭīb* . . . (Breath of Perfumes . . .) [188]
al-Makkī, abū Ṭālib (–996). *Qūt al-qulūb* (Food of Hearts) [189]
Mashāḳa, Mikhā'īl (1800–1888). *al-Risāla al-shihabiyya fī'l-ṣinā'a al-mūsīqīyya* (The Shihabian Treatise on the Art of Music) [194]
al-Mas'ūdī (–956). *Murūdj al-dhahab* . . . Meadows of Gold . . .) [195]
al-Mufaḍḍal ibn Salama (830–905). *Kitāb al-malāhī* (The Book of Musical Instruments) [197]
Muristus. *Ṣan'at al-urghin al-būqī* (On the Construction of the Flue-Pipe Organ) [200]

Muristus. *Ṣan'at al-urghin al-zamrī* (On the Construction of the Reed-Pipe Organ) [201]

Muristus. *Ṣan'at al-djuldjul* (On the Construction of the Chime) [202]

al-Nābulusī 'Abd al-Ghanī. *'Iḍāḥ al-dalālāt fī samā' al- 'ālāt* (The Clarification of Proofs Concerning the Listening to Musical Instruments) [205]

Ṣafī al-dīn, 'Abd al-Mu'min (1230–1294). *Kitāb al-adwār* (The Book of Cycles or Musical Modes) [222]

Ṣafī al-dīn. *al-Risāla al-Sharafiyya* (The Sharafian Treatise) [223]

al-Salmānī ibn al-Khaṭīb (attributed to) (fl. 1294). *Fī'l ṭabā'i' wa'l-ṭubū' wa'l-uṣūl* (On the Natures, Elements and Modes) [227]

al-Shalaḥī, Muḥammad b. Ibrāhīm (14th c.). *Kitāb al-imtā' wa'l-intifā' fī mas'alat samā' al-samā'* (The Book of Joy and Profit in Listening to Music) [232]

Shihāb al-dīn, Muḥammad b. Ismā'īl al-Ḥidjāzī (1795–1857). *Safīnat al-mulk wa nafīsat al-fulk* (The Royal Ship and the Sumptuous Boat) [235]

al-Shirwānī, Mawlana Fatḥ Allah al-Mu'min (15th c.). *Risāla fī 'ilm al-mūsīqī* (Tract on the science of music) [239]

Thābit ibn Qurra (836–901). *Mas'ala fī'l mūsīqī* (A Musical Problem) [254]

al-Ṭurṭūshī, ibn abī Randaḳa (1049/60–1131). *Mas'ala fī'l-samā'* (A Question on the Listening to Music) [257]

al-Ṭūṣī, Nāṣir al-dīn (1201–1274). *Risāla fī'ilm al-mūsīqī* (Treatise on the Theory of Music) [259]

al-Uskudārī, 'Azīz Maḥmud (–1628). *Kashf al-qinā' 'an wadjh al-samā'* (Removal of the Veil from the Aspect of Listening to Music) [263]

Yuḥanna b. al-Baṭrīk (–815). *Kitāb al-siyāsa fī tadbīr al-ri'āsa or Sirr al-asrār* (The Book of Administration, or Secret of Secrets) [267]

Anonymous XVII. *Kashf al-ghumūm wa'l Kurab fī sharḥ ālāt al-ṭarab* (The Unveiling of Grief and Sorrow in Commenting on the Instruments of Music) [285]

Anonymous VII. *Fann al-anghām* (The Art of Modes) [286]

Anonymous LXII. *Sharḥ Mawlāna Mubārak Shāh* (The Mubarak Shah Commentary on the Kitāb al-adwār [330]

Modern editions of additional sources (not included in *RISM*):

al-Bukhārī, *Ṣaḥīḥ*, Cairo, 1932-1938.

al-Birūnī, *Ta'rīkh al-Hind*, Haidarabad, 1958.

Ibn Rushd *Talkhīṣ al-Khiṭāba*, ed. by 'Abd al-Raḥmān Badawī, Cairo, 1960. [Paraphrases in Librorum Rhetoricum Aristotelis]

Ibn al-Muqaffa', *Kalīla wa-Dimna*, ed. by Louis Cheikho, Beirut, 1926.

al-Kisā'ī Muḥammad b. 'Abdallah, *Qiṣaṣ al-anbiyā'*, Leiden, Brill, 1922-23.
al-Shirwānī, Aḥmad b. Muḥammad, *Ḥadīqat al-afrāḥ fī izaḥat al-aṭrāḥ*, Bulaq, 1282.

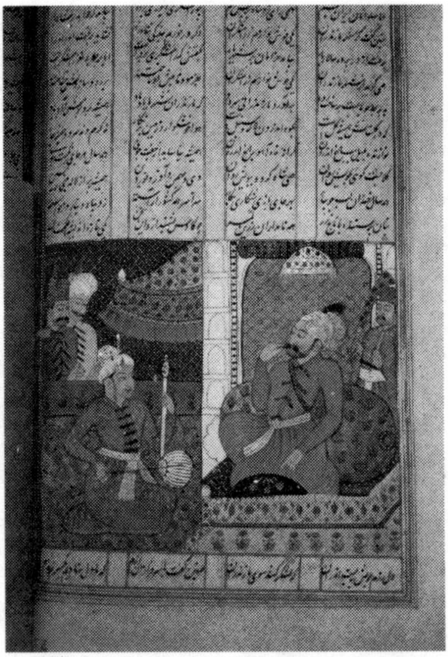

1 A player of a spike fiddle, Nezami, *Khamsa Nameh*, Jewish National and University Library (JNUL), Yah. Ms. Ar. 1119. Indian Ms. Photograph: Noga.

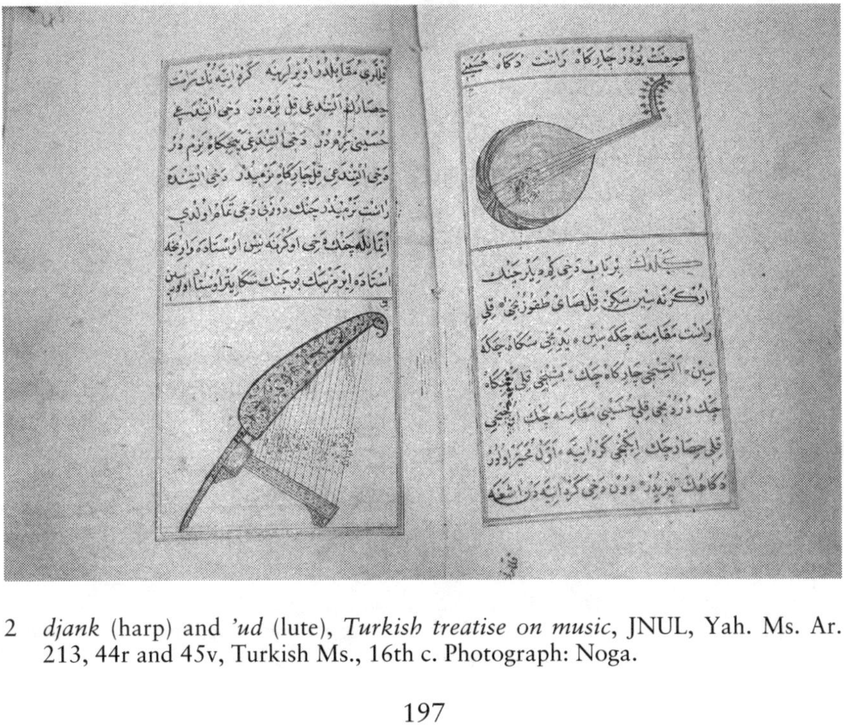

2 *djank* (harp) and *'ud* (lute), *Turkish treatise on music*, JNUL, Yah. Ms. Ar. 213, 44r and 45v, Turkish Ms., 16th c. Photograph: Noga.

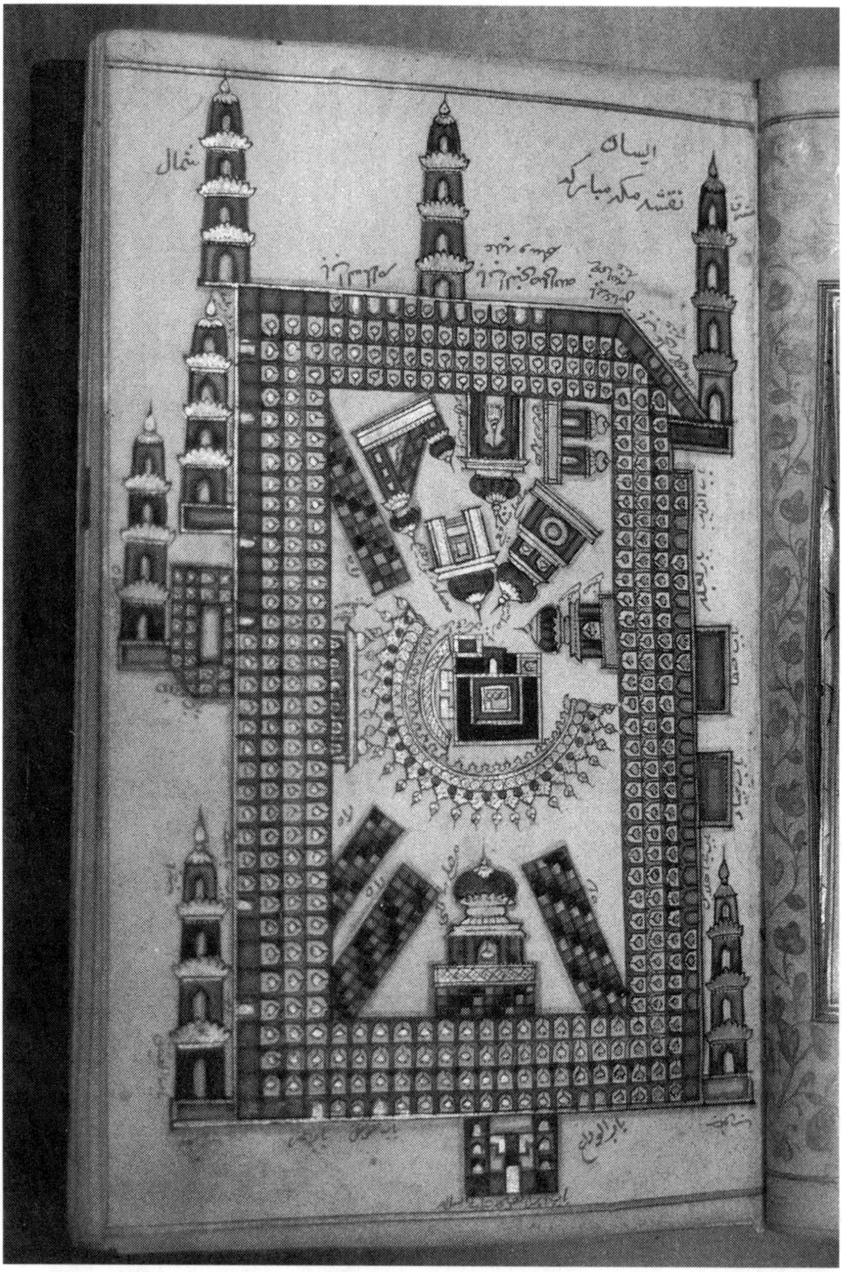

3 The *Ka'ba* from al-Djazūlī's *Dalā'il al-Khayrāt*, [the elements disposed in the half circle surrounding the black stone suggest the dancing of the mystics], JNUL, Yah. Ms. Ar. 863, 28r, Indian Ms. *ca* 1776. Photograph: Noga.

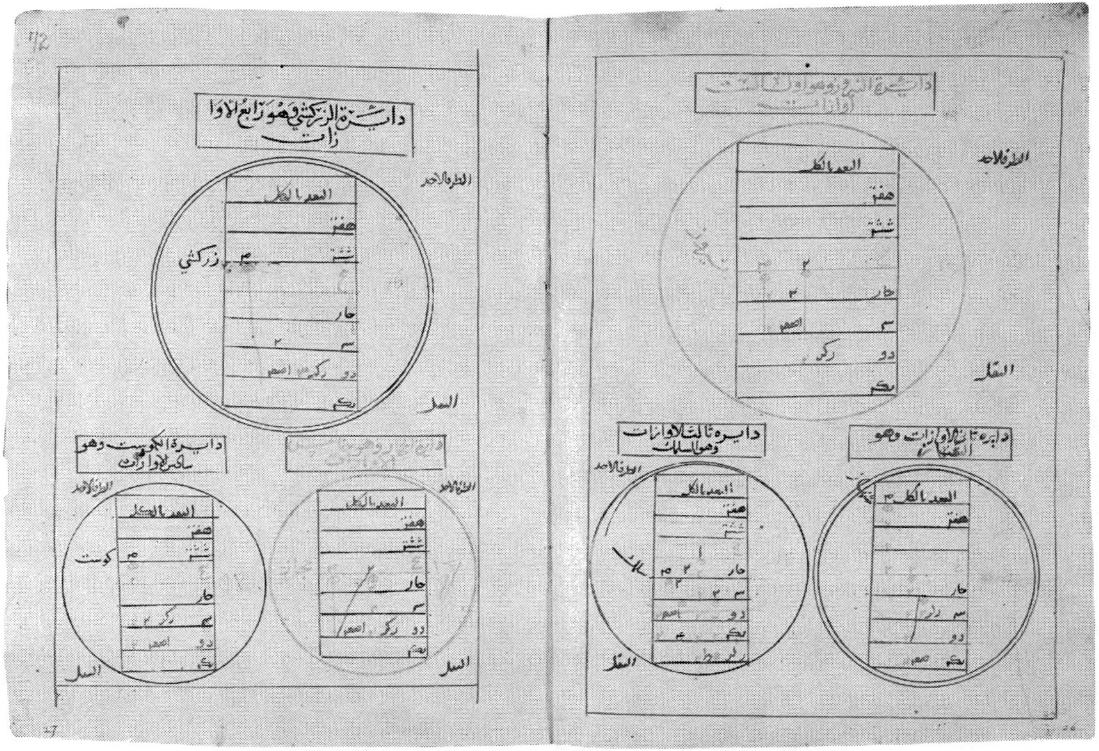

4 A notational system using a colored eight-line stave from the *Epistle on Music* by Shams al-dīn al-Ṣaydāwī, Bodleian Library, Oxford, Ms. March 82, 71v–72r.

5 A musical scene with a harpist and two drummers. Nezami *Khamsa Nameh*, JNUL, Yah. Ms. Ar. 1000, 253r, Persian Ms., 1445. Photograph: Noga.

6 The fox and the double-headed drum hung on the tree, from *Kalīla and Dimna*. Paris, Bibliothèque Nationale, Ms. Ar. 3465, fol. 51v.

7 A bag-pipes player, Paris, BN, Ms. Ar. 6075, fol. 8.

8 Dance of dervishes accompanied by drummers, Paris, BN, Ms. Turc 127, p. 7v.

9 A micrography representing sura 1 and part of sura 2 of the *Qur'ān*, Paris, BN, Ms. Ar. 571, fol. 1. [the reading of sura 1 and a portion of the second is included in music examples 4–6.]

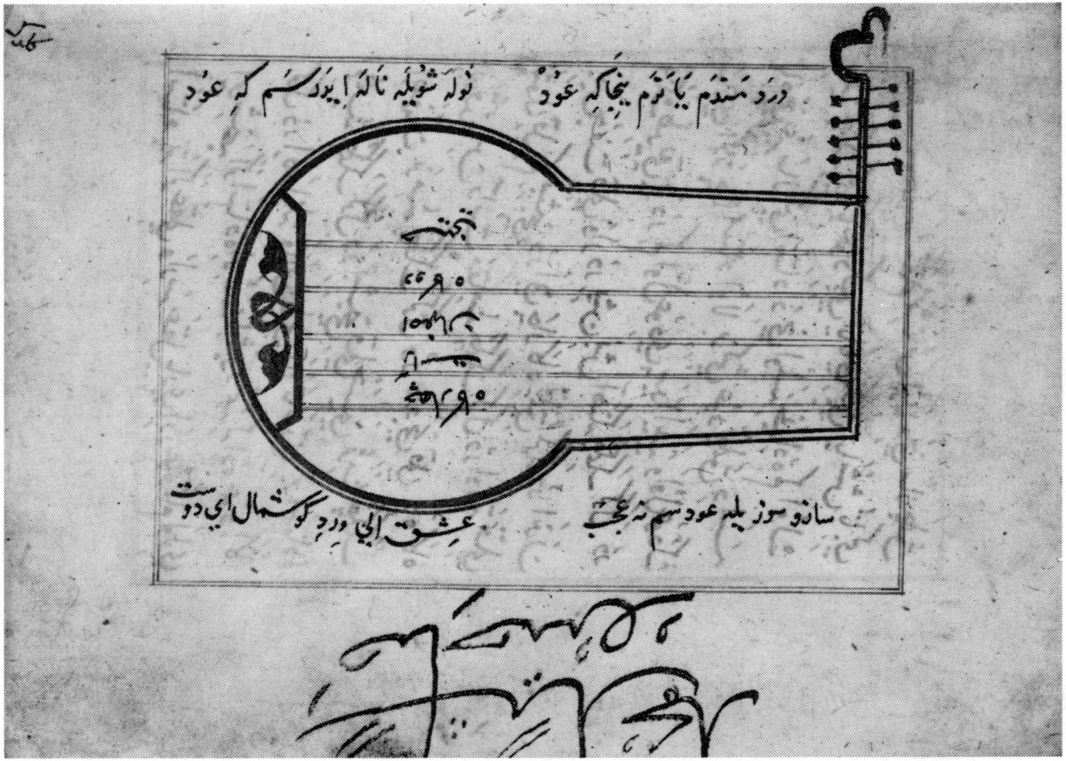

10 Design of a ‘*ūd* in a Turkish treatise on music; the written terms represent the pitches of the five strings, Paris, BN, Ms. Supp. Turc 1424, 29v.

11 Design of a *djank* (harp); Paris, BN, Ms. Supp. Turc 1424, fol. 30v; the written terms represent the pitches of the corresponding strings.

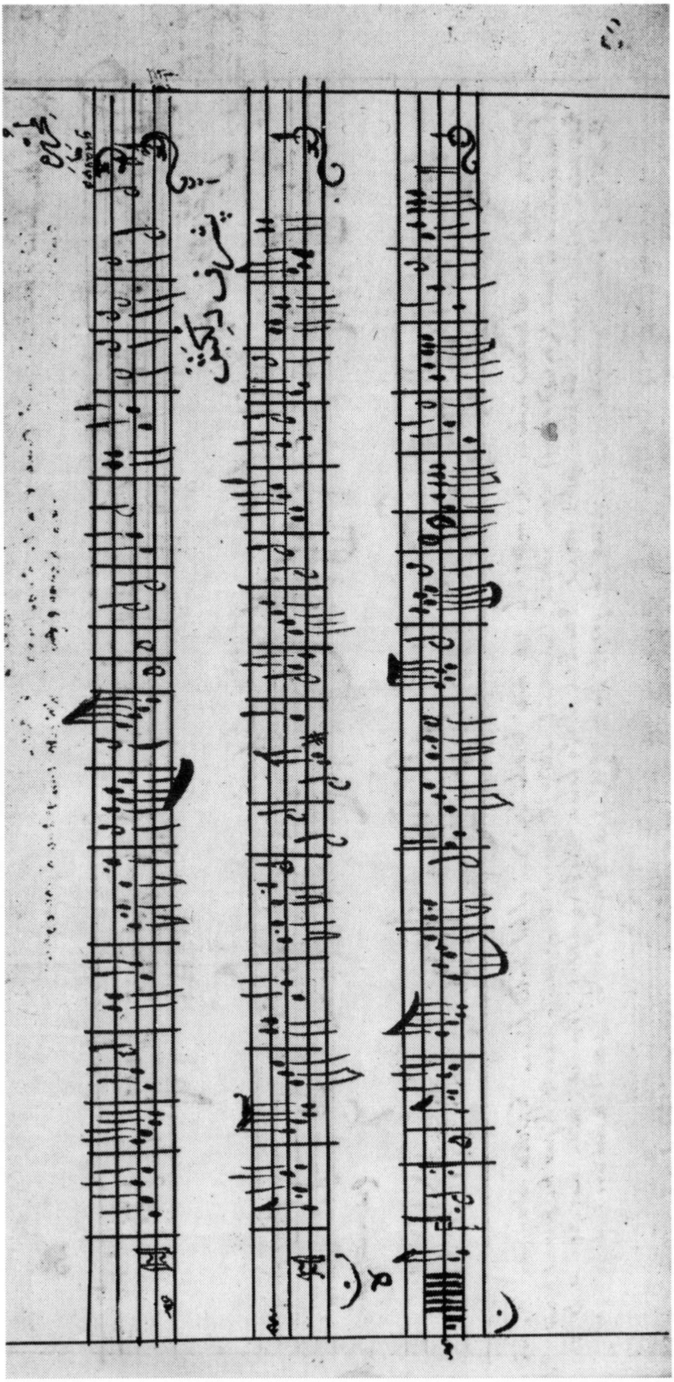

12 The notation of Peshrev dilkash by Albert Bobovsky, alias Ali Ukfi (1610–1675), Paris, BN, Ms. Turc 292, 2v.

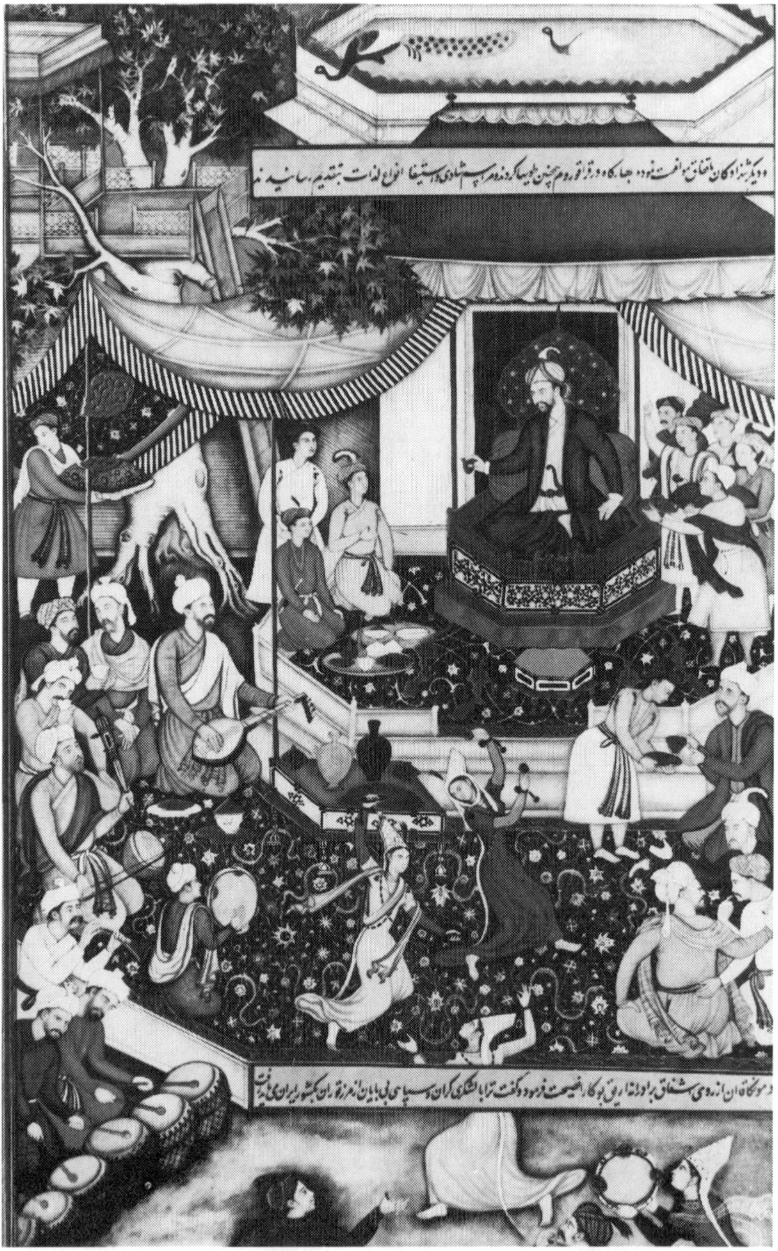

13 A Persian miniature representing a dance scene: three dancers are accompanied by frame drums, kettledrums, an oboe-like instrument, lute and spike fiddle.

14 The adepts of the confraternity Dassoukiyya in Egypt celebrating the *dhikr* [the author is seen in the background while recording the ceremony].

15 An Iranian *santūr* player.

16 A Somalian *'ūd* player.

17 Annotated examples from Thomas Shaw, *Travels or Observations Relating to Several Parts of Barbary and the Levant*. Oxford 1738, p. 272, second edition with Great Improvements, London, 1757, p. 205. The annotated examples represent: 2 Bedouin airs; 2 Moorish airs and a dance; A Turkish air. The same series of musical examples were reproduced identically but without acknowledgement by J. B. Laborde in his *Essai sur la musique ancienne et moderne*, Paris, 1780, p. 380–383.

Ex. 1 *Qur’ān* reading – Saudi Arabia (Sura 20, 1–6).

Ex. 2 *Qur'ān* reading – Tunisia (Sura 63, 1–3).

Ex. 2 concluded

Ex. 3 *Qur'ān* reading – Jordan (Sura 33, 40–42).

ku - rū —— llā —— ha —— dhi —— k-
ran —— ka - thī —— ra —— n wa - sab - bi -
ḥū —— hu buk - ran —— wa - a - ṣī - lan.

Ex. 3 concluded

Ex. 4 *Qur'ān* reading – Syria (Sura 2, 1–5).

Ex. 5 A communal reading of *al-Fātiḥ* (Sura 1) – The Sufi confraternity *al-Shādhilīyya* (Acre–Israel).

Ex. 6 *al-Fātiḥ* (Sura 1) by a Syrian Reader.

Ex. 7 A call to prayer (*ādhān*) – Syria.

Ex. 7 continued

Ex. 7 concluded

Ex. 8 A call to prayer (*ādhān*) – Turkey.

Ex. 8 continued

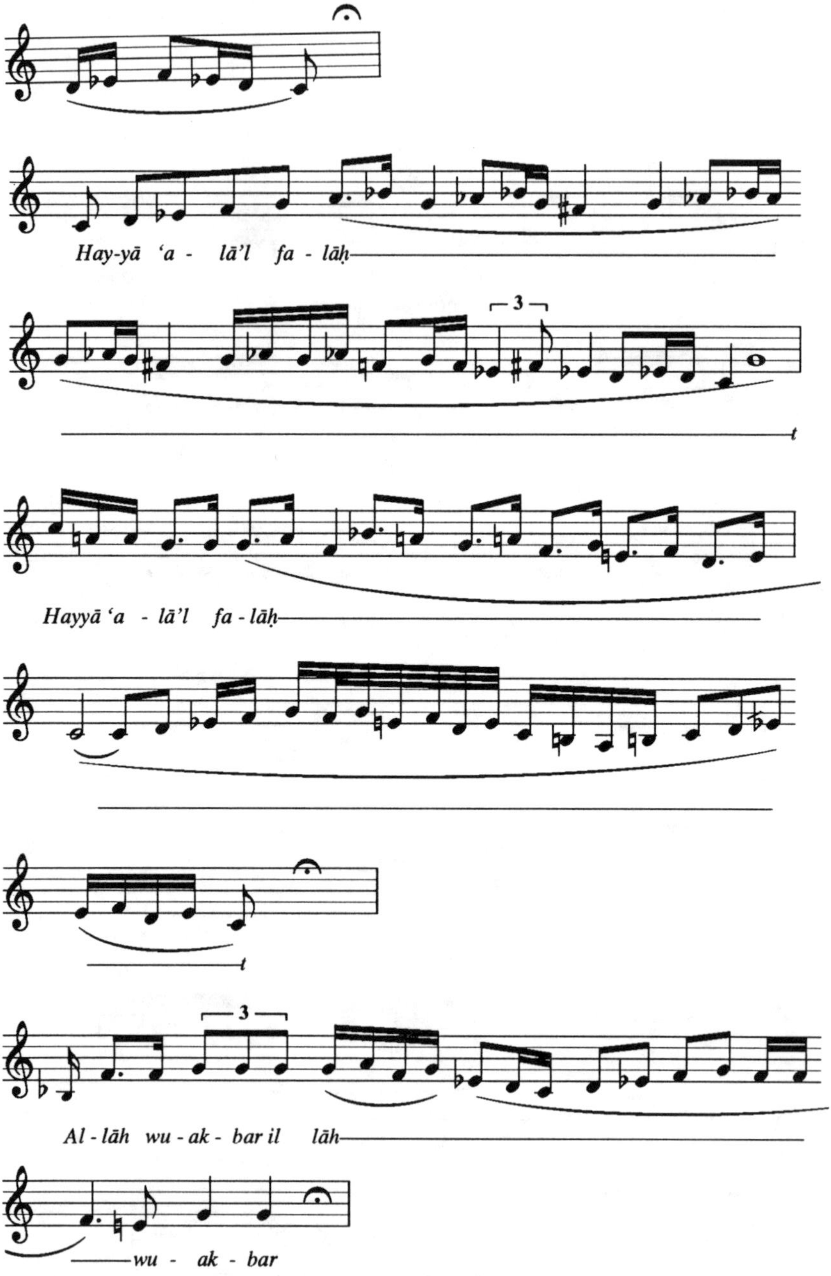

Ex. 8 continued

Ex. 8 concluded

Ex. 9 A call to prayer (*ādhān*) – Bosnia.

Ex. 9 concluded

Ex. 10 *Son peshrev* and *Son Yürük sema 'î* – the concluding parts of the Mewlevi Ceremony of the Whirling Dervishes (Turkey)

Index